LOUDOUN COUNTY, VIRGINIA

MARRIAGE BONDS

1762 – 1850

Compiled by
Mrs. Walter Towner Jewell

CLEARFIELD

Reprinted by Genealogical Publishing Company
with permission of the Virginia Book Company
for Clearfield Company, Baltimore, MD
1993, 1997
International Standard Book Number 0-8063-4699-X
Made in the United States of America

FOREWORD

Loudoun County was formed in 1757 when it was cut off from Fairfax.
It was divided into two parishes, Cameron and Shelburne, the dividing
line between them being Goose Creek. Cameron Parish records are non-
existent, therefore it was thought important to note in this volume
when it appeared on the bond that a participant was from Cameron
Parish.

It is unfortunate that many of the early marriage bonds have been
lost. It is strange too, that many of the marriage bonds in existence
are not followed by the actual marriage records in the Clerk's Office
at Leesburg. For the latter reason, I have compiled this separate
volume of the marriage bonds, believing it to be an invaluable addition
to already published Virginia records.

A few Clerk's fee books were found containing marriage licenses. These
licenses are recorded in this volume. They are not included in the
marriage records.

This work has been in preparation for several years. Searching the
County Archives for possible lost bonds was a major effort. Without
the constant help of my co-worker, Rev. Melvin Lee Steadman,Jr., it
could not have been accomplished. The courtesy and cooperation of the
personnel in the Clerk's Office was also gratifying.

Aurelia M. Jewell

Aurelia M. Jewell

Name of Groom	Name of Bride	Date of Bond

Jacob Fadley   Mary McNeledge   January 5,1799
Sec. Jas. McNeledge

William Ellzey   Frances H. Westwood   March 4,1799
Sec. Robert Armistead. Wm. Westwood, brother & gdn. of bride.

James Campbell   Mary Jackson   February 20,1799
Sec. John Jackson,Jr. Sam'l Murrey test. bride over 21.

John Carr,Senr.   Prudence Collins   January 24,1799
Sec. C. Binns,Jr. Alex. Waugh witness.

William Gallaher   Polly Clarke   September 28,1799
Sec. Samuel Murrey. He test. bride 21 on Sept.29,1799.

William Adams   Linney Willett   January 1, 1799
Sec. William Willett, who test. bride 21.

Aaron Burson   Kitty Burson   March 7, 1799
Sec. Joseph Burson, father of bride. Wit:John Burson, Jesse Burson,
Moses Wilson.

Jacob Huffman   Catherine Koist   June 22, 1799
Sec. Cutloss or Cutlop Koist.

John Neldon   Sebella Smith   April 13, 1799
Sec. Joseph Smith, who test. bride 21. Wit: Alex. Waugh

John Glasser   Sarah Tucker   September 9, 1799
Sec. Nicholas Tucker

Major Hunt   Mary Wilson   November 11, 1799
Sec. Wm. Roberts. C.Binns,Jr. test. bride over 21.

George Chamblin   Mary Davis   September 20,1799
Sec. Van Davis, father of bride

Hanson Johnson   Jane White   June 10,1799
Sec. Samuel Murrey, who test. bride 21.

Wm. Dodd   Hannah Pancoast   October 12. 1799
Sec. John Dodd,Jr., who also test. bride over 21.

James Seaton   Elizabeth Race   October 20,1799
Sec. Wm. Race, father of bride.

Peter Compher   Susanna Stoneburner   March 20,1799
Sec. Peter Stoneburner,father of bride. Wit: Alex. Waugh.

Stephen Beard of   Orpah Lacey   November 4,1799
Cameron Parish
Sec. Meshec Lacey. Joseph Lacey, father, consented.

Name of Groom	Name of Bride	Date of Bond

Philip Cooper   Eliza Addleman   November 5, 1799
Sec. George Cooper, who also test. bride over 21.

Moses Miller   Christeny Shoemaker   October 17,1799
Sec. Daniel Shoemaker, father of bride.

James Stewart   Margt. Whistleman   February 25, 179*
Sec. John Francis, who also test. bride 21.

Joseph Timms   Amelia Presgraves   January 21, 1799
         both of Cameron Parish
Sec. James Giles, who test. bride 21. Wit: Alex. Waugh

William Veale   Linny Horseman   February 25, 179*
         both of Cameron Parish, or Lenah
Sec. Wm. Horseman,Jr., who also test. bride 21.

Charles Veale of Cam.Parish   Juliet Pratt   March 16, 1799
Sec. C. Binns,Jr.

John Wright   Catherine Quick   May 7, 1799
Sec. John Quick, father of bride.

John Craven   Mary Carlisle   February 6, 1799
Sec. David Carlile

Thomas McKinny   Leah Gallaher   May 4, 1799
Sec. William Galleher, father of bride

Jehu Burson   Anna Kent   February 10,1799
Sec. Thos. Kent, father of bride.

John Filler   Catherine Crumbaker   February 1, 1799
Sec. Jacob Crumbacker, who also test. bride 21.

John M Broge (or Bride)   Sarah Watkins   December 25, 1799
Sec. Daniel Tucker

John Lee   Theodosia Warford
Sec. Abm. Warford   of Cam. Par.   September 27,179*

James Whitacre   Elizabeth Randall   November 16,1799
Sec. William Randle

Nathaniel Davison Jr.   Nancy Mcilhany   September 30,179*
Sec. C.Binns. James McIlhany,father of bride test. she 21. Rosannah
McIlhany, mother. (Davison a stranger in County)

John Ellis,Sr.   Nancy Humphreys   December 7, 1799
Sec. John Humphreys,father of bride. Wit: Samuel Handeman

Name of Groom	Name of Bride	Date of Bond
Michael Turner,Jr. Sec. Andrew Betts, father of bride.	Eliza Betts	October 29,1799
William Askins Sec.James Wilson,father of brideCam. Parish	Susanna Wilson of	March 15, 1799
John Griffith,Jr. Sec. Jenkin Oxley	Hannah Homan, called Hannah Stephens,Spinster	December 7, 1799
Edward Muse Sec. William Thrift, who also test. bride 21.	Nancy Jones	April 1, 1799
William Grubb Sec. John Millard	Susanna Tally, widow	April 18, 1799
Thomas Wyatt Sec. David Jay, father of bride.	Henrietta Jay	April 12, 1799
Edward Ellmore Sec. Boley Speaks	Nancy Speaks of Cameron Parish	March 19, 1799
Lewis Amblar Sec.Vincent Hutchison John Hutchison, father of bride, consents.	Sally Hutchison of Cameron Parish	April 1, 1799
Thomas Gregg Sec. John Brown, father of the bride.	Hannah Brown	March 20, 1799
Mahlon Janney,Jr. Sec. James Brown, father of bride.	Sarah Brown	June 26,1799
Frederick Stoneburner Sec. George Reazon, father of bride.	Elizabeth Rasor	March 26,1799
John Johnson Sec. Archibald McMullan	Nancy McMullan	March 22, 1799
Edmond Turley Sec. (Edmond Turley signed)	Elizabeth Edelen of Cameron Parish	November 29,1799
Barton Hawley Sec.Joshua Hutchison (father of bride)	Catherine Heath of Cameron Parish	April 8,1799
Danl. McCluskey Sec. Jonathan Convade	Rebekah Myers, widow	May 13, 1799
Abraham Miller Dec. John Jackson. John Martin, father of girl, consented.	Rachel Martin	December 21, 1799

Name of Groom	Name of Bride	Date of Bond
William Perry	Susanna Turley of	December 24,17
Sec. John H. Gibbs	Cameron Parish	
Giles Turley, father of girl, consents. Wit: Sampson Turley		
Thomas Stephenson	Nancy Green	February 25,17
Sec. Tom Green, father of girl.		
Henry Hall	Sarah Harper of	January 23,180
Sec.Thomas Harper, father of	Cameron Parish	
girl, consented.		
Obediah Clifford	Betsey Couper	September 16,1
Sec. James Hamilton. Alexander Couper, father of girl, consented.		
Peter Koist	Ann Butler	August 12,1799
Sec. Jacob Huffman		
George Berkley	Susanna Bartlett of	December 31,17
Sec. John Linton	Cameron Parish	
Bailey Donaldson, test. bride 21.		
William McGurgan	Rebecca Mellan	March 30, 1799
Sec. John Blaker. John Millan, father of girl, consents.		
George Bussell	Sarah Moore of	June 20, 1799
Sec. Jacob Stump	Cameron Parish	
He test. the girl 21.		
Jacob Wyatt	Morelles Derry	March 15, 1799
Sec. Michael Rymond or Rimond, who also test. the girl 21.		
Sylvester Grimes	Sarah Davis,widow, of	January 21, 17
Sec. Nicholas Grymes	Cameron Parish	
Nathaniel Fitzhugh	Hannah Lane of	February 1st,
Sec. Will Lane, father of	Cameron Parish	
girl, consented. Wt: Joseph Rolly		
Jesse Fox	Sarah Popkins	April 12, 1796
Sec. Asa Fox. John Popkins, father of girl consented.		
Bartleson Fox	Elizabeth Braden	February 11, 17
Sec. William Fox, who test. to ages of both.		
Ambrose Fox	Hannah James of	January 12, 1790
Jonathan Swindler, who also	Cameron Parish	
test. girl 21.		
George Fox	Eliza Walker	March 30, 1791
Sec. Uriah Fox, who also test. both 21.		

Name of Groom	Name of Bride	Date of Bond
Asa Fox Sec. Thornton Kendrick, who also test. girl 21.	Mary Kendrick	February 2, 1795
Joseph Beavers Sec. Willis Legg. Barnet Swarts, father of girl, consented.	Anna Barnett Swarts of Cameron Parish	April 20, 1799
Jacob Shry Sec. Abraham Warford	Catherine Warford of Cameron Parish	October 31, 1799
Thomas Gilham Sec. Abel Triplett, father of girl.	Mary Triplett	December 14,1799
Patk. Dunn Sec. Francis McKimmy, who also test. girl 21.	Eliza McKimmie	November 12,1799
Zach. Holland Sec. Ch. Cushman. Wm. Pack, father of girl Consented. (Park ?)	Mary Pack	November 19,1799
Sampson Littleton Sec. Joseph Marmaduke Cockrill	Kelly Cockrill	December 10,1799
Joseph Shearman Sec. Noble Beveridge. Thomas Chinn, father of girl, consented. Catharine Murray, witness.	Susannah Chinn	November 28,1799
Jacob Spring Sec. John Fally, father of girl.	Elizabeth Fally	October 29,1799
John Shedaker Sec. C. Binns, Jr.	Sally Willis, widow	August 12, 1799
Bazell Street Sec. Harmon Bitzer	Hannah Calor, widow of Cameron Parish	December 11, 1799
Adam Goff Sec. Charles Binns,Jr. Anthony Wright test. the girl 21.	Letitia Delehan	February 19,1799
Cornelius Skinner Sec.Charles Roberts, who also test. the girl 21.	Sarah Smarr, widow, of Cameron Parish	August 17, 1799
Reuben S. Homan Sec. John Griffith	Martha Griffith	February 25,1799
Daniel French Sec. Amos Dunham,Jr., father of the girl.	Eunice Dunham	January 14, 1800
Levy Baggerly Sec. James Lewis, who also test. the girl 21.	Kessiah Guy	December 24, 1799

Name of Groom	Name of Bride	Date of Bond

Thomas Pack,Jr.   Christiana Tucker,widow February 13, 1799
Sec. Jesse Phillips

John Mudd   Patty Gibbs of Cameron March 9, 1799
Sec. John Dowdell   Parish
Henrietta Gibbs, mother of girl, consented.

Daniel Lovett   Rachell Cruthers February 8, 1799
Sec. George McManamay, also test. girl 21.

John West   Elizabeth Dawson February 4, 1799
Sec. Wm. Dawson

Thomas Murphy   Jemima Davis   January 9, 1799
Sec. Finley Murphey. Charles & Bety Davis, parents of girl, consented.
Henley Murphey and John Davis, wit.

Archibald Morrison   Nancy Roper   January 26, 1799
Sec. John H. Canby

James Shore   Sarah Burson   October 10, 1799
Sec. Alex. Waugh. Benj. Burson, father of girl, deceased. Aaron Burson,
son of James Burson, consented.

Edward Milner   Jane Updike   November 3, 1799
Sec. Matthew Orrison, who also test. girl 21.

Wm. Beveridge   Lucy Chinn   November 6, 1799
Sec. Jas. Pickett. Rawleigh Chinn, father of girl consented. Jos. Shearn
wit. Jas. Pickett 2nd, wit.

John Muirhead   Martha Myers   September 28,1799
Sec. Dl. Barecraft. John Myers test. his dau. over 21.

George Seygar   Christiana Firestone October 7, 1799
Sec. Reynolds Hillison, who also test. girl 21.

Gabriel McGeath   Patty Adams   October 20,1799
Sec. Joseph Vandevanter. John Adams, consented and test. girl over 21.

Joseph Shields   Pamelia Scatterday March 11, 1799
Sec. Thomas Davis

Abner Craven   Sarah Sinclair of   November 9, 1799
Sec. George Sinclair   Cameron Parish
Sam'l. Sinclair consented and test. girl over 21.

Samuel Painter   Martha Martin   August 12, 1799
Sec. Luke Green

Name of Groom	Name of Bride	Date of Bond
Smallwood Middleton Sec. Joseph Gore Thomas Lewcas consented and test. girl over 21.	Casey or Thessa Lucas of Cameron Parish	June 12, 1799
Wm. Morris Sec. Edw. Morris	Edy Cantor, widow	June 15, 1799
Conrad Shavor Sec. George Razor	Mary Magdalene Razor	June 10, 1799
Peter C. Rust Sec. Wm. Elgin. Mandley Taylor, father of girl, consented and test. she over 21. Wit: Phebe Elgin.	Elizabeth Taylor	December 1, 1799
George Buffington Sec. Edw. Panter, father of girl.	Nancy Panter	March 4, 1816
Jonathan Bradfield Sec. Uriah McNight	Nancy McNight	November 12, 1804
John Fortney Sec. Alex. Langley, who also test. girl over 21.	Mary Langley	February 26, 1817
George Sullivan Sec. Sampson Hutchison. He also test. girl 21.	Winney Bussell of Cameron Parish	August 20, 1817
James Hamilton Sec. John Bishop	Sarah Gilasby	February 22, 1816
John Newlon Sec. Edw. Carter	Ruth Carter	December 17, 1799
William Furr Sec. Jesse Bates, father of girl.	Nancy Bates	July 23, 1799
George Newlon Sec. John Urton, father of girl.	Winifred Urton	October 5, 1799
Ezra Fox Sec. Michael Shryock	Mary Shryock of Cameron Parish	July 27, 1799
Stephen Gibbins Sec. John Swart He also test. girl 21.	Catherine Swart of Cameron Parish	October 14, 1799
John Seygar Sec. C. Binns, Jr.	Eve Crombacker, widow	October 14, 1799

Name of Groom	Name of Bride	Date of Bond
Samuel Runnels	Elizabeth Davis	

Samuel Davis consented to dau.'s marriage August 29,1801. no bond.

| Abraham Fouch | Nancy Sedgwick, widow | March 31, 1787 |

Sec. John Curry

| Jacob Fouch | Penna McDaniel | March 1, 1786 |

Sec. William Williams

| Isaac Fouch,Jr. | Nancy Coxenals Halling | September 23, 1792 |

Sec. Thos. Fouch, who also test. girl over 21.

| Jonathan Fouch | Chloe McDaniel | May 6, 1795 |

Sec. Aaron Sanders. Stephen Emry test. bride over 21.

| George Fouch | Susannah Moss | April 12, 1796 |

Sec. Thomas Moss, father of girl.

| Eli Janney | Elizabeth White | February 27, 1801 |

Sec. Sam'l Gregg.

| John Shaw | Rebeckah Broomhall | November 26,1799 |

Sec. John H. Canby. John Schooley,Jr., test. to age of girl.

| Ebenezer Grubb | Mary Smallwood | April 4, 1801 |

Sec. Bayn Smallwood, father of girl.

| George Fritz | Mary Hague | August 13, 1802 |

Sec. Stephen Donaldson

| Elijah Hunter | Elizabeth Sexton of | February 3, 1801 |
| Sec.James Solomon | Cameron Parish | |

He also test. both above 21.

| Thomas White | Kitty M. Hamilton | January 6, 1806 |

Sec. James M. Hamilton, who proved ages of both.

| Thomas Carr | Pricilla Wade | January 28, 1807 |

Sec. Robert Waid.

| Ambrose Fox | Sarah McManaman | June 27,1797 |

Sec. James McManaman, also test. girl 21.

| Torrence Tigh (Figh)? | Anne Porton | November 7, 1796 |

Sec. Leon'd Porton

| Michael Fisher | Catharine Ruse | October 11, 1802 |

Sec. Wm. Hamilton

Name of Groom	Name of Bride	Date of Bond

Thomas Fox   Mary Hutchison   August 6, 1795
Sec. Sammuel Riddle. Joseph Fox & Jeremiah Hutchison,Jr. consented.
(Name reads Amos Fox,Jr. in body of bond)

Martin Forbs   Rebekah Wilson   March 31, 1797
Sec. Robert Wilson

Nicholas Feagan   Nancy Stone   August 22, 1796
Sec. Stephen Hatton(?). Nancy Stone test. she bet. 29 & 30 yrs. of age.
Wit: John Hoff

Peter Frye   Sarah Jacobs of   December 10,1796
Sec. Thos. Jacobs   Cameron Parish

John Fearst   Michael Myers   November 1, 1796
Sec. Wm. Harrison, who also made oath girl over 21.

Philip Frye(Frey)   Catharine Virtz   April 1, 1796
Sec. Conrod Verts.

Nicholas Frye   Margt. Ansell   March 11, 1794
Sec. Richard W. John. John Erskins test. bride over 21.

James Neville Fishback   Sarah Harrison,widow   March 17,1795
Sec. Archibald Wilson

Thomas Finch   Nancy Howell of   April 2, 1795
Sec.John Howell,father of girl Cameron Parish

James Fox   Rebeccah Jeans, widow,
Sec. Francis Hereford   of Cameron Parish   June 9, 1794

John French   Catharine Carter   March 13, 1794
Sec. Thomas Lewis,Jr. Richard Carter, father of girl, test. she 21.
Agnes Carter, mother of girl.

James Fitzimmons   Mary Kelly of   February 5, 1793
Sec. Conn O'Neale   Cameron Parish
He test. both over 21.

James French   Nancy Collins,orphan   December 18,1793
Sec. James Bready. Wm.Lane of Farmers Delight,test bride 23 or 24.

Robert Fulton,Jr.   Sarah Powell   September 26,1792
Sec. Elisha Powell, who also consented.

John Flanegan   Betsey Cunnard of   August 29, 1792
Sec. Hopkins Rice   Cameron Parish
He also test. age of girl.

Name of Groom	Name of Bride	Date of Bond
Jacob Falley Sec. John Falley	Barbara Muse	March 26, 1792
William Fowke Sec. Robert D. Fowke, who also test. girl over 21.	Mary Mason Bronaugh	October 2, 1792
William Ford Sec. Thos. Cockerille. Rich'd Simpson of Cameron Par., father of girl, and test. both 21.	Mellion Simson	October 29, 1792
Pat'k Floriday Sec. Richard Allison	Cassandor Allison	March 7, 1792
George Fling Sec. Leven Knolls or Knotts.	Amelia Lattimore of Cameron Parish	April 12, 1791
George Falley Sec. Tho. Shaffar	Mary Wolf	February 18, 1791
Thomas Flagg Sec. Josiah White, Jr.	Martha Ransom	October 9, 1792
Enoch Furr Sec. James Urton	Sarah Clawson	March 5, 1787
Isaac Fleetwood Sec. Michl. Kinjelo, who also test. girl 21.	Sarah Rider	February 13, 1790
William Floyd Sec. Wm. Grimes. James & Margaret Watkins, parents of girl.	Hannah Vance, widow	October 5, 1790
John Filler Sec. William Wenner, Jr., who also test. to age of girl.	Eliz. Bordon	October 23, 1790
Dan'l Farnsworth Sec. Stephen Mahony, who also test. to age of girl.	Sarah Hiskett	December 11, 1780
Thomas Fredd Sec. James Torbert, who also test. age of girl.	Eliza Torbert	August 2, 1788
Moren Fowler Sec. Daniel Moxly, who also test. age of girl.	Susanna Moxley	December 25, 1788
Lewis Tavenner Sec. Benj. Wiggenton Samuel & Robert Scott test. girl 22 first of next June.	Elizabeth Fox of Cameron Parish	February 18, 1781
Hugh Fulton Sec. Joseph Lybough, who also test. to age of girl.	Susannah Lybough	January 19, 1780

Name of Groom	Name of Bride	Date of Bond

Thomas Fouch   Sarah Combs   June 8, 1779
Sec. Joseph Coombs.   Jno. Combs, father of girl, consented.

William Fulton   Hanah Millan of   September 21,1779
Sec. Daniel Howell   Cameron Parish
Wit:Thomas Millan.   William Millan, father of girl, test. age.

William Field   Elizabeth Jones   September 13, 1773
Sec. John Jones, father of girl.

John Field   Margaret Pearle   November 3, 1767
Sec. William Pearle

Daniel Feagins   Violet Combs   February 3, 1767
Sec. Christopher Metcalfe.   Joseph Combs, father of girl, consented.

Benjamin Favor   Pamelia Stephens   March 1, 1787
Sec. Edward Hopkins.   (Edward Faver in body of bond)

John Frye   Susannah Keedar   May 6, 1786
Sec. Nicholas Keedar

John Fidler   Rebeccah Lambert,widow   July 15, 1786
Sec. Stephen Roszel

Joseph Franklin   Elizabeth Smyth   February 25, 1786
Sec. William Terry

John Farlow   Mary Suddoth of   October 23, 1784
Sec. Thomas Fouch   Cameron Parish

Colvin Finch   Sinah Simmonds of   December 3, 1782
Sec. John Ritchie   Cameron Parish

William Francis   Mary Romine   February 6, 1787
Sec. Israel Brown.   John Romine, father of girl.

David Fulton   Rachel Smith   October 29, 1787
Sec. Robert Fulton, who test. to her age.

William Fling   Ann Lattimore   December 13, 1787
Sec. Samuel Jackson

John (James) Fawley   Margaret Wilson   August 10, 1787
Sec. Adam Wolf

William Fox   Mary Braden   February 22, 1790
Sec. James Fox

End of bundle of bonds 1767 - 1816

Name of Groom	Name of Bride	Date of Bond

John Case   Christena Crim   April 6,1809
Sec. Charles Crim, father of girl. wit:Peter Rickard, Thos.F.Jenkins.

Thos. Kiphart   Mary Skinner   March 4, 1809
Sec. Corn's Skinner

Joseph White   Margaret Braden   February 6, 1809
Sec. John Braden, who also test. ages.

Josiah McKnight   Hannah Thomas   April 10,1809
Sec. Uriah McKnight. John Thomas, father of girl, consented.
Wit:Leah Thomas

Job McPherson   Mary Beatty   June 1, 1809
Sec. Isaac Fry, who also test. ages.

John Howell   Patty Reed   December 26,1809
Sec. James Reed

Henry Axline   Catharine Roof   December 26,1809
Sec. John Axline, who also test. ages.

Isaac Shunk   Bethany Oxley   December 23, 1809
Sec. Everitt Oxley, father of the girl.

John Lee   Elenor Wade   December 23, 1809
Sec. Hez'h Wade, father of girl. He test. groom's age.

Nathaniel Triplett   Mary Luckett, widow   December 21, 1809
Sec. Wm. Butler

Daniel McMullen   Barbara Stoneburner   March 13, 1809
Sec. Wm. McMullen, father of groom.

John Stare (Steer)   Elenor Boothe   December 13, 1809
Sec. James Boothe, father of girl, also test. groom 21.

Josiah Winn   Margaret Moore   December 11, 1809
Sec. Samuel Moore, who test. age of girl. William Winn, father. Wit:
John Chamblin

George Troute   Sarah Fisher   December 10, 1809
Sec. Josiah Moffett

Henry B. Downs   Cyntha Beans   December 11, 1809
Sec. James Beans. Jesse Downs test. groom's age.

Nicholas Ropp   Elizabeth Waltman   December 11,1809
Sec. Jacob Waltman, gdn. of girl, he also test. ages.

Name of Groom	Name of Bride	Date of Bond

Marcus Humphrey   Margaret Marks   June 5, 1809
Sec. Bennit Marks. Abel Marks, father, auth. lic. Wit.Thomas Marks.

William Taylor   Euphamy Brown   June 3, 1809
Sec. Mahlon Bewly. Aaron Divine test. age of girl.

James Reed   Rebecca Copeland,widow March 7, 1809
Sec. Henson Vermilion

Joel Osburn   Massey Osburne   March 30, 1809
Sec. James Heaton, gdn. of girl.

Isaac Hughes   Sarah Hixon   April 3, 1809
Sec. James Hixson, father of girl.

Levi Phillips   Rebecah Nutt   April 10, 1809
Sec. Thomas Nutt. Joseph Nutt, father, auth. lic. Wit:Rich'd Matthews.
                                                    Cameron Parish
William Solomon   Henrietta Cullison of/ September 19,1809
Sec. Jermiah Cullison, who also test. groom's age.

Presley Williams   Jane Hixon   May 2, 1810
Sec. Stephenson Hixson

Thomas Renoe   Sarah Beavers   January 18,1809
Sec. James Beavers, who also test. ages.

Jeremiah Harris   Izabella Ewers   January 9, 1809
Sec. Robert Ewers, who test. ages.

Jacob Goodheart   Polley Fawley   March 27,1809
Sec. John Fawley, father of girl, consented & test. groom's age.

William Phillips   Anney Oxley   March 18,1809
Sec. David Philips

Nathan Prince   Mary Ann Ross   March 22, 1809
Sec. Simon Ross, father, consented, and test. groom's age.

Stephen Garrett   Euphame Beans   November 20,1809
Sec. James Beans, who also test. groom's age

Frederick Filler   Elizabeth Cordell   March 22, 1809
Sec. Adam Cordell, father of girl consented, and test. groom's age.

Abel James   Sarah Heath of   March 22, 1809
Sec. James McKim   Cameron Parish
Andrew & Hanah Heath, parents of Sarah, consented.

Name of Groom	Name of Bride	Date of Bond

Lee Cockrell   Delilah Hepburne   November 16,1809
Sec. Mahlon Roach, gdn. of girl. Elias Cockrill test. groom's age.

George Roach   Sarah Cummings   November 11, 1809
Sec. John Cummings, father of girl, he also test. age of groom.

Daniel Bunnell   Nancy Thomas   November 13, 1809
Sec. Wm. Harned, gdn. of girl.

Edward Davis   Mary Tillett   November 22, 1809
Sec. Giles Tillett, father of girl.

John Bumcrots   Christiana Emery   November 28,1809
Sec. Adam Emry, who test. to age of girl.

Michael Reily   Eliza Conden, widow   November 25, 1809
Sec. Thos. Jacobs

John Matthews   Lynda Moreland   November 14,1809
Sec. Philip Moreland

Casper Spring   Elizabeth Slater   December 4,1809
Sec. Jacob Slater, father of girl, he also test. groom's age.

Jesse Evans   Mary Gideon   January 9, 1809
Sec. Peter Gideon, father of girl.

Eli Janney   Sarah Vandevanter   January 23, 1809
Sec. Joseph Vandevanter, who test. the girl's age.

William Hoge   Mary McGeath of   December 11, 1809
Sec. Stephen McGeath   Cameron Parish

Jacob Late   Elizabeth Miller   September 25,1809
Sec. Christian Miller

George Fichter   Sarah Thomas   March 11, 1809
Sec. James McManaman

Joseph James   Rebeckah Garrett   October 30,1809
Sec. Samuel Garrett

George Head   Polly Gover   January 9, 1809
Sec. Joseph Talbott

William Copeland   Lydia Brown   April 17, 1809
Sec. Mahlon Janney,Jr. James Brown and Christiana, his wife, parents
of girl, consent. Wit:James Brown,Jr.

Jeremiah Cloud   Sidney Brown   April 17,1809
Sec. Mahlon Janney,Jr. James Brown & Christiana, his wife, parents of
girl, consent.

Name of Groom	Name of Bride	Date of Bond
George Sheid Sec. Chas. Gullatt	Rebecah Fox, widow of Cameron Parish	April 20, 1809
Eli Nichols Sec. Thomas White, father of girl, test. ages of both.	Elizabeth White	December 9, 1809
Joseph Horseman Sec.William Whaley	Hannah Whaley of Cameron Parish	August 19, 1809
George McKinney Sec. Eli Offutt. Nancy Thomas test. girl over 21.	Elizabeth Thomas	March 4, 1809
Amos Neer Sec. Wm. Paxson, gdn. of girl. Samuel Neer test. groom of age.	Sarah Connard	September 21, 1809
Levi Wilcoxon Sec.John A.Harris,father of girl.	Catharine H.Harris of Cameron Parish	March 9, 1809
James Hill Sec. Charles Taylor	Hannah Taylor	July 1, 1809
John Nieswanger Sec. Christian Nieswanger. Catherine Niswanger consented for her dau.	Mary Ann Nieswanger	June 17, 1809
Thomas Templer Sec. Thomas Lowe. Jas. Templer, father of groom, consented.	Jane Lowe	December 25, 1809
John Dilloe Sec.Frederick Darflinger,father of girl, test. groom's age.	Elizabeth Darflinger	June 24, 1809
John Brown Sec. Moses Dowdell	Elizabeth Davis	June 12, 1809
William Walker Sec. Hugh Wylie, father of girl	Ann Wiley	June 12,1809
Josiah Walraven Sec. Jno. West	Lydia West	September 25,1809
James Collett Sec. William Collett, father of girl consented. Levi Whaley test. her age.	Mary Carter of Cameron Parish	February 16, 1809
Jacob Davis Sec. Thomas Davis, father of groom.	Susannah Beamer	February 13, 1809
Fielder Thomas John Gist, Sec. and father of girl, consented.	Violet Gist of Cameron Parish	February 2, 1809

Name of Groom	Name of Bride	Date of Bond

William Cline   Margaret Carr   July 4, 1809
Sec. Thomas Carr, who test. girl over 21.

Robert Cummings   Mary Carter   January 30, 1809
Sec. Thomas Carter

William Campbell   Jane Wynkoop   January 16, 1809
Sec. Garrad Wynkoop, who test. girl 21. Andrew Campbell, father of
groom consented. Cornelius Wynkoop, father of girl consented and test.
his dau. was born Dec. 14, 1787.

Thomas Collins   Effamah Harper   January 27, 1809
Sec. Valentine Ford. Thomas Harper,father of girl consented. Wit.
Elizabeth Harper.

Henry Howser   Agnes Wildman   May 6, 1809
Sec. Simon Binns. Joseph Wildman consented.

John S. Cranwell   Susan Newton   February 18, 1809
Sec. Jos. T. Newton, gdn. of girl.

Daniel Cooper   Elizabeth Sanders   August 12, 1809
Sec. John Bumcrots

Moses Frazier   Phoebe Race   May 9, 1809
Sec. Phillip Long, who was guardian of both.

John Sample   Lucy Smith   June 12, 1809
Sec. Israel Phillips, who test. girl over 21.

Edward B. Grady   Sarah Taylor   May 19, 1809
Sec. Peter C. Rust, who test. ages.

William McFarling   Rachel Lewis   August 18, 1809
Sec. Samuel Moore, gdn. of girl.

John Fossett   Hannah Batement   August 16, 1809
Sec. John Bartlett

John Poulton   Hannah Marshall   August 14, 1809
Sec. Charles Poulton. John Marshall, father of girl, consented.

William Lafaber   Mary Oatyer of   August 9, 1809
Sec.Peter Oatyar,father of Cameron Parish
girl.

Benjamin Philips   Jemiah Grayham   July 26, 1809
Sec. Israel Phillips. John Grayham, test. age of girl.

Name of Groom	Name of Bride	Date of Bond
Solomon Oden Sec. Hezekiah Athey	Milly Ann Athey of Cameron Parish	July 5, 1809
Thomas Carter Sec. James Pyott. John Pyott, father of girl, auth. license.	Sarah Pyott	January 7, 1809
Charles Brookbank Sec. John Wynn	Hannah Hughs	August 8, 1809
Peter Jett Sec. Joseph Lane, gdn. of girl.	Nancy Lane	October 26, 1809
Henry Freed Sec. Israel Phillips, test. age. John Clyce, father of girl consented.	Catharine Clyce	January 21, 1809
Maky Talton Sec. Israel Phillips. Amos Hague, father of girl, consented.	Plezy Hague	February 20, 1809
Michael Howard Sec. John Ullam, father of girl, who also test. groom's age.	Elizabeth Ullam	February 6, 1809
Thomas Stevens Sec. Joseph Purcel, who also test. girl's age.	Ann Purcel	March 6, 1809
William Forgison Sec. Wm. Woodford	Phoebe Golden	March 13, 1809
David Hixson Sec. Daniel Rawlings	Catharine Ruse	May 27, 1809
Adam Smitley Sec. William Kindal, who also test. to ages.	Jane James	June 8, 1809
Leonard Pinkstaff Sec. Samuel Turner	Delila Glasscock, widow	March 7, 1809
Jacob Gooly Sec. Cornelius Morgan	Margaret Shively of Cameron Parish	January 6, 1809
William Robertson Sec. Jesse Timms	Sarah Fernandis of Cameron Parish	March 8, 1809
Christian Miller Sec. Conrod Near, father of girl.	Sarah Near	January 7, 1809
Lendorus Steel Sec. William Moreland, father of girl.	Mary Moreland of Cameron Parish	August 30, 1809

Name of Groom	Name of Bride	Date of Bond

Lewis Jury   Mary Richards   November 13, 1809
Sec. John Richards

Joseph Fred   Hannah Pierce   December 4, 1809
Sec. Wm. Chambers. Thomas Fred consented for his son.

Thomas Curtis   Fanny Sinclair   January 9, 1809
Sec. Alijah Sands. Hamilton Rogers, gdn. of girl.

Benjamin Hixson   Tacey Humphrey   April 10, 1809
Sec. James Hixson. Abner Humphrey present and gave consent.

Daniel J. Minor   Pleasant Nixon   March 30, 1809
Sec. George Nixon

John Marks   Sarah Powell   December 9, 1809
Sec. John Overfield. William Powell, father of girl, consented.

Richard Carter   Deborah Newlon   April 17, 1809
Sec. Jesse Newlon

Richard Brown   Elizabeth Davis   September 25, 1809
Sec. William Brown, father of groom.

Christopher Howser   Rosannah Lafaber   October 14, 1809
Sec. William Lafaber, who test. the girl's age.

Benjamin Wills   Charrity Furr   April 10, 1809
Sec. Samuel Berkley,Jr. Enoch Furr, father of girl, consented.

Jacob Crim   Susana Abel   May 24, 1809
Sec. George Abel

John Wade   Hannah Myers   September 13, 1809
Sec. Thomas Myers

Richard Riley   Elizabeth McCartor   November 9, 1809
Sec. Moses McCartor

James Heaton   Leah Carter   September 18,1809
Sec. William Carter. James Heaton, father of groom consented. Thomas
Drake, grandfather of groom consented. Deborah Richards, mother of groom
also consented.

Reubin Tumblin   Catharine Smallwood   March 14, 1809
Sec. Ezekiel Chambling

Stephen Ball   Mary Bradon   April 14, 1809
Sec. Mahlon Janney Jr.

Name of Groom	Name of Bride	Date of Bond
John Wyngrove Sec. John Divers	Maria Huldfish	March 23, 1809
John Harbert Sec. James Hutchison.	Lettice Hutchison of Cameron Parish Joseph Hutchison, girl's father, consented.	January 23, 1809
William Brown Sec. Sam'l Gregg	Sarah Walters	April 13, 1809
John Casey Sec. Jeremiah Cloud. George Warner, father of girl, consented.	Hannah Warner	January 16, 1809
Matthew Hays Sec. William Carter, father of girl.	Rhoda Carter	January 16, 1809
Thomas Gheen Sec. James Harrop	Nancy Harrop	January 13, 1809
William Davis Sec. Harmon Bitzer	Catharine Bitzer	March 13, 1809
Michael Ruse Sec. John Bellard	Rachel Bellard	March 13, 1809
William Clendening Sec. Thomas Russell. William Russell, girl's father, consented. Wit: Henry Russell	Ruth Russell	March 28, 1809
James Welsh Sec. Benjamin Walker	Mary Walker	March 5, 1813
Stephen Daniel Sec. Wm. Wright	Catharine McGeath	March 20, 1813
David Alexander Sec.And'rw McMullin, test. both 21	Elizabeth McMullin	May 10, 1813
Thomas Beal Sec. Ford Jacobs	Margaret Jacobs	May 11, 1813
David Newlon Sec. William Richards	Rachel Richards	March 15, 1813
Nathan Prescott Sec. Jas. Lucas. Mary Lucas test. groom over 21.	Mahala Lucas	March 20, 1813
George Gallighar Sec. Joseph Longly,Jr. John Littlejohn test. girl 21.	Catharine McCuan	November 5, 1796

Name of Groom	Name of Bride	Date of Bond
Jacob Gore Sec. John Barruch	Mary Barruck	August 18, 1797
Joseph Garrett Sec. Benjamin Garrett	Margt. Garrett	November 11, 1791
Peter Callihan Sec. Arthur Henderson	Catherine Specht, widow	July 25, 1796
Francis Keen Sec. Thomas Marshall, father	Mary Marshall of Cameron Parish	September 7, 1796
Moses Bartholomew Sec. George Sagar	Elizabeth Sagar	October 22, 1796
William Elgin Sec. Mandly Taylor, father of girl.	Phoebe Taylor	April 10,1797
Nicholas Gray Sec. David Martin	Mary Hall	June 9, 1796
Cornelius Skinner 3rd Sec. Peter Carr, father of girl.	Jane Carr	September 20,1796
Aaron Sanders Sec. Benja. Sanders	Mary Sanders	December 31, 1796

- - - - - -

Name of Groom	Name of Bride	Date of Bond
George Cooper Sec. Jacob Spring, father of girl.	Milly Spring	June 2, 1829
Samuel Thomas Sec. Jno. Mahoney, who also test. as to their ages.	Betsey Mahoney	May 19,1829
John Conard Sec. A. L. Anderson. George Gregg, father of girl consented. Wit:Matilda Jacobs	Eleanor Gregg	May 2, 1829
Henry W. Ward Sec. Samuel Dishman and George Ward	Emily Dishman	April 9, 1829
John Smith Sec. William Grubb. Ebenezer Grubb, father of girl, consented. Wit: Samuel Neer	Sarah Grubb	March 4, 1829
Frederick Roller Sec. Michael Wiard	Rachel Wiard	February 26,1829
Benjamin F. Taylor Sec. Albert Heaton, who also test. ages.	Nancy Taylor	February 14, 1829

Name of Groom	Name of Bride	Date of Bond

Wilson C. Selden Jr.   Eliza A. Lee of   June 10,1828
No Sec. Wit:Chs.G.Eskridge Cameron Parish

William Hammat   Sophia Waters   July 9,1829
Sec. Wm. D. Drish, who also test. age of girl.

James B. Dennis   Harriet McAtee   October 19,1829
Sec. Andrew Beveridge
Harrison McAtee, father of girl, auth. license. Wit:John C.Elgin

Joseph Thomas   Sarah Worthington   September 28,1829
Sec. Craven Osburn, who also test. ages of both.

Jno. Smith   Mary Ann Davis   September 8,1829
Sec. Anthony Davis

Philip Goodridge   Nancy Jacobs   August 21,1829
Sec. John Moore, who test. groom's age. Jno. Rose test. for girl.

Jno. L. Powell   Maria Louisa Grady   October 12,1829
Sec. Wm. O. Chilton
E.B.Grady, father of girl, auth. license.

Presley McDaniel   Mary Lightfoot   November 26,1829
Sec. Robert Moffett, who also test. groom's age, and consented for
girl, he being her guardian.

Peyton Wey   Rachel Mink   November 3,1829
Sec. Lawrence Mink
Thomas H. Wey, test. as to age of groom.

Leroy Balinger   Elizth Ann Gibson   November 3,1829
Sec. Guilford Gregg
Thomas Hatcher made affirmation that groom upward of 21 and Solomon
Gibson, father of girl, gave his consent.

David Beatty   Dicey Polen   November 2,1829
Sec. Adam Barr, who also test. girl's age.

William Jenkins   Elizth. Dove of   December 24,1829
Sec. William Dove,   Cameron Parish
father of girl. He also consented.

John Hunter   Jane Rose   December 18,1829
Sec. Alfred Rose.
Richard Rose, father of girl, auth. license.

Name of Groom	Name of Bride	Date of Bond

Robert Y. Conrad   Elizth. W. Powell   December 8,1829
Sec. Geo. C. Powell
Burr Powell, father of girl, auth.license. Wit: Benj. Smith

William Jackson   Margaret Stoneburner   December 16, 1829
Sec. James Gilmore

Gunnell Saunders   Rachel Ann Saunders   December 17,1829
Sec. Thomas Sanders, also test. ages of both.

Enoch Harris   Elizabeth Davis   December 28,1829
Sec. John Davis, also test. ages of both.

Lloyd N. Rogers   Hortensia M. Hay of   June 24, 1829
Sec. George Hay, father,   Cameron Parish
of girl, who auth. license. Wit:James Monroe, Egbert R.Watson

Charles Shafer   Eve Julian Sackman   July 18,1829
Sec. Samuel Sackman,
J.Martin Sackman, father of girl, auth. license. Wit:Henry Hickman.

Richard Howser   Mary Ann Haig   December 21,1829
Sec. James Haig

Franklin Poulton   Rachel Dowlan   December 21,1829
Sec. Alfred A. Eskridge
Hy.Reed Poulton test. age of groom. Sarah McDaniel of Frederick Co.,
Va., test. she mother of Rachel and test. she 21. Wit:Daniel Gold.

Joseph Potterfield   Elizabeth Ann Alder   December 19,1829
Sec. John Allder

John Janney   Elizabeth Wilkinson of   December 14,1829
Sec. Jno. A. Binns   Cameron Parish
Thos. Wilkinson test. he the father of Elizabeth and that she was born
in the year 1806. Sworn before S.Hough,J.P.

Joseph Cockerill   Jane Poulton, Spinster   December 14,1829
Sec. George Briscoe, who was also guardian of Jane Fulton

Thomas B. Barrick   Hannah McDaniel   December 12,1829
Sec. Coleman R.Brown (Thomas B.Barrett in body of bond)

John P.H. Short   Elizth. J. Atwell   December 14,1829
Sec. James H. McVeigh
Jesse McVeigh, gdn. of girl, test. she the daughter of late Thomas Atwel
and auth. license. Wit:James H.McVeigh, James Surghnor, Town'd McVeigh

Name of Groom	Name of Bride	Date of Bond
Wesley Brabham Sec. Harrison Knight	Elizabeth Orr,Spinster	December 11, 1829
John P. Smart Sec. Joseph Hilliard	Emely Hilliard,Spinster	November 25, 1829
Timothy Conner Sec. John A. Moore	Pleasant R. Dailey	November 16,1829

Jno. Dailey, of Waterford, Loudoun County,Va., test. that Pleasant
was his daughter and consented.

William Wire Sec. Jonathan Potterfield	Catherine Potterfield	November 14,1829
John M. Young Sec. Samuel C. Allen	Teresa Allen,Spinster	November 2,1829
Samuel Baker Sec. Jacob Shriver	Sarah Shriver,Spinster	November 2,1829
George P. Rhodes Sec. S.M.Boss	Catherine Dyer	October 31,1829
Philip Vinsel Sec. Philip Everheart, father of the girl.	Luisia Everheart	October 31,1829
Chelton Parker Sec. John Vandevanter, guardian of the girl.	Sarah Sears	October 13,1829
Robert Cunningham Sec. Wm. Saffer	Eliza Settle	September 14,1829
Daniel T. Mathias Sec. John H. McCabe	Martha Oswald	September 15,1829
Samuel Ullum Sec. Anthony Davis, father of the girl.	Elizabeth Davis	August 10,1829
William Sutherland Sec.William McNabb	Elizabeth Lowe of Cameron Parish	August 10,1829

Bond unsigned. William Sutherland auth. license for his son William
Sutherland,Jr. Wit. Robert Rookard

William Moran Sec.James E.Edwards	Mary Lyne of Cameron Parish	September 15,1829

William Lyne auth. license for his dau. Wit:Hezekiah Ellis, Thomas Lyne

Alpheus Gibson	Harriet A. Aldridge	October 6,1829

Sec.Moses Gibson Sr. father of groom. Jno. Aldridge father of the
girl, auth. license.

Name of Groom	Name of Bride	Date of Bond
Enos Updike Sec. John Wornal. Landon C.Carter test. age of groom.	Barsena White	August 10,1829
Thomas Unglesbee Sec. John Smitly	Mahala Kindall	August 10,1829
Norman Cummings Sec. Jess Lewis, who also test. ages of both.	Hannah Urton	August 10,1829
William Anders Sec. John C. Bozzill. Joseph McDonald test. groom's age.	Mary Griffith,widow	August 10,1829
Adam Barr Sec. David Beatty	Mary Beatty	July 27,1829
Daniel Thatcher Sec. Geo. H. Allder. Calvin Thatcher made oath as to groom's age.	Louisa Palmer	June 11,1829
Maaziah Thomas Sec. Jeremiah C. Furr. Enoch Furr, father of girl, consented. Wit:Thompson Furr.	Elizth. Furr	June 8,1829
Jaquelin A. Berkeley Sec. William Noland	Mary B. Fontaine of Cameron Parish	June 8,1829.
Aaron Russell Sec. Taliferro M.McIlhany. Mortimer McIlhany test. as to ages of both.	Tamson Underwood	June 2,1829
Amos Jenkins Sec.Silvester Jenkins, father of the groom.	Catherine Jenkins of Cameron Parish	May 29,1829
Nathan Gregg Sec. Sam'l Pursel Jr.	Susan B. Gregg	May 16,1829
Thos. E. Hatcher Sec. Samuel Pursel Jr.	Elizabeth P.Gregg	May 16,1829
Lewis Steele Sec. Isaac Workman, father of the girl.	Matilda Workman,Spinster	May 13,1829
John James Sec. David James	Sarah James of Cameron Parish	May 13,1829
James Gibson Sec.Samuel Beans and Solomon Gibson, parents.	Mary Beans, Spinster	May 11, 1829
Henry Greenwood Sec. Henry Stoneburner	Margaret Stoneburner	May 11,1829
James Whaley Sec.Silas Hutchison	Mary Ann Whaley of Cameron Parish	May 11,1829

Name of Groom	Name of Bride	Date of Bond

Daniel Ritchie   Louisa Axline   May 11,1829
Sec. David Axline, father of the girl.

Asa Rogers   Ellen L. Orr   May 2,1829
Sec. W.A.Powell

Alfred D. Offutt   Elizabeth C.Washington   April 21,1829
Sec. E.S.Washington. Eli Offutt test. as to ages of both.

Archibald Atkinson   Elizabeth A.Chilton   April 20,1829
Sec. Wm. L. Powell

Joseph Frye   Margaret Fawley   April 16,1829
Sec. Jno. Fawley, father of the girl.

Edward S. Washington   Ann E. Ellzey   April 14,1829
Sec. M.McIlhany.
L. Ellzey, father of girl, consented. Wit. M.McIlhany

William H. Foster   Rachel Hibbs,widow of   April 14,1829
Sec.Thomas A.Drean   Cameron Parish

Carter Moss   Susan Beveridge of   April 13,1829
Sec. Andrew Beveridge,   Cameron Parish
brother of girl. William Fulton, test. as to age of groom.

Archibald Vickers   Pleasant Nichols   April 13,1829
Sec. Nathaniel Nichols, guardian of girl.

George Plaster   Mary Tracy   May 12,1829
Sec. Col. Ben Mitchell, guardian of girl. Henry Hutchison test. as to
groom's age.

Isaac Torreyson   Mary Baldwin   March 30,1829
Sec. John Baldwin

Rich'd K. Littleton   Keturah R.Carter   March 28,1829
Sec. Fielding Littleton.
Edward Carter, father of girl, auth. license. Wit. Burr Weeks

John W. Littleton   Elizabeth A. Tavenner   March 21, 1829
Sec. James Tavenner, father of the girl.

George Alder   Margaret Filler   March 11,1829
Sec. Samuel Cordell.

Norris Board   Emily Orum   March 11, 1829
Sec. Henry Orum

Name of Groom	Name of Bride	Date of Bond
Joshua T. Hope Sec. William Moss	Massa Gore	March 9,1829
Edon Updike Sec. George Pursel	Kezia Potts	March 9,1829
Isaiah Beans Sec. Carter Moss	Elizabeth Moss	March 9,1829
Elwood Hoge Sec. John Vansickler	Sarah Orrison	March 9,1829
Geo. Smith Marks Sec. L.C.Cunard, guardian of the girl.	Nancy Caroline Conard	March 9,1829
Landon C. Carter Sec. John Wornal. Jacob F.Humphrey test. groom's age. Landon C.Carter gdn. of girl.	Mahala Battson	March 9,1829
Amos Johnson Sec. Lovell H. Middleton who test. ages of both.	Matilda Middleton	March 7,1829
Patrick McGavick Sec. David Orison	Sarah Garner	March 3,1829
Samuel Jenkins Sec. Jno. A. Binns. Samuel Jenkins made oath that above Samuel was over 21 and Bernard Hough, father of girl, consented to license.	Louisa Hough	February 25,1829
George Sagle Sec. John Near	Susan Tower	February 24,1829
James Humphreys Sec. William McClosky, father of the girl.	Rebecca McClosky	February 12,1829
Edward Beard Sec. William Leachman	Dolly Ann Leachman	February 10,1829
Josias Adams Sec. William McClosky, guardian of groom.	Mary Ann Hill	February 9,1829
George Flinn Sec. Levi G. Ewers. John Wilson, consented for his dau. Wit.Julia Ann Hossmon.	Evelina Wilson	February 9,1829
Martin Kizer Sec. Benj. Jackson	Barbara Razer	February 9,1829
Jno. Myers Sec. Wadsworth Shephard	Mary Perry	February 4,1829

Name of Groom	Name of Bride	Date of Bond
Francis R. Simpson Sec. James Merchant, father of girl. Geo.Simpson test. age of groom.	Deborah Merchant	January 24,1829
John Kinsel (Vinsel?) Sec. John Hutchison. James Daymude test. age of groom.	Sophina Daymude	March 9,1829
William W. Hammontree Sec. John S. Manley	Dorcas Manley	January 19,1829
John A. McCormick Sec. Thomas H. Clagett Jacob Fadley,father of girl, consented. Wit. Jas. L. Martin	Ann E. Fadely	January 15,1829
Alfred Jones Sec. Thomas Poulton	Rosetta Gibson	January 12,1829
Lloyd Noland Sec. Benj. Smith	Elizabeth W. Smith	January 19,1829
Samuel Thompson Sec. Jesse Tribby	Sarah Tribby	January 5,1829
Isaac Camp Sec. Andrew Copeland	Sarah Newhouse	January 1,1829

- - - - - - -

James B. Chenoweth Sec. David I. Eaton, who test. both 21.	Eliza Davis	January 2,1830
Harrison Kent Sec. Richard Tavenner	Melinda Henry	January 7,1830
Jacob Shaffer Sec.Jacob Shaffer. Abraham Smith test. both 20 yrs. old.	Malinda Clark	January 9,1830
John Tavenner Sec. John Hesser	Usee Drake	January 11,1830
Francis Piles,Jr. Sec. Francis Piles, who test. both 21.	Catharine Gordon	January 11,1830
George McMullin Sec. Samuel Rogers, who test. girl 21.	Edith Craven	January 11,1830
Luther Cunard Sec. John Chamblin, guardian of the girl.	Amanda Bozzell	January 11,1830
James O. Stonestreet Sec. Thos. Moss, gdn. of the girl.	Amelia Tillett	January 11,1830

Name of Groom	Name of Bride	Date of Bond
Jonas Trenary Sec. Christopher Howser, who test. both 21.	Nelly Wildman	January 12,1830
Joseph Miller Sec. Jonathan Wenner, gdn. of the girl.	Mary A. Waltman	February 8,1830
Francis/King F. Sec. Abel Jones Thomas King, his father, consents.	Hannah Jones	February 15,1830
Wm. L. Craven Sec. Sinclair Craven, who test. to ages of both.	Eleanor H.Craven	February 16,1830
John Shober Sec. John Sarbaugh, who test. her age.	Elizabeth Gower	February 17,1830
Thomas Richards Sec. David Orrison, father of girl, who consented.	Margaret Orrison	February 23,1830
Thomas Beavers Sec. John Beavers, who test. to ages of both.	Delila Jenkins	March 2,1830
Thomas P.Glasscock Sec. Benjamin Rust,Jr. who test. to ages of both.	Catharine McIntyre	March 2,1830
William Taylor Sec. Eskridge H. Torbert Hezekiah Perry,father of girl, consents. Wit. Aaron G. Elwell	Margaret Perry	March 3,1830
Joseph Boxwell Sec. John Chamblin. Nancy Boxwell test. her brother Joseph bound to W.Noland of Winchester till 21, and he is now 21.	Elenor Chamblin	March 8,1830
Jesse Tavenner Sec. Mahlon Morris, father of the girl.	Ceceilia Morris	March 8,1830
John Shafer Sec. John Compher, father of the girl.	Margaret Compher	March 23,1830
Robert S. Saunders Sec. John Veal	Elizabeth Myers of Cameron Parish	March 23,1830
James L. Sampson Sec. James Stedman	Sarah Jacobs	March 25,1830
William Maghay Sec. Henry Miller, who test. both 21.	Catherine Bagent	April 5,1830
Hezekiah Shaw Sec. Jacob Smith	Elizabeth Whitmore	April 5,1830

Name of Groom	Name of Bride	Date of Bond

Samuel Piggott   Sarah Verts   April 6,1830
Sec. William Verts, father of the girl.

Abner Carter   Martha E.Carter of   April 12,1830
Sec.Richard Littleton   Cameron Parish
E. Carter consented to license for his dau. Wit. Landon Carter

William Bolon   Mary Ann Whitacre   April 13,1830
Sec. Thomas Gregg, gdn. of girl. Wit. Amos Whitacre

John Insor   Mary Jane Wooddy   April 15,1830
Sec. Crayton Saunders. M.A.Binns,gdn. of girl consented.

Arthur Rogers   Hannah Nichols   April 26,1830
Sec. Isaac Nichols, who consented for girl.

Jacob Sackman   Sarah winegardner   August 31,1831
Sec. Adam Winegardner, father of girl. J.Martin Sackman consented for
his son.

Burr Smith Walker   Mary Ann Swart   May 3,1830
Sec. James Swart, father of the girl.

Robert W. Power   Arminda Gheen of   May 10,1830
Sec. Walter Power   Cameron Parish

Isaac Fry   Catherine Eakey   May 10,1830
Sec. John Fawley, gdn. of girl.

Samuel Fry   Christena Stoneburner May 10,1830
Sec. Peter Stoneburner, gdn. of girl.

Harrison Cross   Catherine Sutherland of June 8,1830
Sec. Wm. Sutherland, father of girl.

Andrew Beveridge   Rebecca H.L.Race of   June 14,1830
Sec. John W.Race   Cameron Parish

Isaac Workman   Sarah Ann Jane German June 24,1830
Sec. Wm.L.Simpson, who test. girl's age.

Henry T. Franklin   Mary Ann Gear, widow July 17,1830
Sec. Joshua McDonoch

Jonathan Potterfield, wid. Sarah Sackman   July 27,1830
Sec. Jacob Sackman. J.Martin Sackman consented for his dau.

Name of Groom	Name of Bride	Date of Bond

James Morris   Elizabeth Fowler   July 30,1830
Sec. Baldwin Johnson, who test. her age.

Edward Coghlan   Bridget Boland   August 19,1830
Sec. Patrick Boland, who test. age of girl.

Samuel Freed   Elizabeth Trammell   August 9,1830
Sec. Thos. Templar, gdn.of girl. wit. Henry D.Freed

William Spence   Elizabeth Kirk   August 26,1830
Sec. Malcolm C.Kirk, brother, who test. to girl's age. Thomas W.
Dorman test. groom's age.

Henson Combs   Maria Tarperman   August 26,1830
Sec. Cageby Jones, test. to ages of both.

Robert Fulton   Tacey Daniel,widow   September 18,1830
Sec. Joseph D. Taylor

Jno. H. Bennett   Mary I. White   September 22,1830
Sec. John R. White. James W.McIlhany,gdn. gives consent.

Jacob Bartlett   Elizabeth Everhart   September 28,1830
Sec. Peter Derry, who test. they both 21.

Samuel Lumm   Almedia Gibson   October 11,1830
Sec. Solomon Gibson

Philip Reed   Amanda Smallwood   October 14,1830
Sec. John Thomas, who test. to ages of both.

Robin Osburn   Charlotte Miley   October 20,1830
Sec. David Osburn. John Miley gave consent for his dau. Wit.Cuthbert
Powell.

Michael Morrallee   Emily Patience Osborn October 20,1830
Sec. Nicholas Osborn, father of the girl.

Jacob Yackky   Harriet C. Neale   November 8,1830
Sec. Richard Brown, gdn. of girl.

William Trittipo   Louisa Winsel   November 8,1830
Sec. George Winsel, father of the girl.

Gustavus Elgin,Jr.   Elizabeth Cross   November 6,1830
Sec. James Cross, father of the girl.

Thomas Schley Rinker   Ann Feitchler   October 25,1830
Sec. Edward Rinker, father of girl. Jno. Binns her guardian.

Name of Groom	Name of Bride	Date of Bond
James Rogers	Martha Hawling	November 20,1830

Sec. Hamilton Rogers, gdn. of girl.

Issacher Brown — Margaret Griffith — November 22,1830
Sec. Thomas C. Gregg, who also test. to age of girl.

Washington Boteler — M. E. Cordell — December 2,1830
Sec. Presley Cordell

Mandley W. Rust — Rosetta Gibson — December 12,1830
Sec. Alfred Jones, who is also gdn. of girl.

John Allder — Elizabeth Collins — December 20,1830
Sec. Levi Collins, father of girl. John Allder, father of John,
consented. Wit: Albert Alder

Adam Loy — Sarah Frye — December 14,1830
Sec. John Fawley. John Frye, father of girl, consented.

George Donohoe — Sarah Tillett of — December 13,1830
Sec. Thomas Moss — Cameron Parish

James Skinner — Catherine Reid — December 13,1830
Sec. Peter Skinner, who was father of James, and gdn. of girl.

Isaac Nichols — Olivia James — December 22, 1830
Sec. James P.Bradfield. (Groom signed as James Nichols)

Abraham Warford — Elizabeth Piles of — December 20,1830
Sec. Francis Piles — Cameron Parish

Joel Brown — Mahala Barr — December 28,1830
Sec. Thomas C.Gregg. Issachar Brown consented.

William R. Beveridge — Margaret Whitmore — December 22,1830
Sec. Michael Whitmore, father of girl.

Henry Green — Theodota Simpson — December 6,1830
Sec. James Sinclair, gdn. of girl.

George Sinclair — Rutha Ann Belt — December 6,1830
Sec. Alfred Belt, father of girl.

Dolphin Nichols — Anna Tracy — November 18,1830
Sec. Enos Nichols. He test. both 21.

James Hooper — Catharine Adams — November 8,1830
Sec. Henry Adams. He test both 21.

Name of Groom	Name of Bride	Date of Bond

John Byrne   Elizth. Barton   November 4,1830
Sec. Abraham H. Beavers.   Joseph Barton consented for his dau.
Wit: Benjamin Barton

Benjamin Davis   Sarah White   October 25,1830
Sec. Levi White, gdn. of girl. Howell Davis father of Benjamin,
consented.

James Megeath   Margaret Drake   October 25,1830
Sec. John G.Humphrey,gdn. of girl. Lot Tavener test. for groom.

John Brann   Emily Boling   October 20,1830
Sec. Joseph Hope

Thomas L. Hamersley   Emily A. Noland   October 14,1830
Sec. A.G. Waterman

John Magaha   Margaret Magaha   October 2,1830
Sec. Daniel Miller

Townson McBee   Sarah Blaker   September 20,1830
Sec. William Templer

Jeremiah T. Miller   Mary Thompson   September 6,1830
Sec. Mahlon Thompson

Thomas Rogers   Elmina L. Chamblin   September 13,1830
Sec. Fielding Littleton. Charles Chamblin, father of girl,consented.
Wit: Mason Chamblin, Burr Chamblin.

William Presgraves   Mary Ann Presgrave of   September 2,1830
Sec.Lewelin Hutchison   Cameron Parish

Horatio Trundle   Sarah S. Craven   September 1,1830
Sec. Alfred Belt. Sarah Craven consented for her dau. Wit:Sophia
V. Craven.

Phineas Osburn   Margaret Osburn   August 30,1830
Sec. Morris Osburn

Archibald McDaniel   Pricilla Thompson   July 30,1830
Sec. John Thompson

John Walter   Ruah Neale of   July 27,1830
Sec. John Marry   Cameron Parish

Name of Groom	Name of Bride	Date of Bond
Nathan Vail Sec. Smith Gregg	Ann Gregg	July 10,1830
Andrew Towperman Sec. Moses Wilson	Elzth. Moffett	June 24,1830
Thadeus Russell Sec. Jno. Hurdle	Catharine Garrett	May 20,1830
Jas. H. McVeigh Sec. George Cuthbert Powell. Job Guest consented for his dau. named Cynthia Ariel.	C. A. Guest	May 19,1830
Edwin A. Keeble Sec. Richd. Cochran, father of girl.	Susan R. Cochran	April 27,1830
Eben T. Hancock Sec. William Potts, father of girl.	Emma F. Potts	April 3,1830
James Templer Sec. Thomas Gregg, father of girl.	Belsora Gregg	April 3,1830
Josiah Cornwell Sec. Loveless Cornwell, father consented. Isaac Cornwell test. to age of girl. (Name could be Conwell)	Mary Ann Porter	March 31,1830
William Wilkinson Sec. George B. Rogers	Abigail Carter	March 29,1830
Jesse Porter Sec. George Jacobs	Mary Jacobs	March 27,1830
Edward Tillett Sec. John B. Ball	Susan Ball	March 24,1830
Lewis Ruse Sec. Edward Stone, who consented for his dau.	Jemima Stone	March 23,1830
Philip Setzer Sec. John Beach, father of girl.	Emily Beach	March 22, 1830
Isaiah E. Beck Sec. Levi Massey. Samuel Massey req. license. Wit:Isaac Massey, Mordecai Massey, Levi Massey	Phebe Massey	March 17,1830
Benj. Smith Sec. Chas. G. Eskridge	Sarah A.E.Bleman	February 18,1830

Name of Groom	Name of Bride	Date of Bond
Andrew Henderson Sec. Hector Pearce. Wit. Minor Reed	Mahalah Reed Jonathan Reed, father of girl req. license,	February 17,1830
William Dodd Sec. R. G. Saunders	Mary Hunt	February 11,1830
William H. Gray Sec. John Gray	Fanny W. Ellzey of Cameron Parish	January 20,1830
Milburn Palmer Sec. Richard Carter	Rachel Cogill	February 1, 1830
Gilbert Scott Sec. William Wolford	Mary Ann Wolford	January 30,1830
Edward Cochran Sec. Samuel Iden	Emily Iden	January 26,1830
William C. Luckett Sec. William B.Jackson.	Matilda Jacobs Elizabeth Jacobs,mother of girl, consented.	January 11, 1830

- - - -   - - - -

Henry Clapper Sec. Craven A. Copeland	Zillah Copeland	November 28,1831
Maddison C. Klein Sec. Jacob Janney. John A. Klein consented.	Hester B. Janney	November 15,1831
Peter Crim Sec. Jacob Shriver, gdn. of girl.	Mary Wolfe	November 15,1831
Joseph Dixon Sec. William Peacock, father of girl.	Sarah Peacock	November 14,1831
John Schooley,Jr. Sec. Addison H. Clarke	Sarah Roberts,widow	November 12,1831
David D. Merchant Sec. James W. MCDonaugh	Mary Ellen McDonagh	November 10,1831
Joseph Combs Sec. Thomas Brabham, father of girl.	Nancy J. Brabham	December 19,1831
George W. Pettit Sec. Benjamin Stringfellow	Jemima Reed	December 1,1831
James A. Bloxham Sec. Joseph Fredd	Malinda Jury	December 9,1831

Name of Groom	Name of Bride	Date of Bond
James Merchant Sec. Isaiah Romine, father of girl	Rebekah Romine	November 7,1831
Ignatious Elgin Sec. Joshua Lee, father of girl.	Mary Ann Lee of Cameron Parish	November 7,1831
Richard Wynkoop Sec. Lorenzo D. Walker	Frances Thayer	December 26,1831
William Lee Sec. William Peyton, father of girl.	Susanna T. Peyton	November 7,1831
Newton Murphey Sec. Andrew Hesser. Thomas Jones,father of girl, consented.	Mahala Jones	November 3,1831
Mahlon White Sec. William R. Shields	Margaret Wynkoop	November 3,1831
Mahlon Tavenner Sec. Fielding Tavenner. James Brown, father of girl, consented.	Mary Ann Brown	November 2,1831
George G. Armistead Sec. William Noland, gdn. of girl.	Alice Virginia Fontaine	November 1,1831
Joseph P. Grubb Sec. Eli Pierpoint.	Mary Daniel	October 31,1831
James F. Lynn Sec. Abraham Skillman, father of girl. Benj. F. Thomas test. as to age of groom.	Violinda Ann Skillman	October 29,1831
Albert Best Sec. Jacob Goodheart, father of girl.	Eliz'z Goodheart	October 22,1831
Murphey C. Shumate Sec. Francis Elgin	Margaret Elgin	October 22,1831
Thos. S. Hopkins Sec. James Hamilton. Sam'l Harris, father of girl, consented.	Sally L. Harris	October 15,1831
John Byrne Sec. Simon Matthew	Eliza Matthews	September 9,1831
William Gregg Sec. William Brown, father of girl.	Elizabeth Brown	September 5,1831
Charles Noland Sec. William Lodge	Eliza Shipman	September 5,1831

Name of Groom	Name of Bride	Date of Bond
Joseph Carr Sec. William Hall	Mary Hall	September 5,1831
William Fox Sec. William Pierce, father of girl.	Hannah Pierce	August 27,1831
Lawson Vananda Sec. Henry Clapper	Susan Clapper	November 28,1831
Townshend J. Jury Sec. John G. Humphrey, gdn. of girl.	Mary Ann Drake	October 31, 1831
George B. Smith Sec. Britton Saunders. Ann Sanders, gdn. of girl.	Martha L. Gregg	August 9,1831
Thomas M. Winn Sec. John Violett, father of girl.	Nancy L. Violett	August 9,1831
John H. McCabe Sec. C. Binns	Margt. H.D.Tebbs,widow	August 4,1831
Ezekiel Lynn Sec. Michael Lynn	Elizth. Potts, widow	August 8,1831
George Head Sec. Robt. Gover	Hannah I. Gover	July 21,1831
James Osborne Sec. George W. Bartlett, he also test. girl's age.	Nancy Bartlett	July 18,1831
John Baldwin Sec. John Whitacre, gdn. & grandfather of girl.	Mary Vanhorne	July 13,1831
Tilghman Gore Sec. James L. Hamilton	Roana Elgin, widow	July 11, 1831
George K. Fox Sec. Tilghman Gore	Frances Edwards	July 11, 1831
Samuel Jackson Sec. Jonathan West	Susan Grimes	September 9,1831
William Hurst Sec. S.M. Ross	Rebekah Kirk	July 23,1831
William Densmore Sec. Garrett Hough, father of girl, test. she 21.	Sarah Hough	June 1,1831

Name of Groom	Name of Bride	Date of Bond
Philip Saunders Sec. Amos Beale, father of girl.	Amanda Clarissa Bayles	June 18,1831
John Nixon Sec. Sam Tillett	Cassandra Tillett	May 23,1831
James Nixon Sec. Jonas Potts, father of girl.	Susan Ann Potts	May 23,1831
William T. Cole Sec. Sampson Hutchison	Mary E.Taliaferro of Cameron Parish	May 23,1831
Nimrod Newlon Sec. Isaac Richards	Mary Richards of Cameron Parish	May 23, 1831
Peter Stoneburner Sec. John Compher, father of girl.	Cath. Compher	June 20,1831
Thomas Richards Sec. Isaac Richards.	Jane Lynch of Cameron Parish	May 23,1831
Job Morgent Sec. Enoch Shrigley	Susan Shrigley	May 16,1831
William Fry Sec. Henry Fawley, father of girl.	Elizabeth Fawley	May 9,1831
Joseph Pierpoint Sec. James Hague, father of girl.	Rose Ann Hague	April 27,1831
James McDonaugh Sec. David D. Merchant	Elizabeth E. Gardner	April 10,1831
John Fritts Sec. William M. Bollington, gdn. of girl.	Rebecca Chamblin	April 11,1831
Thompson Writt Sec. John Iden	Elizabeth Furr of of Cameron Parish	April 23,1831
Jesse Oxley Sec. Thomas Morris	Sarah Hesser	April 23,1831
Nathan Cochran Sec. William Graham	Mary P. McGavick	March 28,1831
Burr P. Chamblin Sec. V. V. Purcell	Mary V. Purcell	March 14,1831

Name of Groom	Name of Bride	Date of Bond
Bailey Barton Sec. James Wornall, father of girl.	Sarah Wornall	March 14,1831
Jacob Shafer Sec. Jonathan Wenner. Mary Frayser, gdn. of girl.	Charlotte Wenner	March 14,1831
Israel T. Griffith Sec. C.W.D. Binns. William H.Hough test. for girl.	Mary Eleanor Weatherill	April 6,1831
John H. Monroe Sec. John A. Binns	Catherine Eugenia Solomon	February 17,1831
Charles Wright Sec. W. G. Wright. Ashford Violett test. girl 21.	Mary Violett	March 14,1831
Guilford G. Gregg Sec. Enos Nichols	Jemima Gregg	February 15,1831
Peyton Hope Sec. James Wilson	Mary Hope of Cameron Parish	February 14,1831
Harrison Russell Sec. Samuel Wright. Nancy Neale gdn. of girl. (Groom signed William Russell)	Jemima Neile	February 14,1831
William Allen Sec. Thomas Ashby	Nancy Cornell	June 25,1831
William Miller Sec. John Ross	Maria Thomas	January 10,1831
Solomon Kist Sec. Adam Evans	Elizth. Evans	December 27,1831
William Penn Sec. George Hammer. John Copeland,father of girl, req. license.	Mary Ann Copeland	December 21,1831
Philip Morgan Sec. Adam Winegardner	Mary Winegardner	October 21,1831
William H. Noland Sec. Robert Armistead	Harriet M. Armistead of Cameron Parish	September 26,1831
Henson Elliott Sec. L.C. Cunard	Catharine P. Heskell	September 23,1831
Samuel Sackman Sec. Stephenson Hixson, father of girl. John Shafer test. ages.	Susan Mary Hixson	September 20,1831

Name of Groom	Name of Bride	Date of Bond
Abel Jones Sec. Cyrus Burson, gdn. of girl	Julian Vanpelt	February 14,1831
William King Sec. William Gibson	Tacy Daniel	September 15,1831
Silas Havener Sec. Joseph Havenner, father of groom	Julia Ann Rollinson of Cameron Parish	January 10,1831
Joshua Tipton Sec. John Lang	Harriet Lang	February 7,1831
Elias Stream Sec. Jacob Waters	Mary Ann Waters	September 24,1831
Bozzell Havener Sec. William Lefever	Rachel Lafever of Cameron Parish	January 10,1831
Geo. W. Shoemaker Sec. Enoch Shrigley	Mary Shrigley	September 26,1831
Daniel Hirst Sec. Nelson Everhart	Martha Everheart	July 29,1831
Saml. E. Henderson Sec. Ishmal Vanhorn	Matilda Morgan	January 31,1831
John Vandevanter Sec. Presly Saunders	Harriet A. Darne	January 29,1831
Malcom Jameson Sec. David Weatherly Jno. Thompson, father of girl, test. ages.	Julia M.Thompson of Cameron Parish	January 29,1831
Edward Dowling Sec. Edward Harding	Mary Demory	February 1, 1831
Jonathan Myers Sec. William Graham	Malinda Reed	February 10,1831
Edward E. Cooke Sec. W.C.Selden,Jr.	Margaret L.Harrison	February 19,1831
Theodore N. Davisson Sec. Charles G.Eskridge.	Sarah Rogers Asa Rogers test. girl's age	March 14,1831
James Saunders Jr. Sec. Amos Beale	Roena Eleanor Bale	March 19,1831

Name of Groom	Name of Bride	Date of Bond
Zedekiah Kidwell Sec. Nelson B.Everhart.	Mary Ropp Nicholas Ropp,father of girl, test. age.	March 21,1831
Benj. F. Filingame Sec. Catesby Jones	Elizth. Jane Thyer	April 7,1831
Henry M.Dowling Sec. David Ogden	Harriet J. Haslett	April 13,1831
Samuel Bowles Sec. John Wornal	Amelia Wildman	June 16,1831
Lewis Dennis Sec. William A.Dennis, father of girl.	Olivia F.Dennis of Cameron Parish	April 28,1831
John Abraham Sec. Adam Karn.	Mary Wenner Magdalena Frazier, mother of the girl.	June 4,1831
Jacob Divine Sec. S. Dodd	Elizth. Dodd	April 25,1831

- - - -   - - - -

Samuel Carter Sec. Enos Updike.	Elisabeth Ann Batson Sam'l West test. her age.	March 12,1832
Edward T. Lowe Sec. C.W.D.Binns. Joshua Pusey, gdn. of girl, consented.	Amelia Smallwood of Cameron Parish	February 13,1832
Robert E.Beall Sec. Alfred Wright	Susan Wright	March 6,1832
Samuel Ball Sec. Sebastion McPherson, father of girl.	Catharine McPherson of Cameron Parish	February 29,1832
John James Sec. Henry Mershon	Sarah B. Mershon	February 28,1832
John Moore Sec. John Fulton, gdn. of girl	Martha Ann Lathrum	February 14,1832
Edmund Allen Sec. John Butler, gdn. of girl.	Margt. B. Jenkins	February 13,1832
John L.Chamblin Sec. Mahlon Baldwin, gdn. of girl	Mary Ann Baldwin	February 13,1832

Name of Groom	Name of Bride	Date of Bond
Samuel R. Beveridge Sec. Carter Moss	Harriet C. Moffett of Cameron Parish	February 13,1832
John Worson Sec. Henry Mills George Mills,father of girl,consented. Wit.John Lacy & Francis W.Kendall	Frances Mills of Cameron Parish	February 11,1832
John Moore Sec. William Smith	Elizabeth Ritacre	February 10,1832
John A.W.Smith Sec. Wm. F. Phillips. Rev.John A.Collins,test. girl's age.	Sally Odell Hall	February 7,1832
George Price Sec. Samuel Dawson	Elizabeth Clapham	January 30,1832
Joseph Gochnauer Sec. William Davis, father of girl.	Harriet Ann Davis of Cameron Parish	February 3,1832
James J. Major Sec. Jno. A. Binns	Hannah Ann Harris	January 13,1832
James B. Dodd Sec. S.Dodd. Dr.Joseph B.Fox test. girl 21.	Delila B. Fox	January 23,1832
Jeremiah Lalor Sec. Samuel Marmaduke	Eliza Marmaduke of Cameron Parish	January 12,1832
John R. White Sec. Lewis Ellzey, father of girl.	Mary Cecelia Ellzey	January 4,1832
William B. Price Sec. Fielding Littleton Jno. Lanphier, gdn. of girl, consented.	Sarah P.S.Martin of Cameron Parish	January 9,1832
Charles Fenton Downs Sec. Eli Pierpoint	Hester Daniel	August 25,1832
John H. Kaighn Sec. Wm. Mershon	Mary E. Triplett of Cameron Parish	August 4,1832
Melville B.Hutchison Sec. Geo. Rose. Richard Hutchison test. groom's age.	Lucinda Presgraves of Cameron Parish	July 23,1832
Enos Potts Sec. Solomon Ruse. Jonas Potts test. groom's age.	Martha Tavener	June 25,1832

Name of Groom	Name of Bride	Date of Bond
Wm. Sutherland Sec. John H.Beatty. Wm.H.Beatty test. girl 21.	Eliza Beatty	June 21,1832
Beverly Hutchison Sec. Benjamin Hixson, father of girl.	Mary P. Hixson	April 23,1832
Joseph Blincoe Sec. George W.Hunter	Lucinda Jones of Cameron Parish	April 16,1832
Levi Collins Sec. Joseph Allder	Elizabeth Fawley	April 2,1832
Parkinson L. Lott Sec. Simon Smale, father of girl. Miss Frances Lott test. groom's age.	Mary Smale	March 20,1832
William R. Shields Sec. Benjamin Saunders	Susan Blaker	March 6,1832
John Curry Sec. Andrew Graham, father of girl.	Elizth. Graham	March 1,1832
Samuel E. Taylor Sec. Jams McKim, father of girl.	Alcinda McKim	February 27,1832
Wilson Gregg Sec. Presley McDaniel	Margaret Lightfoot	June 27,1832
David J. Eaton Sec. Wm. Dailey	Mary I. Eaton	July 18,1832
Thomas Edwin Thompson Sec. Notley C.Williams. Richard Thompson,father of groom,consented.	Margaret M.A.Williams	June 22,1832
Benj. Poling Sec. William O. Stocks	Elizabeth Woolford	February 21,1833
Malcolm Horton Sec. Oliver Denham, who also test. girl's age.	Margaret A. Denham	February 25,1832
Jacob Anderson Sec. William Lafaber, father of girl.	Rachel Lefever of Cameron Parish	February 10,1832
James Best Sec. M. Janney	Rosannah M. Janny	February 4, 1832

Name of Groom	Name of Bride	Date of Bond
Arthur L. Robinson Sec. William D. Robinson	Mahala Snyder	February 2,1832
Presley Orrison Sec. Andrw Grayham, who test. groom 21.	Mary Grayham	February 2,1832
James Kittle Sec. Amos Carr. James Carr test. her age.	Nancy Carr	February 7,1832
John Slack Sec. William Lickey, father of girl.	Juliet Lickey	February 20,1832
William Vickers Sec. Jacob Crim, father of girl.	Catharine Crim	February 27,1832
Sam'l Beavers Sec. Price Jacobs	Hannah Fulton	January 12,1832
Presley Davis Sec. John Griffith	Mary Ann Gladhill	January 12,1832
James Gowings Sec. John S. Gordon	Catharine A.Jordan of Cameron Parish	January 2,1832
Thomas Johnson Sec. Otho Riggs (Riffs?)	Louisa Palmer	September 4,1832
Jeremiah Davis Sec. Ashford Weadon	Catharine Weedon	December 31,1832
Daniel Feagans Sec. William Virts, father of the girl.	Jane Virts	December 26,1832
Sam'l Buffington Sec. Joseph Wheatley	Nancy Ann Wheatley	January 14,1832
George W. Thompson Sec. Benjamin Thompson	Sarah Pursell	December 20,1832
Thomas Sanders Sec. Chas. Shriver	Mary Meade	December 3,1832
Thos. W. Brooks Sec. A.M.Kitzmiller. Thos. Saunders consented.	Sarah H.Saunders	November 7,1832
John Gaunt Sec. William Davis. Ann Brown, mother of girl, consents. Samuel Gant consented for his son.	Sarah Ann Watkins	November 5,1832

Name of Groom	Name of Bride	Date of Bond

Alex'r Kilgour   Margaret Ann Stribling   November 1, 1832
Sec. John Janny. M.M.McIlhany, gdn. of girl, consented. Wit. John A.
Washington & Daniel Stone

Ryland Jacobs   Elizabeth Thomas   October 29,1832
Sec. Wm. Chamblin

Charles C. Newton   Mayden Hammerly   October 24,1832
Sec. Parkerson L.Lott. Jane Hammerly, mother of girl, consented.

Herod Thomas   Mary Ann Robinson   June 12,1832
Sec. Thomas Littleton

Washington Jenkins   Edah Howell   September 22,1832
Sec. Jesse Howell

Isaac S. Hough   Mary Jane Paxson   March 12,1832
Sec. Samuel Paxson, father of girl.

Fielding Harvey   Ruth Trayhorn   March 12,1832
Sec. Stephen McPherson, gdn. of girl.

Benjamin Filler   Mary Hines   March 12,1832
Sec. John Wine

John B. Young   Eliza Aldridge   March 20,1832
Sec. John Aldridge, father of girl.

Harrison Anderson   Catherine Anderson   April 2,1832
Sec. Elijah Anderson, father of girl.

Richard Baker   Mary Ann Baggot   April 3,1832
Sec. William Tavenner

Josiah Burchett   Sarah Ann Burchett   April 7,1832
Sec. William Burchett, father of girl. Eli Janny test. groom's age.

Moses D. Wilson   Ann Lloyd of   September 6,1832
Sec. Armistead M.Howell   Cameron Parish

Wm. Smallwood   Eliza Harden   September 8,1832
Sec. Joseph Harden
Thomas Harding, test. he is father of girl. Polly Smallwood test.
she the only surviving parent of groom.

James Chappell   Susan Slack   August 18,1832
Sec. Tunis Slack, father of girl.

Name of Groom	Name of Bride	Date of Bond
Hansford White Sec. Jesse Triplett	Charlotte Grimes	August 13,1832
William Bagent Sec. Joseph Keist	Nancy Keist	August 13,1832
Arthur Orrison Sec. Thomas G.Dowdell	Elizabeth Harris	June 13,1832
Edwin Rogers Sec. John Elgin	Ann Elgin	September 15,1832
Alfred Bolon Sec. Ferdinando Bolon.	Sarah Roach Henry S.Taylor, test. girl's age.	June 5,1832
Thomas Oden Sec. Sam'l M. Edwards	Barbara Drish	May 31,1832
William F. Simpson Sec. John C.Newton, father of girl.	Mary A. Newton	May 24,1832
Zadock Hempstone Sec. Samuel B.Harris, father of girl.	Mary M.Harris	May 21,1832
John Norris Sec. Thomas Birkby	Hannah Sophia Birkby	May 17,1832
Frederick A. Davisson Sec. William Wickes, father of girl.	Eliza D. Wickes	May 18,1832
Lemuel Watson Sec. Thomas Birkby	Lucy H. Birkby	May 10,1832
William Fulton Sec. Walter Elgin, father of girl.	Mary B. Elgin	April 9,1832
William Taylor Sec. Chs. G. Eskridge.	Mary R. Timms Jesse Timms, father of girl, consented.	April 14,1832
James Woody Sec. John A. Binns	Betsey Tifford	May 9,1832
Woodford Galloway Sec. Luther C.Cunard	Harriet Andrews	August 5,1832
Henry Fish Sec. John Burson. Laban Burson, father of girl, consented. Wit. Cyrus Burson.	Mary Ann Burson	September 10,1832

Name of Groom	Name of Bride	Date of Bond
Powell Sry Sec. Solomon Heater	Nancy Heater	September 7,1832
Jefferson Fritts Sec. Hector Osburn	Jane Day	September 15,1832
Thornton F. Offutt Sec. John B. Young. Joseph Conner test. girl 21.	Eliza Clayton	September 22,1832
Israel Burke Sec. J. A. Binns. James H.Chamblin test. for groom. Mary Hains test. for girl.	Elizabeth Garner	October 1,1832
Levi Winegarner Sec. Levi Collins, father of girl.	Cath'e Collins	October 8,1832
And'w Hoskinson Sec. R'd Houser	Eleanor Wilson of Cameron Parish	October 11,1832
William Ball Sec. Thomas Davis. George Davis, father of girl, consented. Wit. William Davis and James Davis.	Anna Davis	December 3,1832
James M. Wallace Sec. William Johnson, father of girl.	Adelaide Johnson	November 23,1832
Sanford McNeeley (McNelea) Sec. Richard Houser	Sarah Moran of Cameron Parish	December 31,1832
William Tarlton Sec. William Bitzer. Macka Tarlton, father of groom,consented. Sarah Bitzer, mother of girl, consented. Wit. Lydia C.Reed & John D.B. Savage.	Catherine Reed	October 11,1832
Solomon Calvert Sec. William Davis. William Willis, father of girl, consented. Wit. John A. Gaunt.	Elizabeth Willis	October 15,1832
Charles W. James Sec. Jos. Richardson. Daniel Brown, father of girl, consented. Wit. Eleanor Watkins. Elijah James consented for groom.	Martha Brown	October 29,1832
James W. Nixon Sec. Mahlon Thomas, gdn. of girl.	Martha Thomas	November 12,1832
John Winner Sec. George Whitmore	Sarah Everheart,widow	November 27,1832
Adam Cooper Sec. Charles G. Edwards, father of girl.	Harriet Edwards	December 3,1832

Name of Groom	Name of Bride	Date of Bond
John Yaky Sec. George Beamer, father of girl.	Mary Beamer	December 3,1832
William Horseman Sec. Benjamin Johnson	Sarah Johnson	December 3,1832
Coleman Kidwell Sec. George W. Thompson, gdn. of girl.	Emeline Simms	December 10,1833
James Thornton Sec. Jesse McConaha	Octavia Vanhorne	December 4,1832
- - - -	-	- - - -
Richard Carter Sec. Charles Carter	Lavina Craven	September 23,1833
Thomas Hogue Sec. John Simpson, father of girl.	Mary Anne Simpson	September 23,1833
William Gardner Sec. Geo. Head	Ann Gover	September 19,1833
Lorenzo D. Nixon Sec. S.M.Boss. John F.Barrett test. groom's age. Rebecca Shaw, mother of girl, auth. license. Wit. Mary Shaw.	Eliza A.Shaw	September 10,1833
Daniel Adams Sec. Levi Winegarner	Susanna Smith	September 9,1833
Samuel Megeath Sec. James Hoge	Mary Ann Handy	September 9,1833
William Long Sec. William Divine, gdn. of girl.	Lucinda Crooks	September 9,1833
Isaac G. Bowles Sec. William Young, father of girl.	Ann Young	September 6,1833
Landon Jolly Sec. Elisha Smallwood. Jesse Richards and Jacob Jolly, father of groom, auth. license.	Margaret Lynch	August 17,1833
Jesse Sibbett Sec. David Carlisle, gdn. of girl.	Rachel H. Cummings	August 14,1833
John Potts Sec. Jacob Shriver	Ruth Talley	August 12,1833
Jonah Hatcher Sec. Enos Nichols	Adeline S.Gregg	August 12,1833

Name of Groom	Name of Bride	Date of Bond
George Beamer Sec. Samuel Cordell	Elizabeth Dixon	April 26,1833
Jacob Zinn Sec. Wm. Ambler	Elizth. Halley of Cameron Parish	May 6, 1833
John W. Seaton Sec. Stephen Lewis	Nancy Lewis	July 11,1833
Joseph H. Robinson Sec. Hugh Campbell. Wit. Elias Robinson.	Flizth. F. Blackwell William Robinson,father of groom, auth. license. Benjamin Blackwell, father of girl, auth.license.	July 15,1833
Bennet Francis Sec. Seth Smith	Mary Ann Crupper	July 15,1833
Mortimer Poulson Sec. Richard Brown.	Olivia McFaden John McFaden consented for his dau.	August 7,1833
John Briel Sec. George Vinsil	Sally Filler	July 22,1833
Thomas T. Wheeler Sec. Geo. M. Chichester.	Hester A. McLeod John M. Edward test. girl's age.	August 8,1833
William Hamilton Sec. George W. Hunter	Jane Daily	August 8,1833
Logan Osburn Sec. Herod Osburn, father of girl.	Hannah Osburn	August 9,1833
Reubin Jenkins Sec. Herod Osburn, gdn. of girl.	Eleanor Rector	August 9,1833
John F. McAtee Sec. Levi Ewers	Julia A.Horsman	August 31, 1833
Mason Rutter Sec. Jonathan Andrews	Ann Andrews	August 31,1833
Peyton Robinson Sec. Samuel Carter, father of girl, consented.	Elizabeth Carter	September 2,1833
James Martin Sec. Peyton Taylor	Margaret Taylor	September 2,1833
William B. Moffett Sec. Lewis Klein, father of girl. Robert H.Gover test. ages of both.	Louisa Klein	September 14,1833

Name of Groom	Name of Bride	Date of Bond
Russell Bracket Sec. Washington Jenkins	Frances Ann Jenkins	September 17,1833
Henry Oram Sec. William Wise	Jane Wise	September 23,1833
Harvey Evans Sec. John Earnest. John Grubb test. girl's age.	Nancy Grubb	October 23,1833
Jonathan Cooper Sec. Mahlon Myers	Mary Ann Myers	November 5,1833
Gabriel Vandevanter Sec. John Braden	Mary E.Braden	November 9,1833
James F. McKnight Sec. Enos Nichols. Joseph Hough, father of girl, consented.	Harriet E. Hough	November 27,1833
John Gross Sec. John Ramsey, father of girl. Daniel Wine test. groom's age.	Patience Ramsey	November 30,1833
John H. White Sec. John George Jr. who also test. girl 21. Wit. John George Jr. and Solomon George.	Malinda S.George	December 2,1833
Alfred J. Dorsey Sec. Allen M. Dorsey. Isaac Moon test. for girl.	Eleanor Moon	December 7,1833
Amos Fouch Sec. Wm. Rollings	Sarah McGuygan of Cameron Parish	January 1, 1833
Reuben French Sec. Samuel Beavers	Catherine Watkins	January 3, 1833
Leroy Gheen Sec. Henry Young	Rachel Young	January 7, 1833
Michael Trittipo Sec. Henry Fawley	Margaret Fawley	January 14,1833
Gabriel Kidwell Sec. James Welsh, father of girl. Andrew Hesser test. ages.	Sophia M. Welsh	January 14,1833
Joseph A. Lloyd Sec. Charles T. Denham	Margt. Gheen	January 12,1833
Ferdinando Bolon Sec. William Vanhorn. Amy W.Bradfield auth. license. Wit. James P. Bradfield.	Harriett Bradfield	January 22,1833

Name of Groom	Name of Bride	Date of Bond

Robert Munday   Rosanna Frye   February 11,1833
Sec. Nich's Frye, father of girl.

Albert B. Florance   Catherine L.Skinner of   February 14,1833
Sec. Amos Skinner,   Cameron Parish
father of girl.

Thomas Moreland   Sarah Rinker   March 11, 1833
Sec. Edward Rinker, father of girl.

Reuben Triplett   Eleanor Williams   March 16,1833
Sec. James Williams

John H. Hughes   Martha Ann Rogers   March 25,1833
Sec. Samuel Rogers. Dinah Rogers, mother of girl, consented.
Wit. T. Rogers. J. Hughes, father of groom, consented. Wit.
William Adie & Samuel Canby

Thomas M. Humphrey   Lydia Whitacre   April 17,1833
Sec. James Whitacre

James M. Heskett   Martha M.Barton   January 21, 1833
Sec. James A. Bloxham

John Snow   Scivilla Slates,widow   April 20,1833
Sec. Emanuel Waltman

Dennis McCarty   Ann Eliza Skinner   April 22,1833
Sec. Gabriel Skinner, father of girl.

Wm. R. Abbot   Eleanor J. Harris   May 6,1833
Sec. Samuel B.Harris, father of girl.

Samuel C. Luckett   Mary B. Hamilton   May 13,1833
Sec. C.B.Hamilton,Jr.

William Wynkoop   Catherine Clever   May 13,1833
Sec. William Smith

Matthew Lee   Ann Berkley of   May 13,1833
Sec. Nath'l S.Oden   Cameron Parish
Ann Berkley req. license for herself & W.Matthew Lee. Wit. N.S.Oden
and Alexander D. Lee

James Randall   Sarah Petit   October 8,1833
Sec. Jonathan J.Pettit. Joseph Randall test. his son over 21.
Wit. Jonathan Palmer and Harison D. Pool

A. M. Kitzmiller   Anne E. Hilliard   October 1, 1833
Sec. Joseph Hilliard, father of girl.

Name of Groom	Name of Bride	Date of Bond

Robert Fish — Mary Ann Lumm — October 1,1833
Sec. John Lumm, father of girl. Joshua Nichols test. age of groom.

James Skilman — Elizabeth Carter — September 24,1833
Sec. Abraham Skillman. Wm. Wilkison test. girl's age.

James Hoge — Phila Holmes — October 10,1833
Sec. John Holmes. William Holmes, father of girl, auth. license.
Wit. Elisha Holmes.

James Washington Hill — Mary Humphrey — October 18,1833
Sec. Laban Lodge

Middleton Smith — Clarissa Towner — October 24,1833
Sec. Henry Newton

Washington Myers — Margaret McIntosh — December 7,1833
Sec. Lambert Myers

George Barr — Mary Coe — October 29,1833
Sec. Wm. M. Herrick

Ebenezer Tally — Lavinia Gregory — November 1,1833
Sec. Samuel Buffington

Barton Garrett — Mary McFaden — October 30,1833
Sec. Walter Woodyard. John McFaden test. girl's age.

Isaac Wilberforce Moon — Eliza Sullivan — October 19,1833
Sec. Alfred J. Dorsey. Samuel Sulivan test. girl's age. Henry Moon,
of Waterford, father of girl, consented.

James Booth Jr. — Sarah Arnold — November 8,1833
Sec. Philip Boger, gdn. of girl.

James or Jesse Fox — Sarah Ann Pierce — November 11,1833
Sec. Charles Binns

Josiah Tally — Ann Gore — November 11,1833
Sec. Mark Gore, father of girl.

William Dove — Elizabeth Whaley — November 11,1833
Sec. William Whaley, gdn. of girl.

John G. Miller — Amanda Russell — November 12,1833
Sec. John Miller, gdn. of girl.

Horatio Drish — Elizabeth Weadon — November 15,1833
Sec. F. Weedon, who also test. ages of both.

Name of Groom	Name of Bride	Date of Bond
Howson Hooe	Nancy Reed	November 20,1833

Sec. John Reed, father of girl.

Henry D. Magill	Ann Elizabeth Mason	November 21,1833

Sec. William T.T.Mason, father of bride.

Mahlon Basford	Elizabeth Near	December 9,1833

Sec. John Near, father of girl.

Mahlon Myers,Jr.	Margaret Cooper	December 10,1833

Sec. P.K. Dorsey

George M. Green	Mary Miller	December 10,1833

Sec. John Miller, gdn. of girl.

William Davis	Elizabeth Gaunt	December 10,1833

Sec. Samuel Gant, father of girl, auth. license. Wit. John Gaunt and
Rachel Ann Gaunt. Gary Davis auth. license for his son. Wit. Thomas
Davis.

Francis Protzman	Mary Connor	December 23,1833

Sec. Hugh Connor. Ann Baker test. girl 21.

Bernard Simpson	Dewanner Wildman	December 10,1833

Sec. C. Binns

John Timms	Elizabeth Emory	December 14,1833

Sec. Jacob Arnold

Lewis Jackson	Eleanor Carrico	December 19,1833

Sec. James Carrico, father of girl.

Samuel Beavers	Sarah Hough	December 26,1833

Sec. Samuel B. Caldwell

Jacob Bontz	Ann Prince	December 30,1833

Sec. Mathias Prince, father of girl.

William Brumley	Elizabeth Gray	December 31,1833

Sec. George Craig. Jno. G. Gray, father of girl.

Isaac Richards	Hannah Triplett	December 30,1833

Sec. Humphrey Richards

Christian Gottleib Ludwick	Susanna Derry	December 30,1833

Sec. Mathias Prince

Henry Rickard	Elizabeth Farought	December 21,1833

Sec. Beil, Jacob

Joseph Stone	Ruth Tribby	January 21,1833

Sec. Reed Poulton. Tamar Tribby gave permission for her dau. to
marry. Wit. James Tippett

Name of Groom	Name of Bride	Date of Bond

Lott Purcell — Hannah Taylor — January 28,1833
Sec. Joseph Taylor, father of girl. Manly Atwell test. both 21.

George W.Washington — Sarah Ann Wright — July 18,1833
Sec. Alfred D. Offutt. John Wright test. his dau. 21. Wit. Robert D. Wright.

David Stedman — Elizabeth Dawson — February 18,1833
Sec. John B. Rathie

David Beard — Mary Ann Beach — March 6,1833
Sec. John Beach

William Nelson — Virlinda Ann Anderson — February 21,1833
Sec. John P. Smart

William Tavenner — Malinda Gaines — April 18,1833
Sec. Arthur Gaines. Richard Tavenner auth. license for his son. Wit. Lewis Torreyson and Jonathan Tavenner.

William B. Jackson — Rebecca T. Dulin — April 8,1833
Sec. Benj. Jackson, father of groom.

Henry Morrison — Mary Ann Reed — April 6,1833
Sec. Thomas Reid, father of girl.

John Ellmore — Elizth. Ann Rose of Cameron Parish — April 13,1833
Sec. George Rose, father of girl.

Edward Baker — Elizth. R. Biscoe — April 13,1833
Sec. J. B. Biscoe. Harrison Pool test. groom's age. James B. Biscoe test. for girl.

John L. Rinker — Susannah Johnson — April 4,1833
Sec. William Johnson. Simon Smale test. groom 21.

James Hope — Sarah Vanpelt — April 2,1833
Sec. John H. McCabe. Jotham Wright test. ages of both.

Thomas P. Matthews — Jane P. Hughes — March 25,1833
Sec. Samuel Canby

George W. Hough — Mary C. Shawen — March 25,1833
Sec. J. A. Braden. Mary Shawen consented for her dau. Wit. F.Hixon

George Fleming — Ann Otley — March 7,1833
Sec. Wm. Fleming. James Otley auth. license for his dau. Wit. Joseph Fleming.

Name of Groom	Name of Bride	Date of Bond

Israel Potterfield   Elizabeth Lyons   March 23,1833
Sec. Elam Jacobs

Samuel Winsell   Elizth. Keen   February 26,1833
Sec. Jacob Keen, father of girl.

William R. Ellis   Rebecca Skinner of   August 19,1833
Sec. Alexander Skinner   Cameron Parish
He test. girl 21.

Benjamin Case   Ann Oden   July 9, 1833
Sec. Thomas Oden, father of girl.

Philip Ritchie   Nancy McGaha   June 29,1833
Sec. William McGaha. David McGaha auth. license for his dau.
Wit. F. M. Bond and Hannah Brown

James Madison Thornton   Sarah Cath'e Hicks   June 22,1833
Sec. Abram Hiskett, who test. both 21.

Thomas Noble   Marian Reed   June 21, 1833
Sec. Elijah Barnes. Catharine Reed, mother of girl, auth. license.
Wit. Elias Triplett.

John Whitacre   Nancy Hope,widow   June 20,1833
Sec. Israel Dyer

Jacob Wenner   Eliza Ritchie   June 19,1833
Sec. John Snow, who test. both 21.

John Wesley Hall   Sarah E. Rice   June 12,1833
Sec. Thirza Rice, mother of girl. The girl's father, Jesse Rice,
is dead. No gdn. chosen.

Arthur F. Lane   Catharine L.Crain   June 10,1833
Sec. Peter Gregg

Samuel Terman   Ann Elizabeth Dunn   June 10,1833
Sec. William D.North, test. ages of both.

Anthony Addison   Mary Juliet Thompson   June 4,1833
Sec. William M. Thompson, father of girl.

Reuben Cockrill   Mary E. Coe   June 3,1833
Sec. Mary Coe, gdn. and mother of girl. John L.Tillett test.
groom's age.

Name of Groom	Name of Bride	Date of Bond
William A. Stephenson Sec. George Mason Grayson	Mary B. Grayson	May 30,1833
John Lacey Sec. John H. McCabe. Josephus Powell test. girl above 21.	Betsey Ann Vanpelt	May 27,1833
Leven Thomas Sec. John Graham, gdn. of girl. Joseph Thomas test. groom 21.	Rebecca Philips	May 25,1833
James White Sec. Enos T. Best, who test. girl (Eliza R.) over 21.	Elizabeth M. Best	May 15,1833
Thomas Flowers Sec. J. A. Binns	Margaret Smith,widow	May 15,1833
John Kelley Sec. George Briscoe, who test. girl's age.	Louisa Dennis	May 14,1833

- - - - - - - - -

James W. Brawner Sec. Samuel C. Rose	Sarah Rosseau of Cameron Parish	August 5,1834
Nimrod Claspey Sec. Henry Orum, father of girl.	Mary Orum	June 19,1834
Edward Ellmore Sec. William L.Timms Benjamin Hatton, father of girl, test. her age. Wit. Nat'l S.Oden	Elizabeth Hatton of Cameron Parish	June 21,1834
Thomas S. Hall Sec. Edmund Tyler, gdn. of girl.	Angeline R. Boyle	June 18,1834
Solomon Derry Sec. George Derry. William Derry auth. license. Wit. Jacob Derry	Maria Derry	June 18,1834
Samuel Breitenbagh Sec. Jn. Nicholas Kline, father of girl.	Maria L. Kline	June 16,1834
Henry A. Ball Sec. Wesley S. McPherson, gdn. of girl.	Elizabeth Ann Thrift	June 16,1834
John M. Harrison Sec. James Rust	Susan E. Bailey	August 4,1834
Michael Sagle Sec. Adam Jacobs, who test. girl's age.	Eliza Jacobs	August 4,1834

Name of Groom	Name of Bride	Date of Bond

Wilson C. Duvall   Harriet Jennings   June 10,1834
Sec. Jno. A. Binns. Betsey Jennings, mother of girl, consented.

Horace W. Dowden   Eleanora Smallwood   May 22,1834
Sec. T. L. Jones, who test. ages of both.

Craven Osburn Van Horn Mary Emberson   May 17,1834
Sec. Judson Emberson, father of girl, consented.

James A. Johnson   Nancy Clowes   May 16,1834
Sec. C.B.Hamilton. (Groom signed James A.Taylor)

Solomon Smitley   Mary Bumcrotz   May 9,1834
Sec. John Bumcrotz, father of girl.

Benjamin M. Brocchus   Isabella G.Armistead   March 24,1834
Sec. Jno. Graham, who test. girl over 21.

Sam'l Ruser   Nancy Turner   March 17,1834
Sec. George Sager, who test. groom 21. Robert Turner, father of
girl, auth. license. Wit. Thos. Wright.

George W. Mock   Mary Ann Russell   March 15,1834
Sec. William Russell, father of girl.

Jonah Potterfield   Clarissa Amanda Thrasher March 14,1834
Sec. Sarah Thrasher, mother of girl, auth. license, father dead.
Wit. Samuel Price and Archibald Thrasher.

Joseph Garrett   Elizabeth Harden   March 10,1834
Sec. Levi Gulick, who test. groom's age. Elizabeth Harden, mother
of girl, auth. license. wit. Stephen Garrett.

Simon Mathew   Susanna Fritts   March 10,1834
Sec. George Frits, father of girl.

Harod Glasscock   Edith Chamblin   March 10,1834
Sec. A. G. Chamblin. Mary Chamblin auth. license. Relationship not
shown. Wit. Mahlon Baldwin.

Jonathan Wiard   Catharine Harper   February 22,1834
Sec. James Harper, father of girl, auth. license.

Solomon George   Sarah Ann Everhart   February 22,1834
Sec. Solomon Everhart, who test. groom 21. Philip Everhart, auth.
license. Wit. John Conard Jr.

Archibald Henderson Jr. Henrietta Gray   February 20,1834
Sec. Charles G. Eskridge

Name of Groom	Name of Bride	Date of Bond

Thomas Athey   Mary Thompson   February 15,1834
Sec. French Thompson, who test groom's age. Benjamin Thompson, father
of girl, auth. license. Wit. Daniel Grimes.

John A. Carter   Richardetta T. DeButts   February 11, 1834
Sec. Robt. McIntyre. Alexander Moore, Reg. of Wills of Alexandria,
test. John P. Dulany,gdn. of girl as appears by will of Mary DeButts,
dec'd. John P.Dulany auth. license. Wit. Julia A.B.Dulany and Samuel
W.DeButts. Louisa F. Hall, auth. license for her dau. Richardetta T.
DeButts. Wit. Margaret A.Hereford.

George T. Hunt   Maria West   February 11,1834
Sec. M.McIlhany

John Conner   Lucinda Rice   February 10,1834
Sec. James Thomas

Hiram McVeigh   Mary E.White   December 22,1834
Sec. Theodore Davisson. John White, father of girl, auth. license.
Wit. Sam C. White.

Presley K. Dorsey   Hannah Reed   December 22,1834
Sec. A. M. Dorsey

Joseph R. Lynn   Pamelia Carrell   December 22,1834
Sec. John H. Hixson, who also test. to ages of both.

Nelson Fisher   Mahulda Brooks of   December 17,1834
Sec. Benjamin Brooks   Cameron Parish

Leonard Frye   Susanna Spring   December 15,1834
Sec. Nicholas Fry, father of groom. Henry Spring test. girl 21.

Josiah Ulum   Elizabeth Waters   December 15,1834
Sec. Samuel Waltman, who test. groom 21. Jacob Waters, father of girl,
auth. license. Wit. John Snow

Seth D. Robertson   Christiana Mason   December 15,1834
Sec. Adam Mason, test. girl 21.

Absalom Beans   Maria Gooden   December 13,1834
Sec. David Reece

John Orrison   Sarah Sherb,widow   December 9,1834
Sec. Minor Bartlett

Caleb Aduddell   Ann Wilson   December 29,1834
Sec. Edward Wilson, father of girl. Wm. H.Francis, test. groom's age.

Name of Groom	Name of Bride	Date of Bond

Fenton Vandevanter — Mary A.L. Saunders — December 6, 1834
Sec. Britton Sanders, father of girl. Washington Vandevanter test. groom's age.

Lewis Hunt — Mary Garner — December 8, 1834
Sec. W.W. Kitzmiller

Philip Moyer — Carey Peirce — December 5, 1834
Sec. C. Binns

Vivian Beck — Emily Huffman — December 3, 1834
Sec. John Huffman, father of girl.

Joseph G. Gray — Mary E. Ellzey — December 3, 1834
Sec. John Gray

Moses O. Galleher — Evelina Lovett — December 2, 1834
Sec. William H. Galleher

Henderson Bishop — Juliann Nicewanger — December 1, 1834
Sec. John Nisewanner, father of girl.

William F. Adam — Adelaide Osburn — December 1, 1834
Sec. Joel Osburn, father of girl.

Bernard R. Atwell — Jane A. Hammerly — November 27, 1834
Sec. John A. Klein

Landon O. Reed — Rebecca G. Fleming — December 1, 1834
Sec. George Fleming. Dinah Fleming, mother of girl, auth. license. Wit. John C. Thompson and Joseph Gibson.

James Orange — Susan Fichter, widow — November 26, 1834
Sec. C. Binns

John W. Dodd — Rachel Young — November 26, 1834
Sec. John Young. Ludwick Luckett auth. license for groom. wit. J.W. Bronaugh and Thomas A. Hereford.

Elam C. Veale — Mary E. Hough of Cameron Parish — November 24, 1834
Sec. Joseph Hough, father of girl.

Benjamin Saunders — Mary Catherine Blaker — November 24, 1834
Sec. Amos Beale

Cephas Hempstone — Mary Eleanor Belt — November 19, 1834
Sec. Alfred Belt, father of girl.

Name of Groom	Name of Bride	Date of Bond

Samuel B. Taylor   Sarah E. Hogue   November 15,1834
Sec. Benjamin F. Taylor. Elizabeth Hoge consented to marriage of
her dau. Wit. John G. Hoge

Claiborne Lang   Elizabeth A. Richards   November 10,1834
Sec. Samuel R. Newlon

Samuel T. Canby   Julietta Cookus   November 3,1834
Sec. John G. Hoge

Mason McKnight   Thurza Romine   November 3,1834
Sec. Isaiah Romine, father of girl.

Daniel Dever(Deaver)   Catherine Ritchie   October 29,1834
Sec. John Filler

John George Jr.   Rosanna M. White   October 27,1834
Sec. John H. White

Samuel C. Jackson   Margaret Ann Donohoe   October 25,1834
Sec. E. Hammat

James Harper   Elvina Mahonny   October 13,1834
Sec. Jacob Shriver

George L. Moore   Ann Amanda Russell   October 6,1834
Sec. Henry Russell, father of girl.

William H. Rogers   Mary Jane Rogers   September 22,1834
Sec. Hamilton Rogers, who also test. ages of both.

Daniel Brown   Sarah A. Smith   September 20,1834
Sec. William Wright

Hiram Cockrell   Eleanor Falley   September 10,1834
Sec. Amos Hanvy. Isaac Falley test. ages.

Samuel W. DeButts   Julia A. Dulany   September 13,1834
Sec. John P.Dulany, father of girl and gdn. of groom.

Alfred Young   Emily Worthington   September 9,1834
Sec. Craven Osburn

Thomas Powell   Hester Ann Lum   September 8,1834
Sec. John Lum, father of girl. Peyton Powell test. age of groom.

William McCullough   Clarissa P. Dagg   September 6,1834
Sec. Francis T. Grady

Name of Groom	Name of Bride	Date of Bond
Jacob Saurbaugh Sec. Mathias Prince, father of girl.	Elizth. Prince	September 6,1834
Joseph Helm Sec. William Carr	Mary E. Carr	September 3,1834
George W. Grayson Sec. Landon L. Carter, gdn. of girl.	Juliet A. Murray	September 1,1834
Richard Trenary Sec. Robert Cunningham. Nelson Settle test. girl's age.	Matilda Settle	September 2,1834
Thomas Jones Sec. John L. Chamblin	Lucinda Baldwin	September 1,1834
Bernard Watkins Sec. John W. Littleton	Charlotte Littleton	September 1,1834
James Adams Sec. Daniel Ott. John Cranwell, father of girl, auth. license.	Jane S. Cranwell	May 8,1834
Sampson Hutchison Sec. Edward Harding. Thomas Harding, father of girl, auth. license. Wit. Jackson Harding.	Rachel Harding	May 8,1834
William W. Ball Sec. S. M. Ball. John H. McCabe, father of girl, consented.	Dorothy H. McCabe	May 6,1834
John Heffner Sec. Philip Swank, father of girl.	Sarah Swank	April 22,1834
James B. White Sec. T.M. McIlhany	Agnes B. White	April 15,1834
Redding Hutchison Sec. William Ambler	Catharine B.Hutchison of Cameron Parish	April 10,1834
John Stevens Sec. Alfred H. Shields. Joseph P.Grubb test. ages of both.	Hannah L. Daniel	April 8,1834
Curtis R.Saunders Sec. E. Hammat	Edith Saunders	April 8,1834
John Campbell Sec. John Saunders	Sarah Ann Saunders	March 31,1834
John Johnson Sec. Jacob Staley, father of girl.	Caroline Staley	March 31,1834

Name of Groom	Name of Bride	Date of Bond
William Rollison Sec. Sandford Fling	Henrietta D.Solomon of Cameron Parish	August 30,1834
Jacob Snoots Sec. John Bontz	Catharine Bontz	August 25,1834
William Lanham Sec. James Gibbs. William Gibbs, father of girl, test. ages of both.	Rebecca Gibbs	August 25,1834
Bayliss Trussell Sec. Aaron Chamblin, father of girl. Moses Trussell auth. his son's license. Wit. Thomas Trussell & C.B.Nalls.	Angelina Chamblin	August 19,1834
John Vermilen Sec. William Divine, father of girl, auth. license.	Margaret E. Divine	August 16,1834
John Adams Sec. Bernard Watkins. Ann Brown, mother of girl, auth. license.	Eleanor Watkins	August 1,1834
Samuel Moreland Sec. Joseph H. Fred. George Moorland of Frederick Co. auth. license.	Sarah Fredd	August 11,1834
Urial Triplett Sec. Joseph H. Fred, who test. Elizabeth Fred is girl's mother.	Sarah Ann Fred	February 10,1834
Oscar Fitzallen Reed Sec. Elam C. Veale, who test. ages of both.	Eveline Fleming	February 3,1834
David Brown Sec. John Brown, who test. ages of both.	Kezziah Wiley	February 1,1834
Joshua Gibson Sec. James H. McVeigh. Jesse McVeigh, father of girl, auth. license. Wit. Francis McVeigh.	Mary Ann McVeigh	December 26,1834
Samuel Price Sec. Wm. Burchett. Kitty Burchett test. girl in 22 yr. and auth. license.	Amanda D. Smith	January 1, 1834
Lyman L. Lane Sec. Samuel Pursell, test. ages of both.	Nancy Cost	January 6,1834
Benjamin Melvin Sec. Joseph Cockrel, father of girl.	Isabella Cockrel	January 10,1834
Thomas Kidwell Sec. Townsend J. Jury, who test. girl's age.	Mary Jury	January 8,1834
Thos. K. Humphreys Sec. Presley Cordell, father of girl.	Helen A. Cordell	January 14,1834

Name of Groom	Name of Bride	Date of Bond

Samuel Barker   Rebeckah Bazell   January 15,1834
Sec. Joseph Eidson. John Bazill, father of girl, auth. license.
Wit. Catharine M. Church.

John Widdicombe   Louiza Tavenner   January 18,1834
Sec. Eli Tavenner, father of girl.

Robert J.C.Thompson   Eliza Steadman   January 28,1834
Sec. Parkerson L. Lott, who test. ages of both.

Noble S. Braden   Mary Ann Pusey   January 29,1834
Sec. Joshua Pusey, father of girl.

- - - -   -   - - - -

Moses Thomas   Ann Fox of   January 1, 1835
Sec. Joseph Fox.   Cameron Parish
Benjamin D. Cockran made oath that Moses Thomas is over 21 and that
Joseph Fox is father of Ann.

David H. Lovett   Jane L. Green   January 3,1835
Sec. James H. Bennett. John C. Green augh. license for his dau.
Jane Laurens Green to Dr. David Harrison Lovett.

George Willett   Elizabeth Rhodes   January 6,1835
Sec. Samuel Rhodes, who proved her age. Joseph Orrison proved groom's.

James A. Reed   Mary E. War   January 7,1835
Sec. John War, father of girl.

David Ruse   Sarah Vermillion   January 12,1835
Sec. Garrison Vermillion, father of girl.

Benjamin F. Taylor   Sarah Morris   January 13,1835
Sec. Mahlon Morris, father of girl.

Levi Athey   Agnes Coats   January 23,1835
Sec. Walter Brabham, test. girl's age.

Joshua Hatcher   Sarah Ann Gregg   January 26,1835
Sec. David Reece.

Ephraim Bloxham   Clarissa Fred   January 26,1835
Sec. Joseph H. Fred, who auth. license. Wit. Samuel Moreland.

James Torbert   Maria Humphrey   January 27,1835
Sec. William Little, who test. her age.

Bushrod C. Washington   Maria P.Harrison of   January 27,1835
Sec.Thos.B.Washington   Cameron Parish

Name of Groom	Name of Bride	Date of Bond

Rodney Braden   Eliza A. Vandevanter   February 3,1835
Sec. Gabriel Vandevanter, gdn. of girl.

Humphrey Richards   Hannah Milburn   February 3,1835
Sec. William Milbourn, test. both 21.

Clauson Bond   Susanna C. Rowles   February 3,1835
Sec. Amos Janney

Sandford I. Cockrel   Nancy Schryock of   February 9,1835
Sec.Presley Saunders   Cameron Parish

Benja. Newman   Eliza Newman   February 9,1835
Sec. Sam'l Core or Gore, gdn. of girl.

William Foly   Abigail James of   February 9,1835
Sec. David James,   Cameron Parish
who test. girl and groom, both 21.

Thomas Gheen   Amey Gheen of   February 9,1835
Sec. Robert Power,   Cameron Parish
gdn. of girl.

William Powell   Hannah H. Galleher   February 11,1835
Sec. Moses O. Galleher, test. both 21.

Samuel Orrison   Margaret Field   February 11,1834
Sec. Thomas J. Hanes, who test. both 21.

Joseph Vandeventer   Mary E.Greenlease   February 16,1835
Sec. C.H.F.Greenlease. James Greenlease, father of girl, consented.
Wit. W.H.Cassady.

Thomas A. Lovett   Harriet Atwell   February 18,1835
Sec. James P. Lovett, test. for groom. Manly Atwell test. girl 21.

James Buck   Sarah Vanhorn   February 24,1834
Sec. Bernard Vanhorn, who test. girl 21.

Erasmus Ball   Elizth. Chilton   February 26,1835
Sec. John T. Mulikin, test. ages of both.

George Kabrich   Jane Morrison   February 27,1835
Sec. Edward Morrison, test. their ages.

Ebenezer Brooks   Edith Young   March 2,1835
Sec. John I. Young. David Young, father of girl, consented. Wit.
Edith Hatcher and Hariet Davice

Name of Groom	Name of Bride	Date of Bond

John Carruthers   Malinda E. Nixon   March 3,1835
Sec. Joel Nixon, father of girl.

Samuel Stone   Elizabeth A. Frank   March 10,1834
Sec. Thos. P. Marlow. Josiah Janney affirmed groom 21.

A note signed by M.Bayly,Jr. requesting Mr. Binns furnish him with
fees against George Bayly for recording deed and copy of an agreement
or marriage contract between Thos. Buck & his wife dated March 10,1834.

John Young   Eliza Ann Gheen   March 16,1835
Sec. Leroy Gheen. Narcissa Gheen consented for her dau. Elizabeth
Ann to marry. Wit. John Gheen, Lemuel Gheen & Ebenezer Brooks.

Frederick Miller   Elizabeth Stream   March 23,1835
Sec. Henry Ruse, who test. girl's age.

James Mason   Olivia Hill   March 23,1835
Sec. James Hill, father of girl.

Roger Chew   Sarah W. Aldridge   March 25,1835
Sec. Joseph W. Aldridge

Augustus G. Smith   Ann Maria Johnston   March 25,1834
Sec. Charles A.Johnston, who test. her age.

William McMullen   Ann Wildman   March 30,1835
Sec. Jacob Wildman, father of girl. Daniel McMullen test. groom's age.

John W. Lickey   Euphama Fred   March 31,1835
Sec. William Lickey, father of groom. John Van Sickler test. girl's ag

Burr Piggott   Hannah J. Nichols   April 13,1835
Sec. Tho. Nichols, father of girl.

Abner H. Settle   Isabella S. Hixon   April 13,1835
Sec. Benjamin Hixson, father of girl

James W. Smith   Permillia Osburn   April 28,1834
Sec. Joel Osburn, father of girl.

Sampson Harper   Polly Cox, widow   April 30,1835
Sec. Augustin McDaniel. Stasee Harper, mother of groom, test. he over

Ferdinand Butler   Lydia Cloud   May 11, 1835
Sec. Asa Brown, test. both 21.

Francis W. Powell   Harriet Harding   May 6,1835
Sec. John J. Harding, father of girl.

Name of Groom	Name of Bride	Date of Bond

Andrew Shank   Emily R. Smith   May 18,1835
Sec. Josiah J. Janney, test. ages of both.

George Warner Jr.   Alcinda D. Loveless   May 25,1835
Sec. Thos. Loveless, father of girl. Mahlon Warner test. groom's
age.

Solomon Everhart Jr.   Mary Ann Wenner   June 1,1835
Sec. William Wenner, father of girl. Thomas Everhart test. son's age.

William Norred   Elizabeth E.Dowdell   June 13,1835
Sec. Charles William, gdn. of girl.

Isaiah Simms   Elizth. Darne of   June 20,1835
Sec. Gunnell Darne,   Cameron Parish
test. both 21.

Joseph Gore   Catharine Lightfoot,widow   June 30,1835
Sec. Thomas R. Saunders

William Harper   Tamar Brooks, widow   August 17,1835
Sec. Sam'l Harper

Thomas J. Stedman   Amy Phillips   July 25,1835
Sec. Edmund Phillips. Js. Steadman made oath for T.J.Steadman.

Charles H. Thornton   Ann Eliza Adams   July 21,1835
Sec. Meriweather T.Ashby. Henry Adams, father of girl,consented.
Wit. Thomson Ashby.

Peter Cooper   Rachel Myers   July 27,1835
Sec. Mahlon Myers, father of girl.

Joshua Rodrick   Mary Hamilton   July 30,1835
Sec. Solomon Derry

Joseph Hawkins Jr.   Mary Ann King   July 29,1835
Sec. William King, father of girl. John Nixon test. groom over 21.

John Akers   Stelly Swarts   August 3,1835
Sec. John Palmer, who test. both 21

Martin Fry   Susanna Davis   August 10,1835
Sec. John Talley, who test. girl over 21.

Sampson L. Jenkins   Julia Birch of   September 1,1845
Sec. Lewis D.Birch,   Cameron Parish
who test. girl 21. Barbary Birch test. her dau. Julia's age also
and stated she is her gdn. Wit. Thomas Hunton

Name of Groom	Name of Bride	Date of Bond
Herod Osburn Sec. John Janney,who test. girl over 21.	Pricilla Osburn	August 25,1835
John Mahoney Sec. Jonathan Conard, who test. girl over 21.	Catharine Miller	September 5,1835
John Littleton Sec. Jn. A. Binns	Rebecca Elgin	September 11,1835
Ellwood B. James Sec. Jos. Richardson	Elizth. Ann Richardson	September 11,1835
William Combs Sec. Joshua Nichols, who test. both 21.	Barbara E. McCray	September 14,1835
John Anders Sec. Silas Garrett, gdn. of both.	Susan Beavers	September14, 1835
Alexander Johnston Sec. James Craven, father of girl.	Moranda Craven	September 22,1835
Samuel Palmer Sec. Samuel Palmer Jr. who test. girl's age.	Mary Porter	September 18,1835
Miles Hilton Sec. William Carmel, who test. girl over 21.	Rebekah Mansfield	September 23,1835
Peter Myers Sec. Casper Spring, father of girl.	Catherine Spring	September 20,1835
Daniel Potterfield Sec. E. Garrett. Enos Garrett father of girl.	Eliza Garrett	September 23,1835
R.W.A.Power Sec. Ananias Orrison.	Susanna E.Davis of Cameron Parish	September 30,1835
Addison Chappell Sec. Jonah Steer who test. girl over 21.	Mary Anderson	October 5,1835
John M.Moran Sec. Jesse Timms. Jordan B.Luck test. his dau. of age and consented. Wit. Margaret Speller.	Drusilla Ann Luck	October 6,1835
Lial Beech Sec. Joseph Hough. Mary Ball gave consent for her dau. Wit.H.G.Butler	Charlotte E. Ball	October 12,1835
Shadrich Thompson Sec. John W. Payne, who test. both over 21.	Elizabeth Payne	October 10,1835

Name of Groom	Name of Bride	Date of Bond

Solomon Everhart   Sarah Ann Edwards   October 12,1835
Sec. Joseph Edwards, father of girl. Israel Edwards test. for groom.

James West   Judah Jackson   October 15,1835
Sec. C. Binns

George Carter   Elizabeth O. Lewis   October 30,1835
Sec. Jesse Timms

Henry Grimes   Ann Elizabeth Cridler   October 22,1835
Sec. John Cridler, father of girl.

Alfred Glascock   Margt. Carrington,widow   October 31,1835
Sec. Roger Chew

Nimrod Trussell   Susan Fleming   November 2,1835
Sec. George Fleming, who test. both over 21.

Lewis Livingston   Amey Powell   November 3,1835
Sec. Levin H. Powell, father of girl.

David Conner   Jane Ann Merchant   November 9,1835
Sec. William Merchant, father of girl.

Charles Gulatt   Eleanor Sinclair   November 17,1835
Sec. Geo. Sinclair, who test. to ages of both.

Matthew McKennie   Sarah E. Torbert   November 19,1835
Sec. William Settle, who test. girl's age.

Washington Beavers   Delila Anderson   November 25,1835
Sec. John A. Beavers. Alfred Anderson test. girl's age. John Asby
Beavers test. groom's age. Samuel Beavers, father of groom.

John Bayley Jr.   Lucy Hutchison of   December 7,1835
Sec. Chapin Bayly   Cameron Parish

Gibson Gregg   Mary R. Cochran   December 14,1835
Sec. Tholemiah Cochran

Geo. W. Shuman   Harriet P. Surghnor   December 14,1835
Sec. William L. Bogue. James Surghnor test. gor his dau. Wit. Rev.
Cochran.

Algernon S. Tebbs   Julia E. Coleman   December 23,1835
Sec. John A. Waggaman

Elias Cooper   Margaret Cooper   December 27,1835
Sec. John Crim.

Name of Groom	Name of Bride	Date of Bond

John Talbert   Eliza Perry   March 21,1835
Sec. Marshall B. Perry. Hezekiah Perry, father of girl, consented.

- - - -   -   - - - -

John P. Hough   Hannah A. Schooley   May 2,1836
Sec. Samuel Hough. Elizabeth Schooley consented for her dau.
Wit. Presley Neale Schooley.

Samuel Brown   Mary Jane Bradfield   October 31,1836
Sec. John Brown, father of groom. Wm.Bradfield, father of girl.

Martin Yeaca   Amanda Russell   October 31,1836
Sec. Thomas Russell, father of girl.

George W. Wynkoop   Nancy Reese   October 31,1836
Sec. Reed Poulton.

Jefferson Lockheart   Margt. Waltman   October 26,1836
Sec. Joseph Miller. Wm. Lockheart test. that Jefferson Lockheart of
Hampshire County, his son and over 21. Wit. Asa Hiett & Madison Lockhea

Samuel Tavenner   Sarah Jane McCray   November 12,1836
Sec. John Purcell. James McCray auth. license for his dau. Wit.Presley
Orrison. Richard Tavenner auth. license for groom.

Jacob Householder   Catherine Compher   November 14,1836
Sec. Peter Compher, father of girl.

Samuel Rogers   Jane E. Adams   November 14,1836
Sec. Richard Adams, father of girl.

Stephen T. Chamblin   Susannah Marmaduke   November 15,1836
Sec. Alfred G. Chamblin, gdn. of girl.

Abraham E. Nichols   Sarah Miller   November 22,1836
Sec. George Miller, father of girl.

Richard L. Rogers   Nancy H. McVeigh   November 26,1836
Sec. James H. Gulick. Jesse McVeigh test. for dau. Wit. Angeline
McVeigh, Jesse H. McVeigh.

Harrison Cummings   Ansey Cummings   November 26,1836
Sec. William Lyons, who test. to ages of both.

Luke S. Forrest   Mary Ann Middleton,widow November 28,1836
Sec. John M. Wilson

Name of Groom	Name of Bride	Date of Bond

Samuel P. Murray   Elizabeth Carrol   November 29,1836
Sec. Abraham Sinkfield.

Israel Everhart   Maria Ropp   November 29,1836
Sec. Solomon Ritchie. Nicholas Ropp, father of girl, consented.
Wit. Nelson B. Everhart.

Marcus Dishman   Mary Ann Violett   December 12,1836
Sec. Thomas W. Winn. John Violett, father of girl, consented.

William McPherson   Nancy Ann Brown   December 6,1836
Sec. George Brown, brother of girl, who test. she 21.

William T. Hart   Emiline Frances Thatcher December 3,1836
Sec. G'e Richardson. Mary Thatcher consented for her dau. Wit. George
Richardson and Thomas E. Brandon.

Samuel Evans   Mary Ann Myers   December 12,1836
Sec. Jonathan Painter. Washington Myers, gdn. of girl. Jesse Evans
test. that groom was born in yr. 1813, Mar.2 - which will make him
23 yrs. of age last March.

John L. Parsons   Jane Timms   December 12,1836
Sec. Jesse Timms, father of girl.

Samuel Laycock   Matilda Blaher   December 12,1836
Sec. William Shields, who test. to girl's age.

Joseph Orrison   Jane E. Whaley of   December 13,1836
Sec.John G.Whaley   Cameron Parish
James Whaley,father of girl,consented. Wit.Bailys Foley.

Jonah Steer   Mary E. Brown, widow   December 15,1836
Sec. C. Binns. Ephraim Schooley test. girl his dau. and widow of
John Brown,dec'd. and she is 22 yrs. of age.

Mahlon Taylor   Amanda M.Gore   December 15,1836
Sec. Thomas Gore, father of girl.

Solomon Heater   Caroline H. Wunder   December 16,1836
Sec. Harry S. Wunder, father of girl.

James Feagans   Mary Ann McCrae   December 17,1836
Sec. Joseph Nichols, test. the girl over 21

William Gideon   Frances Booth   December 17,1836
Sec. James Boothe, test. girl over 21.

Name of Groom	Name of Bride	Date of Bond

Manly Mead   Mary Ann Nichols   December 17,1836
Sec. Jacob Nichols, father of girl, consented. Wit. Jonathan Nichols, & Jacob Nichols,Jr.

Josiah Bennett   Eliza Ann Lowe   December 19,1836
Sec. Joseph Wood, who test. girl's age.

John Sexton   Alcinda Parker   December 21,1836
Sec. Chilton Parker, who test. girl's age.

Richard Triplitt   Sarah A. Tavenner   December 19,1836
Sec. James Tavener, who test. both 21.

Abner H. Hixson   Harriet R.Reebleman December 24,1836
Sec. William M. Lynn, who test. both 21.

Thomas Muse   Sydney Jane Havener December 26,1836
Sec. Michael Havener

Lawson Kelly   Amanda I. Clowe   December28, 1836
Sec. L.Worthington, who test. for groom. William H.Clowe, father of girl, test. her age.

Thomas Lemon   Mariah Bodine   December 31,1836
Sec. Joseph H. Bodine

David Boren   Elizabeth Sexton   December 28,1836
Sec. Edward Hooper, who test. both 21.

Jonathan Ewers   Phoebe Gregg   October 19,1836
Sec. Townsend J. Jury. Abner Jury test. girl over 21.

Joseph W. Alder   Lucy A.Alder   October 17,1836
Sec. Albert Allder, who test. girl over 21.

P.H.W.Bronaugh   Eleanor A.Wildman   October 10,1836
Sec. Francis W.Luckett. Jane D.Wildman, mother of girl, consented. Wit.Rachel Wornal & I.B.H.Wildman.

Mahlon James   Rachel Ann Paxon   October 8,1836
Sec. Elijah James, father of groom. Samuel Paxson, father of girl.

Andrew H. Kalb   Ann James   October 8,1836
Sec. Elijah James. Absalom Kalb, test. his son past 21.

Richard Tavenner   Sidney Copeland   October 25,1836
Sec. Eli Hunt

Presley Parker   Lucy Ellen Perry   October 20,1836
Sec. John D. Perry, father, consented.

Name of Groom	Name of Bride	Date of Bond
John C. Filler	Ann Riley	October 4,1836

Sec. Jacob Shafer, who test. girl over 21.

Joseph H. Wright	Catherine Rinker	September 19,1836

Sec. Edward Rinker, father of girl.

Henry Timms	Castara Hesser	September 19,1836

Sec. John L. Parsons. Nancy Morris or Morrison, mother of girl,consented.
Wit. John Hesser.

Fenelon Slack	Margaret G. Tucker	October 6,1836

Sec. Margaret Tucker, mother of girl. Father is dead.

Isaiah B. Janney	Hannah S. Hirst	September 12,1836

Sec. William Brown, who test. girl over 21.

Isaiah Beans	Sophronia Morris	September 15,1836

Sec. John Hesser, gdn. of girl.

George W. Smith	Mary Esther Rice	September 13,1836

Sec. Thirza Rice, mother of girl.

John Goodheart	Lucinda Rhodes	September 12,1836

Sec. Spence Minor, who test. girl over 21.

George W. Tavenner	Mary Ewers	August 22,1836

Sec. Samuel A. Jackson, who test. girl over 21.

William S. Ward	Mary Blincoe	August 9,1836

Sec. George Adie

Jesse Attwell	Mary Peugh,widow	August 9,1836

Sec. C. Binns

Samuel S. Downey	Nancy Fiechter of	September 7,1836
	Cameron Parish	

Sec.George Fechter,
father of girl.

George William Dorrell	Mary Ann Boszell	July 25,1836

Sec. Susan Boszell, mother of girl, father is dec'd.

Montgomery Blair	Caroline R. Buckner	July 12,1836

Sec. Spencer A. Buckner.

Israel Garrett	Mary Young	June 13,1836

Sec. David Young, father of girl.

Name of Groom	Name of Bride	Date of Bond
Solomon Gibson Sec. William Galleher	Jane W. Cooper	June 13,1836
Peter O'Brien Sec. Arthur Orison, who test. girl's age over 21.	Mary Donohoe	June 13,1836
Samuel Darr Sec. Geo. W. Shoemaker, who test. girl's age. Sam'l Cooper test. groom's age.	Margaret Shoemaker	June 8,1836
Francis Elgin Sec. William Ball. Amos Fouch, father of girl, consented.	Mary Fouch	June 4,1836
Samuel Trittipo Sec. Andrew Fry, who test. girl over 21.	Mary Frye	May 28,1836
Sebastian McPherson Sec. E. Thompson	Sally Felby,widow	May 25,1836
William Graham Sec. Thompson Stone, who test. girl over 21.	Sarah Stone	May 21,1836
Daniel Miller Sec. John A. Klein, who test. both 21.	Mary A. Klein	May 20,1836
John L. Gill Sec. John C. Humphrey. Minor Furr auth.license for his dau. Wit. Mahlon Fulton.	Cath'e M. Furr	May 17,1836
John Latimer Sec. Newton Keene	Lydia Ann Dulin of Cameron Parish	January 11,1836
William Beatty Sec. Jacob Smith, father of girl.	Cath'e Eliza Smith	May 17,1836
William T. Hereford Sec. Henry H. Hutchison, father of girl. Thos. A.Hereford test. groom over 21.	Julian Hutchison	May 16,1836
Sydnor Williams Sec. Charles Williams, who test. girl over 21.	Eleanor V. Craven	May 16,1836
James McNealy Sec. Henry Lowe. William Rice test. groom over 21, and that Henry Lowe the father of girl.	Mary Lowe of/ Cameron Parish	April 21,1836
John Crain Sec. John Wornal	Elizth. Wornal	April 11,1836
John Bartlett Sec. John Compher, father of girl.	Sarah Compher	March 19,1836

Name of Groom	Name of Bride	Date of Bond

Addison Osburn   Lydia Ann Osburn   March 14,1836
Sec. Joel Osburn, father of girl.

Benjamin Graves   Mary Compher   March 14,1836
Sec. Peter Compher. Francis Simpson test. groom over 21 and
that Peter Compher is father of girl.

James Gheen   Winifred Bodine   March 28,1836
Sec. John Bodine, father of girl.

David Young   Phebe R. Donohoe   March 29,1836
Sec. Stephen J.Donohoe

James Fields   Maria Richardson   March 1, 1836
Sec. William Taylor. Marthy Fields consents. Wit. Th.L.Humphrey &
Mahlon Tavenner.

William Compher   Mary Fawley   February 22,1836
Sec. Henry Fawley, father of girl.

John Wheatly   Eliza Kippon   February 19,1836
Sec. William Rippon.

Geo. W. Hunter Jr.   Mary A. Conrad   February 8,1836
Sec. David Conrad, father of girl.

Lewis French   Eliza Marshall   February 8,1836
Sec. James Whitacre. James French test. both over 21.

Thomas Ward   Hannah Fox of   January 25,1836
Sec. Jacob Fox   Cameron Parish

Washington Stone   Mary Houser   January 23,1836
Sec. Thompson Stone, who test. groom over 21. Wit. Jacob Houser.
Abraham Houser consented for his dau.

William Fawley   Elizabeth Compher   January 25,1836
Sec. John Compher, father of girl.

George N. Tavenner   Elizabeth Hann   January 20,1836
Sec. Mathias Hann, fater of girl. Eli Tavenner test. groom over 21.

Alexander Newton   Eliz. Hinton, widow January 19,1836
Sec. John C. Newton.

Thomas Jefferson Young Mercy Smith   January 16,1836
Sec. Manly Mead, who test. both over 21.

Henry Corbin Blincoe   Mary Ann Solomon   January 15,1836
Sec. William Solomon, father of girl.

Name of Groom	Name of Bride	Date of Bond

Henry Adams   Mary McGaha   January 13,1836
Sec. David McGaha, father of girl.

Benjamin Barton   Harriet G.Fletcher January 11,1836
Sec. Samuel Richards, who test. groom over 21. Joshua Fletcher
auth. license for his dau. Wit. A.G.Chamblin.

Jesse W. Mobberley   Catharine T.Moore January 7,1836
Sec. John Hough test. both over 21.

- - - -   -   - - - -

Leven D. Smallwood   Juliet Ann Perry October 30,1837
Sec. Abner Carter. Mary Smallwood,mother of groom, auth.license.
Wit. Thornton Walker. Presley Parker test. girl's age.

John H. Thompson   Nancy Tavener   December 26,1837
Sec. Elisha Janney. Joseph Tavenner, father of girl, auth. license.
Wit. Mahlon Tavenner and John Tavenner.

Israel Myers   Mary Titus   December 19,1837
Sec. Mahlon Myers, who test. ages of both.

Albert G. Chamblin   Eveline B.Maddux December 19,1837
Sec. John Francis, who test. ages of both.

George W. Noland   Ruth H. Taylor   December 19,1837
Sec. Barney Taylor, who test. girl's father dec'd. Ruth C.Taylor
mother of girl, auth. license. Wit. Mahlon K.Taylor.

Moses Arnett   Ruth Hannah Gibson December 13,1837
Sec. Jonas Janney, who test. ages of both.

Archibald Thrasher   Emily Jane Alder December 30,1837
Sec. William Allder. Latimer Allder, father of girl, auth. license.
Sec. Leonidas Allder.

William Gadsby   Jane K. Smith   December 7,1837
Sec. Edmund Taylor

Murphey C. Shumate   Diadama Elgin   October 7,1837
Sec. Levi T. Roller. Oliver Edwards test. girl's age. Francis Shreve.

Aaron Roller   Eliza Jane Cole   December 4,1837
Sec. Levi T. Roller

John H. Bennett   Hannah Ann Frank April 11, 1837
Sec. Thos. J. Marlow

Name of Groom	Name of Bride	Date of Bond

Joseph S. Hough   Mary M. Hough   April 29,1837
Sec. Benjamin Hough, who also test. ages of both.

Bernard Hough   Sarah Ann Clendening   July 27,1837
Sec. William Clendening Jr.

John Wm.Jeffries   Eliza Johnston   July 17,1837
Sec. Braxton B. Jeffries. Baldwin Johnston, father of girl, auth.
license. Wit:Thomas B.Johnston & John Drish.

Armistead Quick   Margaret Ann Powell   August 28,1837
Sec. Catesby Jones.

John McKimmy   Sarah Walters,alias Thornton September 22,1837
Sec. Alfred Belt.

James Shaw   Anna Mumphred   October 24,1837
Sec. John Bontz

Amos Fouch   Ellen Stephens   October 17,1837
Sec. Isaac Torreyson, who test. girl's age.

Amos Fouch   Ellen Stephens   October 7,1837
Sec. Lewis Cross. Gustavus Elgin ack. girl over 21.

Bannister P. Stevens   Elizabeth Carns   December 2,1837
Sec. Warner W. Shackleford, who also test. ages.

Alexander Skinner   Sarah Ann Cochran   November 25,1837
Sec. William B. Cochran, who test. ages.

William Long   Mary Hurdle   November 13,1837
Sec. Amos Neer, who test. ages.

Mason James   Patience Nichols   November 13,1837
Sec. Nathaniel Nichols, gdn. of girl.

Theo'd Leith   Veturia A. Plaster   November 1,1837
Sec. L.L.Carter. Henry Plaster,father of girl, auth. license.
Wit. Townsend Howell.

Washington Harper   Debby Roberts   October 30,1837
Sec. William Harper. Jonathan Harper test. ages.

Joseph Davis   Amey Powell   November 20,1837
Sec. Peyton Powell. Benjamin Davis test. groom's age.

Name of Groom	Name of Bride	Date of Bond
Daniel Mason Sec. Peter Mason. George Waller, father of girl.	Elizabeth Waller	October 23,1837
Mahlon Morris Sec. Andrew Ogden, who test. age of girl.	Ann Ogden	October 18,1837
George Vinsel Sec. Samuel Potterfield, who test. groom's age.	Catharine Shover,widow	October 13,1837
Howard C. Freeman Sec. Daniel J.French	Courtney W.E.M.French of Cameron Parish	October 13,1837
Hiram McKenna Sec. George Fitcher, father of girl.	Amanda Fitcher of Cameron Parish	October 10,1837
Isaac Sinclair Sec. Francis Moxley & Lucian Fitzhugh	Elizabeth Ann Moxley of Cameron Parish	October 18,1837
Jason Wilmarth Sec. Hugh F. Rutter, gdn. of girl. Wit. Edmund R.Gantt.	Mary Ann Jane Rutter	October 9,1837
Harley Cockeril Sec. Alfred H. Shields	Harriet Craig	October 9,1837
William Weedon Sec. David Brown, who also test. ages.	Lavina Wiley	October 7,1837
John A. Beavers Sec. Washington Beavers, who test. ages.	Christian Anderson	September 23,183
Henry Neer Sec. Michael Derry	Lydia Ann Derry	October 2,1837
Joseph Carr Sec. James M. Carr, who test. ages.	Martha Ann Carr	October 3,1837
William Davis Sec.B.Shreve Jr. (William Adams in body of bond)	Darcus Preston	September 19,183
Joseph Hart Sec. Enoch Glascock	Sarah Rawlings	September 15,183
John McCarty Sec. Reuben Cockrill & Mary Coe	Emily Jane Coe	September 14,183
Elisha Chamblin Sec. Lawson Osburn, who test. ages.	Mahala Romine	September 11,183

Name of Groom	Name of Bride	Date of Bond
Joseph Carter Sec. Stephen Gregg	Martha Ann Lucas	September 6,1837
Washington Williams Sec. Peter Skinner. Jas. Thomas test. groom's age.	Sarah E. Skinner	August 29,1837
Thomas Cole Sec. Peggy Cole, mother of bride, consents, and test. groom's age.	**Elizabeth Cole**	August 29,1837
Thomas Brown Sec. George Brown, who test. ages.	Louisa Whiting	August 14,1837
William H. Francis Sec. Uriel Glasscock, father of girl.	Mary E. Glasscock of Cameron Parish	August 10,1837
John Conner Sec. Levi Ewers, who test. ages.	Susan Lyne	August 5,1837
James Long Sec. James Boothe, who test. ages.	Malinda Davis	August 4,1837
Laurence P. Bayne Sec. A. M. Gibson. Bushrod Rust, father of girl, auth. license. Wit. Wilman Cole. Jesse McVeigh test. age of groom.	Delia Elizabeth Rust	July 6,1837
Charles Scott Sec. Noble S. Braden	Cynthia Comstock	June 28,1837
David H. Galleher Sec. Edmund R.Gantt, who also test. girl's age. Sarah Galleher, mother of girl, auth. license. Wit. Jonathan Lovett.	Caroline Norton	June 13,1837
Joseph Arundel Sec.Wm.Lafever William Mershon test. groom's age.	Honour Lafever of Cameron Parish	June 7,1837
John Fawley Sec. Tunis Titus, who test. girl's age.	Edith Titus	June 6,1837
Joseph Fred,Sr. Sec. Joseph H. Fred, who test. girl's age.	Elizabeth Peyton	June 1,1837
William Harper Sec. John Umbaugh, who test. girl's age.	Ann Mondy	May 29,1837
Benjamin F. Carter Sec. Ro. L. Wright.	Rebecca M. Wright	May 17,1837

Name of Groom	Name of Bride	Date of Bond

George D. Hicks   Jane Morrison   May 4,1837
Sec. Horatio Styles. (Girl was dau.of Archibald Morrison,dec'd)

Eli C. Albaugh   Sarah Ann Gray   April 28,1837
Sec. John A. Moore. Phebe Gray, mother of girl, auth. license.
Wit. D. Shawen.

Richard H. Carter   Mary Welby DeButts   April 25,1837
Sec. Saml. W.DeButts. John P.Dulany, gdn.of girl, auth. license.
Wit. Robert Carter & Mary Dulany. Edward Carter auth. license for
his son. Wit. S.S.Scott.

Marcus Anderson   Mary Ann Brown   April 11,1837
Sec. William P.Brown, father of girl, consented, and test. to groom's ag

William Newman   Mary Biscoe of   April 10,1837
Sec. Edward M. Baker   Cameron Parish

Calvin Coats   Elizabeth Robey   April 10,1837
Sec. Abel Jones, who test. ages. Jane Robey, mother of girl, auth.
license. Wit. Mahlon Baldwin.

Richard Adams   Anna Dyer   April 10,1837
Sec. Chs. G. Eskridge

Edwin Rogers   Alice Ann Cross   April 10,1837
Sec. Harrison Cross, father of girl, consented.

Malcolm Brady   Sarah Ann Pierce   March 31,1837
Sec. Wallace Brady

John Pyott   Ann Nixon   March 28,1837
Sec. James T. Vermillion, who test. girl's age.

Samuel D. Rice   Mary Rhodes   March 14,1837
Sec. Lewis H. Saunders. Randolph Rhodes, father of girl, consented.
Wit. John Boley,Jr.

Fenton M. Love   Elizabeth Morris   March 13,1837
Sec. Jonah Nichols. Mahlon Morris,father of girl, consented.

Hugh Rutter   Elizabeth Rivers   March 13,1837
Sec. D. Galleher

Lacey Peyton   Eliza Jones   March 13,1837
Sec. Abel Jones. Elizabeth Peyton, mother of groom, consented. Father
not living, no gdn. and he is a minor. Wit. Jas. Alexander. Thomas
Jones, father of girl, consented. Wit. Francis F. King.

Name of Groom	Name of Bride	Date of Bond

Jacob Nichols — Ianthy Smith — March 13,1837
Sec. George McMullen. Saml. Nichols test. girl's age.

Matson James — Hannah Thomas — March 13,1837
Sec. Mahlon Thomas

John Vermilion — Hannah Pomroy — March 13,1837
Sec. John Simpson. Burr Pomroy auth. license for his dau. James T.
Vermilion test. groom's age. Wit. John McCarty.

Richard L. Hipkins — Elizabeth Jacobs — March 13,1837
Sec. J.L.Sampson, who test. ages.

William S. Greenlease — Mary Ann Hughes — March 13,1837
Sec. Thomas P.Matthews, who test. girl's age.

William H. Cassady — Mary Jane Denham — March 1,1837
Sec. D.B.Denham

John Compher — Susan Fawley — February 14,1837
Sec. Henry Fawley

Jas. Beaumont — Caroline Eliza Johnson — January 12,1837
Sec. Amos W.Johnson, father of girl. (Ack. Feb.12)

Samuel Ellis — Effie Ann McKim — February 7,1837
Sec. James McKim, who test. groom's age.

Thomas A.H.Evans — Mary Elizth.Forrest,widow. February 2,1837
Sec. Bushrod Grigsby

Edward Rhine — Nancy Cole — February 27,1837
Sec. Peter Cole, who test. girl's age.

Wesley White — Jane Harden — February 2,1837
Sec. Edward Harding, who test. groom's age. Thomas Harding, father of
girl, auth. license. Wit. Jackson Harding & Calvin Coats.

Nelson B. Wilson — Rebecca B.Hoskinson — February 20,1837
Sec. Thomas L.Hoskinson, who test. girl's age.

Elijah M. Smittey — Catherine Davis — January 30,1837
Sec. John Spring, who test. ages.

Edward Jenkins — Martha S. Keene — January 27,1837
Sec. Richard Keen, who test. ages.

Name of Groom	Name of Bride	Date of Bond
John Weadon Sec. A.G.Chamblin	Harriet Palmer	January 24,1837
Thomas Hutchison Sec. Charles W. Gist, who test. girl's age.	Mary Ellen Gist	January 16,1837
Jacob Ropp Sec. William Derry, who test. ages.	Isabella Crowen	January 15,1837
Eli F. Cooper Sec. William Commerell	Susanna Commerell	January 15,1837
John Brown Sec. William Brown, who test. girl's age.	Margt. Whiting	January 10,1837
Jacob Short Sec. George Vinsel, gdn. of girl.	Eliza M. Smith	January 15,1837
Robert Strother Sec. Hiram McVeigh, gdn. of girl.	Caroline Howard	January 9,1837
Robert Gooding Sec. Joseph Shugars, who test. ages.	Lettuce Vermillion	January 6,1837
John N. Bumcrots Sec. Jacob Bumcrots	Catharine Cooper	January 5,1837
Joel White Sec. William Shields, who test. ages.	Harriet Blaker	January 2,1837
- - - -	-	- - - -
James F. Divine Sec. Aaron Divine. Middleton Smith test. girl 21.	Hannah E. Towner	January 22,1837 (Ack.Jan.22,1838)
Israel Dulany Sec. Geo. Miller	Catharine Miller	August 2, 1838
Henry Spring Sec. Jno. Williams, who test. ages.	Charlotte Carne	May 18,1838
Mahlon Myers Sec. Jno. Crist, who test. Ages.	Elizth. Davis	January 29,1838
John Davis Sec. Presley Davis, who test. ages.	Malinda Davis	August 6,1838

Name of Groom	Name of Bride	Date of Bond

Bernard Simpson   Ann M. Perry   May 14,1838
Sec. Alfred Spates, who test. ages.

John L. Green   Mary Elizabeth Moore   May 7,1838
Sec. Jesse W. Mobberley. Mary Moore, mother of girl, test. that
girl's father, Abner Moore, is dec'd. and she consented to marriage.
Sec. Garret Hough.

George F. Crim   Matilda Filler   January 2,1838
Sec. Jacob Filler, who test. ages.

John Cross   Elizabeth Bussey of   September 3,1838
Sec. Daniel Ackers.   Cameron Parish
Henry Lowe test. ages.

James Speaks   Sally Gheen of   May 19,1838
Sec. Henry Hatton   Cameron Parish

John C. Williams   Elizabeth Spring   September 18,1838
Sec. Henry Spring, who test. ages.

William B.Sullivan   Susan King   February 19,1838
Sec. William King, who test. to groom's age.

Leven Richards   Evaline Jinkins   March 21,1838
Sec. John T. Jinkins. John Jinkins, father of girl, auth. license.
Wit. Jesse Richards.

Albert Harding   Ellen E. Fox of   October 25,1838
Sec. James Hutchison   Cameron Parish

Samuel Virts   Hannah Elizabeth Brown   January 22,1838
Sec. Joseph Fox, who test. Jas.Brown, father of girl,dec'd. Mary
Brown, mother, auth. license. Wit. Arthur Orison & John E. Poulton

Francis J. Stribling   Amanda Mary Ann Heaton   October 23,1838
Sec. Jonathan Heaton. Thos.W.Edward test. age of groom.

Benjamin T. Chinn   Edmonia R. Carter of   January 26,1838
Sec. Alfred Ball   Cameron Parish

Michael Twomey   Sarah E. Handy of   October 2,1838
Sec. Geo. Adie   Cameron Parish

Philip Hopkins   Joannah A. Carter   October 4,1838
Sec. John C. Murry

John Ault   Mahala Campbell of   June 5,1838
Sec. William Ault,father   Cameron Parish
of groom. John Campbell, father of girl.

Name of Groom	Name of Bride	Date of Bond

Samuel Shoemaker   Mary C.E.Beall   September 28,1838
Sec. David L. Beall.   David F.Beall, father of girl, auth. license.
Wit. Susan Beall.

James Smith   Mary Ann Eliza Price   January 29,1838
Sec. Geo. Price.

Jacob Potterfield   Sarah Ann Rebecca Johnson   March 26,1838
Sec. Robert Johnston, who test. ages.

Samuel G. Gordon   Martha Margaret Clarke   June 11, 1838
Sec. John H. Clark

Robert A. Ish   Pamelia H. Hixson   November 1,1838
Sec. Benjamin Hixson

Isaac G. Nichols   Louisa White   January 22,1838
Sec. Thomas Nichols.   Consent given by both fathers, unnamed.

Henry Reid   Lyda Dillehay   March 19,1838
Sec. Hyram Reid, who test. ages.

Elias Davis   Charlotte Everhart   October 22,1838
Sec. Philip Everhart.

Benjamin Hummer   Dorothy R. Noble   February 23,1838
Sec. John S. Noble   (Signed Benjamin Hoummer)

John Souder   Mary M. Filler   March 23,1838
Sec. Jacob Housholder

Warner Holmes   Elizabeth Smith   March 26,1838
Sec. William Smith, who test. groom's age.

James M. Carr   Elizabeth Cost   March 10,1838
Sec. Peter Cost.   Mary Cost, mother of girl, auth. license. Wit.
David McIntosh.

Edward T. Green   Malinda Darne   March 28,1838
Sec. James W. Darne.   James Darne, father of girl, auth. license and
his son James W., affirmed same.

Andrew Campbell   Martha Ann Campbell   January 15,1838
Sec. John Campbell

Jacob Smith   Mary Amich   March 26,1838
Sec. Abraham Smith.   Geo. Vincell test. girl 21 and Solomon Smith
test. groom 21.

Name of Groom	Name of Bride	Date of Bond
Jackson D. Jennings	Mary Ann Margaret Rogers	April 28,1838
Sec. Sanford Rogers		

Noah Arnold   Emeline Filler   November 13,1838
Sec. Jacob Filler, father of girl, test. ages.

Solomon George   Mary Denges   November 14,1838
Sec. H.S. Wunder, who test. ages.

George Rhodes   Mary Ann Brown   March 27,1838
Sec. Joseph Brown. (Bond signed Joseph Rhodes, not George)

Garrett Wynkoop   Mary S. Hunt   June 6,1838
Sec. Eli Hunt. John Wynkoop test. groom's age.

Philip Pendleton   Virginia M. Tutt   June 6,1838
Sec. N.C.Mason, who test. her age.

John Yakey   Elizabeth Crumbaker   October 26,1838
Sec. Solomon Crumbaker, father of girl, consented.

Griffith E. Thomas   Rebecca B. Wright   November 23,1838
Sec. W.O. Wright

Jonathan Mathew   Rebecca C. Copeland   May 7,1838
Sec. David Copeland

Jeremiah Titus   Susan Goodheart   October 1,1838
Sec. John Goodheart, who test. ages.

William J. Wertenbaker   Sarah A. Thomas   June 26,1838
Sec. Absalem R. Replor, who test. groom's age.

Albert Wright   Elizabeth Ann Davis   November 26,1838
Sec. Elias Davis, who test. ages.

David Conner   Elizabeth E. Anderson   September 8,1838
Sec. Robert S. Anderson

David Shriver   Amelia Ropp   February 26,1838
Sec. Samuel Ropp, who test. ages.

John C. Thompson   Sarah Adams   October 27,1838
Sec. Landon Worthington. Alfred Works test. both 21.

William H. French   Mary Ann Hanes   January 22, 1838
Sec. Thomas W. Hart. Mary Hanes auth. her dau.'s license. Wit. C.W.
Vandeventer.

Name of Groom	Name of Bride	Date of Bond
Charles A. Johnston Sec. S.M.Boss	Mary R. Boss	September 13,1838
Cyrus Burson Sec. Presley Saunders	Ansey Thompson	January 4,1838
William W. Wenner Sec. Emanuel Waltman	Susan A. Waltman	January 4,1838
Sampson Lickey Sec. James A. Reid, who also test. ages.	Mary Carson	January 1,1838
Jonas Potts Sec. William Silcott, who test. ages.	Amanda Silcott	January 17,1838
Samuel Young Sec. Samuel Craven, who test. ages.	Sophia V.Craven	August 30,1838
Presley Beach Sec. Abel Orrison. Mary Thiare auth. dau.'s license. Wit.Michal Lynn.	Frances Lane	April 23,1838
John S. Pancoast Sec. Samuel C. Russell,Jr.	Louisa Smith	November 12,1838
William C. Cocke Sec. John Riley. Hester Hines, mother of girl, auth. license. Wit. William Anjel.	Lucy Ann Hines	March 21,1838
Peter Wire Sec. Luther A. Thrasher. Elizabeth Stoneburner, mother and gdn. of girl, auth. license. Wit. Jonathan Wenner.	Mary Louisa Ann Stoneburner	February 3,1838
Robert W. Henderson Sec. John Campbell, who test. groom's age.	Elizabeth Campbell	February 6,1838
William H. Rice Sec. George Rhodes	Jane Rhodes	May 29,1838
Charles A. Balthrope Sec. James E. Dawes, test. ages. Eli Crupp, gdn. of girl, auth. license. Wit. A.H. Little.	Mary A.M.Dawes	February 13,1838
James Skinner Sec. James Priest. C.Turner of Millsville, father of girl, auth.license. Wit. Henry Priest. Gabriel Skinner test. groom 21 on Feb. 6 last. Wit. George Turner.	Jane Elizabeth Turner	January 10,1838

Name of Groom	Name of Bride	Date of Bond

Thomas M. Wrenn   Julia Ann Cockerell   July 4,1838
Sec. William Amblar.

Bailey Crain   Huldah Cockerill   June 16,1838
Sec. Luther O. Sullivan, who test. girl's age.

William C. Luckett   Mary Virts   March 12,1838
Sec. John Virts, who test. girl's age.

David L. Beall   Luclemma E. Gibson   May 25,1838
Sec. Levi G. Ewers, who test. ages. Rebecca Gibson, mother of girl,
auth. license. Wit. Leonora J. Ewers.

Ferdinand A.F.Carter   Pammelia Jane Swart   November 7,1838
Sec. Samuel Swart. Elizabeth Swart, mother of girl, auth. license.
Wit. John Rose.

John B. Dutton   Emma Schooley   September 1,1838
Sec. T.M. Bond

Jonah Tavenner   Sarah Jane Baldwin   August 13,1838
Sec. Isaac B. Baldwin. Ruth Baldwin, mother of girl, auth. license.
Wit. John D. Baldwin.

Oswell Carter   Emily Combs   October 8,1838
Sec. Thomas Powell, who test. ages.

Geo. W.Carlyle Whiting   Mary Ann Dulany   December 22,1838
Sec. Chs. G. Eskridge. John P.Dulany, auth. license.

James McDowell   Sarah Ann Prince   February 14,1838
Sec. Mathias Prince, test. ages.

John Hough   Mary Ann Grubb   December 24,1838
Sec. John Grubb, father of girl, test. ages.

Daniel Fry   Susan Anderson   December 24,1838
Sec. Geo. Anderson, who test. ages. Wm. Galleher, test. groom over 21.
John Anderson, father of girl, auth. license. Wit. John Tumblin.

William Ball   Sarah Ellen Lee of   December 17,1838
Sec. Joshua Ball, who   Cameron Parish
test. ages of both.

Joseph Eidson   Mary Skinner   August 13,1838
Sec. Gabriel Skinner. (girl's name could be Nancy)

John Tavenner   Rebecca M. Nichols   December 29,1838
Sec. Levi Tavenner. Saml. Nichols test. girl's age.

Name of Groom	Name of Bride	Date of Bond

William H. Feagins   Elizth. Thompson   December 26,1838
Sec. James Feagins, who test. groom's age. Lorenzo Thompson test. girl's age.

Vincent Miley   Rachel Marts   November 17,1838
Sec. John Marts who test. ages.

William Everhart   Catharine Deakins   August 13,1838
Sec. Philip Everhart. Oliver Edward test. girl's age.

James Craig   Louisa Gulick   January 7,1838
Sec. John Gulick, who test. ages.

John Varnes   Hetty Kirk   May 28,1838
Sec. William Hart.

James Sexton   Mary Ann Riley   May 2,1838
Sec. Rich'd Riley, father of girl, consented.

William Hart   Eliza Sutherland   May 28,1838
Sec. John Varnes, who test. girl 21.

George Newlon   Amanda F.Cockerill   January 11,1838
Sec. John H.Cockerill, test. ages. Sarah Newlon,mother of girl, auth. license. Wit. Mason Newlon. Sanford W.Cockerill, father of girl, also auth. license. Wit. William B.Wynkoop. Josiah Tidball test. groom's father George Newlon,Sr. dec'd.for not less than 18 or 19 yrs.

John A. Hope   Lydia Catherine Reed   April 9,1838
Sec. Richard Brower, who test. ages.

Nimrod Tavenner   Sarah Grimes   November 26,1838
Sec. Eli Tavenner, father of groom. George Grimes, father of girl.

John Rivers   Harriet Beavers   May 19,1838
Sec. John Allison, who test. ages.

John Ferno   Sarah Antes   September 6,1838
Sec. Samuel Orison,Jr., who test. ages.

Abner Conard   Mary C. Axline   November 13,1838
Sec. David Axline, who test. girl's age. Jacob Filler test. groom's age.

- - -   -   - - -

Name of Groom	Name of Bride	Date of Bond

Andrew Balmain Jr.   Amey Ellen Denham   February 6,1839
Sec. Chs. T. Denham, who test. girl's age.

Bushrod Osburn   Elizth. V. Clowes   December 2,1839
Sec. Thomas J. Clowes, who test. ages.

Thomas P. Hereford   Matilda W. Lacy   August 9,1839
Sec. B.B. Beard

Sydnor B. Johnson   Rosanna R. Heskit   April 16,1839
Sec. Joseph B.Gourley test. ages.

Alexander R. Milton   Ann Cecelia White   May 10,1839
Sec. F.A.Davison, who test. groom's age.

Lorenzo D. Thompson   Mary Francis Feagins   December 9,1839
Sec.Wilford Feagens, gdn. of girl (her name may be Martha)

Temple Fouch   Rebecca Torrison   January 21,1839
Sec. William Torrison, who test. ages.

Charles E. Chinn   Rebecca Elgin   June 6,1839
Sec. William Card,Jr., who test. age of girl.

William Weedon   Mary Wright   June 28,1839
Sec. Benjn. Rust, who test. girl's age.

William Prosser   Mary Ish of   August 12,1839
Sec. Robert A.Ish   Cameron Parish

Thomas Trammell   Mary Catharine Jenkins   April 5,1839
Sec. William Cooper, who test. ages.

Craven Popkins   Catharine Colbert   August 29,1839
Sec. John Mead, who t est. ages.

Jonathan Harper   Jane Woodard   August 1,1839
Sec. J. Woodard. Mrs. Harper, mother of Jonathan, test. his age &
Jabez Woodard test. for his dau.

James Gulick   Ann V. Simpson   February 11,1839
Sec. Friench Simpson, father of girl. Sanford P.Rogers test. groom's age.

Robert Wade   Amelia Ann Myers   July 29,1839
Sec. Robert S. Saunders, who test. girl's age. John F.Barrett test.
groom's age.

Charles McFarland   Catharine Hughes   July 26,1839
Sec. Thomas Hensey, who test. ages.

Name of Groom	Name of Bride	Date of Bond
James W. Taylor Sec. John Moore, who test. ages.	Elizabeth Swart	April 15,1839
Nathaniel Prince Sec. George Jay, who test. age of groom.	Sarah W. Dakins	April 8,1839
Isaac Vandevanter Sec. John Braden	Caroline S. Braden	September 9,1839
Solomon Ritchie Sec. Nelson Everhart. Nicholas Ropp, father of girl, auth. license. Wit. Samuel Ropp.	Eliza Ann Ropp	September 10,1839
D. W. Porter Sec. C.W.Gassaway	Mary E. Catlett	April 23,1839
John Haley Sec. John Hunt	Emily Hunt	February 23,1839
Christopher C. Head Sec. John McDonough, who test. ages.	Emily J. Steadman	September 5,1839
John Tally Sec. James Sexton, who test. ages.	Barbara Wolf	August 26,1839
Albert Ryan Sec. William McDonagh, who test. groom's age. Elizabeth Garrissin, late Solomon, mother & gdn. of girl, auth. license. Rachel Garner, late Solomon, also mentioned as gdn. Wit. John T. Derry.	Emeline Solomon	March 14,1839
William G. Furr Sec. Thomas C. Humphrey, who test. ages.	Mary Agnes Furr	January 14,1839
Philip Vaunters Sec. Sanford Fling	Eliza Jane Fling of Cameron Parish	February 4,1839
Benj. Simmons Sec. William Harrison, who test. ages.	Catharine Legg	August 19,1839
Periander L.Bussard Sec. Newton Keene Martina B. Hummer, Mother (?) of girl, auth. license.	Caroline Amanda Sheid of Cameron Parish	November 11,1839 Wit.Wm.Mershon.
Samuel Boger Sec. John Shafer	Mary Shafer	November 26,1839

Name of Groom	Name of Bride	Date of Bond

Benjamin Grubb   Rebecca Grubb   September 18,1839
Sec. Curtis Grubb, who test. ages.

Richard Bennett   Nancy Grubb   October 19,1839
Sec. Reed Poulton, who test. groom's age. John Grubb, father of girl,
auth. license.

Elisha Holmes   Hester Thomas   January 19,1839
Sec. Levi White, who test. groom's age. Mahlon Thomas test. girl's age.

Ellmore Waters   Frances Kidwell   January 21,1839
Sec. John Coe, who test. groom's age & cert. that the statement of
Elizabeth Kidwell, widow of Thomas, mother of Frances, is true. She
was 21 on May 9,1838. Wit. Zedekiah Kidwell.

Luther A. Thrasher   Elizabeth Margaret Cooper   March 16,1839
Sec. John Souder, gdn. of girl, test. groom 21.

James Madison Campbell   Margaret Wynkoop   August 17,1839
Sec. Samuel C. Wynkoop. Sarah Campbell, mother of groom, auth. license
to Margaret, dau. of Joseph Wynkoop of Loudoun. Wit. Isaac Eaton &
Thomas Smitson.

Caleb Barnhouse   Sarah Ann Thomas   June 3,1839
Sec. George Thomas, who test. ages.

James Heaton Chamblin   Octavia Keppler   March 2,1839
Sec. Chs. G.Eskridge. Saml. Keppler test. girl's age.

Samuel McGaha   Julian Sanbower   March 30,1839
Sec. George Hefner. Michael Sanbour test. girl's age. Margaret
McGaha, mother of groom, auth. license.

Hudson Bennett   Lucy Moxley of   April 11,1839
Sec. Lucian Fitzhugh   Cameron Parish

Abraham Young   Susan B.Janney   February 9,1839
Sec. Charles F. Sangster. Jno. Janney test. ages.

John H. Hunton   Amanda M. Butcher   September 10,1839
Sec. Martin O. Butcher. John H.Butcher, father of girl, auth. license.
Wit. John Butcher.

Samuel Compher   Hannah Williams   October 28,1839
Sec. Israel Williams, father of girl, test. ages.

Name of Groom	Name of Bride	Date of Bond

Charles W. Simpson   Emily M. Luck   December 3,1839
Sec. Jordan B. Luck, who test. ages.

Samuel P.Thompson   Elizth. Hough   January 17,1839
Sec. Samuel Zimmerman, who test. groom's age. Bernard Hough, test.
bride's.

William Triplett   Mary James,widow   October 24,1839
Sec. E. Hammat

Levi Tavenner   Susan Young   February 25,1839
Sec. William Young

William Franklin   Mary Jane Lowe   November 13,1839
Sec. R.Lowe. Rector Lowe, father of girl, cave consent. Benjamin
Franklin test. to groom's age.

Solomon Cooper   Emeline Titus   November 4,1839
Sec. Tunis Titus

Samuel R. Newlon   Elizabeth Jane Kile   November 21,1839
Sec. George Kile, father of girl, test. ages.

Thomas Potts   Mary Ann White   May 22,1839
Sec. Nathan White, who test. ages.

Hamilton Cross   Matilda Brown   February 5,1839
Sec. Fielding, Brown, father of girl, test. ages.

Albert Allder   Mary Catharine Locker   February 11,1839
Sec. G. Locker, who test. ages.

Alexander Milton   Ann Cecelia White
  No bond but cert. signed by Nancy White, dated May 8,1839, auth.
marriage of her dau. Ann Cecelia to Alexander R. Milton, Wit. F.A.
Davisson & R.J.T.White.

John A. Throckmorton   Mary B. Tutt   March 14,1839
Sec. N.C.Mason, who test. ages

John W. Minor   Louisa Catlett   June 20,1839
Sec. W.C.Selden. Charles S.Catlett, father of girl, auth. license.
Wit. Thomas Herttell & John Selden.

Richard Francis   Maranda Jane Lewis   January 5,1839
Sec. James Hill, who test. ages.

Name of Groom	Name of Bride	Date of Bond

Jno. Alexander Stevens   Roxanna Burgess   October 7,1839
Sec. William Burgess & Warner W. Shackelford. Margaret Burgess,
mother of girl, auth. license. Wt. Louisa Burgess.

Philip Howser   Betsey Vaughters   January 23,1839
Sec. Richard Vaughters, father of girl. Wm. Lafeber test. ages.

Johnathon Wist or Wilt Maria Tribble   January 9,1839
Sec. Adam Cooper, who test. ages.

Griffith M. Paxson   Dewanner Rickard   March 21,1839
Sec. George Rickard, who test. groom's age.

William Adams   Mahala Wolford   February 26,1839
Sec. William Wolford, test. ages.

William W. Poston   Sus'n Hamilton   September 9,1839
Sec. John Beavers. Roger Chew test. girl lived at John Beavers and
was 21.

John Riticor   Elizth. Jane Lee of   March 13,1839
Sec. Joshua Lee   Cameron Parish

Henry Bidenger   Margaret E. Rust   June 1,1839
Sec. George Rust

John K. Hoskinson   Sarah Ann Benedum   December 2,1839
Sec. Henry Benedum

Landon Shipman   Catharine Tillett of   January 28,1839
Sec. William Kent, who   Cameron Parish
test. groom's age. James Goram test. girl's age.

Francis McCormick   Rosannah Mortimer Ellzey November 20,1839
Sec. Jas. Sinclair. Lewis Ellzey auth. license for his dau.

Burr Weeks   Ann B. Gibson   December 10,1839
Sec. A. M. Gibson. A.Gibson auth. license for his dau. Wit. Thos.
W.Gibson.

Lewis Thompson   Elizabeth Ann Burke   January 28,1839
Sec. John Orrison, who test. girl's age.

Daniel A. Sowers   Martha Rogers   May 27,1839
Sec. Wm. Rogers who test. ages.

William Titus   Mary Jane Brown   April 1,1839
Sec. Tunis Titus. M.Brown, mother of girl, consented.

Name of Groom	Name of Bride	Date of Bond

Benjamin H. Benton   Margt. J. Gulick   August 12,1839
Sec. William Benton, who test. groom's age. William Gulick, father
of girl.

Richard L.Harris   Sallie Beales   December 14,1839
Sec. John Johnson, who test. ages.

James Burch   Ann Lawson Rutter   October 28,1839
Sec. Landon Jones. Groom signed as William Burch. Barbary Burch
mother and gdn. of groom, auth. license. Wit. Joseph Blincoe

Fenton Furr   Susan E. Gill   November 2,1839
Sec. Leven P. Chamblin. John L.Gill, father of girl, auth. license.
Wit. Richard C. Littleton.

Josiah Burke   Lucinda Davis   January 28,1839
Sec. Joseph Davis, who test. ages.

Thomas J.Harding   Susan Latham   November 16,1839
Sec. W.W.White. Nancy Latham, widow, and mother of girl, auth. license
Wit. Wm. Taylor

Thomas Bales   Catharine Ballenger   October 23,1839
Sec. John Ballenger, who test. ages.

Wilson C. Sanders   Sarah Ann Gregg   September 14,1839
Sec. James Sinclair, who test. ages.

Joab Osburn   Emily J.Gibson   November 2,1839
Sec. Leven P.Chamblin, Israel Gibson, father of girl, consented.

Abner H. Settle   Mary Ann Kile   December 3,1839
Sec. Alexr. Edmonds. Geo. Kile, father of girl, auth. license.
Wit. Mason S. Adams

William Hickman   Ann Eliza Everhart   November 18,1839
Sec. Philip Everhart. Elias Davis test. groom's age.

Thomas Smitson   Eliza Ann Campbell   October 15,1839
Sec. Samuel C. Wynkoop. Sarah Campbell, mother of girl, auth. license.
Wit. James M. Campbell.

- - - -   -   - - - -

David Gochenauer   Elizth. Blakely   September 5,1840
Sec. William Blakely, test. girl's age.

Name of Groom	Name of Bride	Date of Bond

George Hickman   Eleanora M. Kalb   September 14,1840
Sec. Samuel Hall, who test. ages.

Nimrod Ashby   Mary Agnes Smallwood   September 15,1840
Sec. John Smallwood. John Wesley Smallwood, father of girl, test. ages.

William Jackson   Julia Ann Woodard   October 8,1840
Sec. Wm. McDonough test. ages. Groom was 21 on Oct. 8,1840.

Andrew M. Cridler   Rachel Jane Smallwood   June 13,1840
Sec. Joseph H. Bodine, who test. ages.

Josiah F. Moore   Julia Ann Knott   August 17,1840
Sec. William F. Moore, who test. groom's age. Alfred Belt test.
girl's age, from the record of her father, she will be 21, Nov. 4,
1840. Wit. James Belt.

Jacob Lemmon   Mary Jane Bodine   April 13,1840
Sec. Andrew M. Cridler, who test. ages.

Henry Williams   Rebecca Johnson   October 8,1840
Sec. Thomas J. Stedman, who test. ages.

John Richard Skinner   Sarah B. Stover   February 24,1840
Sec. Lorenzo D. Walker. Edwin A.Stover consented to marriage of his
dau. Sarah Burril Stover. Wit. Wm.L.Bogue & Peter Skinner.

James W. Lawson   Evelina Frye   November 28,1840
Sec. Joseph Frey. Philip Fry auth. license for his dau.

James Cross   Elizabeth Lowe of   January 29,1840
Sec. Henry Lowe, father   Cameron Parish
of girl, test. ages.

William A. Harris   Frances Murry   November 16,1840
Sec. E.C.Murray. Elizabeth Murray auth. license for her dau. Wit. Emma
Murray & Edward C. Murray.

Thomas Claxton   Caroline Fichter   February 6,1840
Sec. George Fichter

James Benjamin   Ann Wilson Hardy   January 20,1840
Sec. John P. Dickey, who test. ages.

Robert W. Gray   Mary Elizabeth Bentley   June 16,1840
Sec. Rob. Bentley

Name of Groom	Name of Bride	Date of Bond

William Myers   Mary H. Donaldson   February 29,1840
Sec. Mahlon Myers. Elizabeth Donaldson, mother of Mary Hannah, auth.
license. Wit. Noble S. Braden and Samuel Davis.

Oliver Milbourn   Mary Jane Jones   January 6,1840
Sec. William Milbourn. Jonathan Milbourn test. ages.

Charles E. Speaks   Sarah Ann Crim   May 6,1840
Sec. George W. McKim.

John Logan   Mary Ann Walker   February 20,1840
Sec. Benj. Walker, father of girl. Samuel Logan test. ages.

William Wynkoop   Mary Franklin   January 7,1840
Sec. B.T.Franklin, who test. girl's age. Joseph Wynkoop, father of
groom, test. his age and consented.

Elisha P. Phelps   Mary W. Bennett   October 27,1840
Sec. Sydnor Bennett.

William W. Divine   Eliza Ann Orrison   February 12,1840
Sec. William Milbourn, who test. groom's age. Catharine Orrison,
mother of girl, consented. Wit. Jonathan W. Nixon.

William Lamb   Elizabeth Gregg   September 12,1840
Sec. C.F.Anderson, who test. ages, and that Nancy Lamb, mother of
William, cert. he 21. George Gregg, father of girl, consented.
Wit. Samuel Virts.

Garrett B. Walker   Adaline B. Skinner of   February 24,1840
Sec. Lorenzo D.Walker   Cameron Parish

Archibald Morrison   Rachel Morrison   November 19,1840
Sec. Edward Morrison, who test. girl 21.

Rich. H. Edwards   Ann E. Edwards   March 2,1840
Sec. Chs. G. Edwards

Ludwell Tinsman   Geraldine Slack   July 2,1840
Sec. J.L. Slack. Nancy Tinsman, mother of groom, says no father
living, she consents. Wit. James Chappell. Sigmunda Slack, mother
of girl, says girl not of lawful age, has no father living, she her
gdn. and consents.

William Harrison   Sarah Riley   April 28,1840
Sec. Richard Riley, father of girl. James Harrison test. groom's age.

Name of Groom	Name of Bride	Date of Bond

Luke Fields   Catharine Shell   May 11,1840
Sec. Alfred Jones, who test. ages. Wit. James P.Wilson.

Peter Carter   Mary Ann Harrison   December 24,1840
Sec. James Harrison, father, auth. license for his dau. Wit. Caleb
Russell.

Thomas Jenkins   Ann Whaley of   July 23,1840
Geo. W. Hunter, Sec.   Cameron Parish
Wit.John Wines.

John Snoots   Susan Cordell   February 3,1840
Sec. William McCoy

John Vanhorn   Sarah Carter   July 27,1840
Sec. Richard Carter, father of girl, test. ages.

Washington Haines   Mary Elizabeth Sample   December 25,1840
Sec. Armistead T.M.Hough, who test. ages.

Steward Darr   Tabitha Ann Collins   February 19,1840
Sec. Thomas Davis, who test. ages.

Samuel Dixon   Eliza Smitley   April 14,1840
Sec. Henry S. Williams, who test. groom's age. Jane Smitley, mother
fo girl, auth. license. Wit. Jacob Stoutsenberger.

Uriah Steadman   Louisa Carpenter   September 15,1840
Sec. B.R. Sampson, who test. girl's age. ----Glasgow test. groom's age.

John E. Fulton   Massey Warner   August 10,1840
Sec. Israel Warner, father of girl. Wm. Butler, test. groom's age.

Henry Holliday   Mary Ann Lewis   September 7,1840
Sec. William Kent, test. ages.

Nathaniel Everhart   Darcus Frits   August 10,1840
Sec. Daniel Miller, who test. ages.

Mortimer Cockerill   Sarah Ann Evans   June 15,1840
Sec. Jesse Evans, father of girl, who test. ages.

William Collier   Mary Styles   June 4,1840
Sec. Columbus Hickman, who test. ages.

Benjamin D. Ridgeway   Ann Elizabeth Kent   August 24,1840
Sec. William G. Kent, test. ages.

Name of Groom	Name of Bride	Date of Bond

Jas. T. Vermillion   Nancy Carruthers   December 28,1840
Sec. Joel S. Nixon, who test. ages.

John McLenen   Mary Nancy McDaniel   December 14,1840
Sec. John Tavenner. Thomas Rogers, gdn. of girl, auth. license. Wit.
John H. Crimm

John Arnet   Mary E. Reed   November 2,1840
Sec. Moses Arnet, who test. ages.

Braxton B. Jeffries   Tacy H. Daniel   December 17,1840
Sec. Sampson G. Dowdell, test. ages.

John George   Sarah Long   June 13,1840
Sec. John Everhart, who test. ages.

John W. Seaton   Frances A. Eaches   November 28,1840
Sec. John Newlon. Hiram Seaton, father of groom, auth. license.
Wit. James S. Carter. Thomas Eaches, father of girl, auth. license.
Wit. Wilmon Cole.

George Hefner   Hannah Fawley   August 4,1840
Sec. William Fry. Henry Fawley, father of girl, auth. license.
Wit. Jacob Fawley.

John Prince   Matilda Cole   August 11,1840
Sec. Jacob Bontz, who test. groom's age. Priscilla Cole, mother of
girl, auth. license. Wit. Michael Amick.

Thomas J. Brabham   Martha Stephenson of   August 20,1840
Sec. James Whitacre   Cameron Parish
James Stephenson, father of girl, auth. license. Wit.Edwin A.Stover.

John Keen,Jr.   Amanda L.Broaddus   January 31,1840
Sec. Lewis D. Means, who test. his age.

Erasmus Perry   Adeline M. Sheid   December 14,1840
Sec. W. Hammer, who test. ages.

John Wynkoop   Mary Campbell   October 12,1840
Sec. Garret Wynkoop, who test. ages.

John Bontz   Mary Merchant   October 11,1840
Sec. James Merchant, father of girl.

Name of Groom	Name of Bride	Date of Bond

John S. Bascue   Matilda Hammer   December 21,1840
Sec. Thomas Hammer, father of girl, test. ages.

Alexander W.Johnson   Sarah Ann Fichter   August 24,1840
Sec. James Orange, who test. groom's age. Mrs. Orange, mother of
girl, consented.

Frederick L. Crissey   Mary Elizabeth Surghnor   June 23,1840
Sec. John Surghnor, father of girl. James H.Benedum, test. groom's age.

Alfred Lee   Margaret M. Peyton   August 10,1840
Sec. Squire Lee, who test. ages.

Enoch Hoffman   Delila Conard   October 19,1840
Sec. David Conard, father of girl, test. ages.

James Henry Bitzer   Mary Jane Gochnauer   August 8,1840
Sec. David Gochnauer, who test. girl's age. James Harvey Bitzer
gdn. of Wm. Bitzer's children at Septr.6,1839 Court.

Fenton Johnson   Elizth. Jane Stephenson   February 17,1840
Sec. Thomas J. Brabham, who test. ages.

William B. Paxson   Henrietta C. Hough   February 12,1840
Sec. Benjamin Hough, who test. ages.

Mandley Hammerly   Eliza A. Brown   December 9,1840
Sec. Asa Brown

John A. Brooks   Elizth. McMullen   November 10,1840
Sec. John Smith, who test. to groom's age. Mary McMullen, widow of
Robert, mother of girl, auth. license. Wit. Jacob Shriver.

John J. Mobberly   Mariah Underwood   November 11,1840
Sec. George Lay

Robert H. Kercheval   Unity Keene   March 9,1840
Sec. Willis A. Kercheval, test. groom's age. George Keen, father
of girl, auth. license. Wit. John Keen,Jr.

Samuel Boggess   Eliza Jane Rust   March 30,1840
Sec. R.W.Latham, who test. ages. Bushrod Rust, father of girl,
auth. license(Home named "Green Gardens") Wit. T. W. Rust.

Samuel Nichols   Harriett Handley   January 31,1840
Sec. David Hanley, father of girl, who test. ages.

Name of Groom	Name of Bride	Date of Bond

Asbury M. Nixon   Hannah Brown   November 16,1840
Sec. Benjamin Brown.

William Thomas   Elizabeth Hanley   November 25,1840
Sec. David Hanley, father of girl. He test. groom was 21 and was
bound without having been discharged from his apprenticeship, has for
several years been doing for himself and that he has known him
personally for many years.

John Turner   Juliet Ann Wildman   November 13,1840
Sec. David Brown, who test. ages.

Nimrod Triplett   Susanna E.Saffer of   May 14,1840
Sec. Wm. Gilmore.   Cameron Parish
William Saffer, father of girl, auth. License. Wit. George Briscoe
and John W. Saffer.

Albert Francis   Icey Blaker   February 3,1840
Sec. William Shields who test. ages.

Wesley Pearce   Jane Fox, alias Pearce   January 4,1840
     widow of Edward Pearce
Sec. James Leslie (This couple may be free negroes)

George W. McKim   Martina Merchant   April 15,1840
Sec. John Merchant, father of girl, who test. ages.

Craven James   Catharine Louisa Morris   March 9,1840
Sec. Mahlon Morris, who test. ages.

Jesse D. Kalb   Mary Eliza Virtz   December 12,1840
Sec. Conrad Virtz, father of girl, consented and test. groom's age.

William Thomas   Elizabeth Stewart   June 3,1840
Sec. Richard Thomas

Tunis Titus   Mary Ann Hunter   September 15,1840
Sec. William Titus. John Hunter test. girl 21.

John Henry Scanhan   Elizabeth Short   July 29,1840
Sec. Frederick Miller. Henry Grubb test. groom would be 22 on
Sept.10,1840.

Benjamin Hammer   Emily Havener of   February 17,1840
Sec.Orlando K.Sheid   Cameron Parish
Joseph Havener test. ages.

Name of Groom	Name of Bride	Date of Bond

James Landon McFarling   Mary Ann Tarleton   March 2, 1840
Sec. John E. Fulton test. ages.

Hiram Stephenson   Ruth Sarah Walker   June 23,1840
Sec. Lorenzo D. Walker, test. ages.

John Hamilton   Permelia Graham   March 22,1840
Sec. Chs. G. Eskridge. Elijah Peacock test. girl's age.

John William Bell   Mary Catharine Jones March 3,1840
Sec. Seth D.Robertson, who test. ages.

- - - -   -   - - - -

Garrett Hough   Mary Moore   July 5,1841
Sec. George Head, who test. girl's age.

Benjamin D. Rathie   Sarah D. Fadely   November 24,1841
Sec. Chs. G. Eskridge. Jacob Fadely, father of girl, consented.

Robert Costelo   Mary Ann Triplett   March 9,1841
Sec. Jesse Fleming. James Costelo, father of groom, auth. license.
Wit. Lemuel Hutchison. Lucy Gray, mother of girl, auth. license.
Wit. Thomas Germain Gray & Joseph Fleming.

Elijah Peacock   Mary Jane Wright   December 28,1841
Sec. Jacob Cruson, test. girl's age.

John S. Tillett   Harriet Ann Poulton   November 13,1841
Sec. Reed Poulton

Charles Wm.Schooley   Mary Hough   August 3,1841
Sec. Garret Hough, father of girl, test. her age.

Joseph S. Harden   Frances Jane Dennis   December 29,1841
Sec. Thomas Bell, Henry Dennis test. ages.

William Clendening Jr.   Elizth. Ann Thompson   November 16,1841
Sec. Samuel P.Thompson test. ages.

Enoch Foley   Martha Skinner of   November 23,1841
Sec. Nath'l Skinner,   Cameron Parish
test. girl's age.

James H. Benedum   Sarah A. Hammatt   September 2,1841
Sec. E. Hammat.

Name of Groom	Name of Bride	Date of Bond

George W. Ryon   Catharine Dorrell   December 6,1841
Sec. Alfred Spates, who test. ages.

Benjamin Hough   Rachel Umbaugh   December 2,1841
Sec. William Worsley, who test. ages.

Arthur Shackelford   Susannah Fulton   November 6,1841
Sec. Benjamin Boles, who test. groom's age. Margaret Fulton, mother
of girl, test. Susannah an illeg. child, and she auth. license.

William Carruthers   Louisa White   November 16,1841
Sec. Adin White, father of girl, test. ages.

Joseph C. Mock   Mary James   November 16,1841
Sec. Elijah James. George W.Mock test. groom's age.

Jonas M. Best   Nancy Young   December 27,1841
Sec. David Young, who test. ages.

Sydnor Bennett   Sarah E. Russell   October 25,1841
Sec. Henry Russell

David Hall   Nancy Chin or Chew   December 6,1841
Sec. Roger Chin or Chew?

Azariah Kinder   Mary Jane Kidwell   July 21,1841
Sec. Hezekiah Kidwell, who test. ages.

William S. Gray   Sarah Ann Orrison   December 6,1841
Sec. David Orrison. Margaret Orrison, mother of girl, auth.license.
Wit.Arthur Orrison.

Absalom Johnson   Louisa Jane Hough of   June 10,1841
Sec.James M.Carr   Cameron Parish
Ann M.Whaley test. girl's age. William Johnson, father of groom
test. his age and consented.

George L. Ayres   Mary Ann Benton   April 23,1841
Sec. William Benton, father of girl, test. ages.

Lewis D. Means   Alcinda A. Paxson   November 23,1841
Sec. G.W.Paxson, who test. ages.

Thomas S. Rice   Lucelia C. Gibson   April 2,1841
Sec. A.M.Gibson, who test. groom's age. A.Gibson,father of girl,
auth. license. Wit. S.M.Gibson.

Name of Groom	Name of Bride	Date of Bond

Robert C. Bowman   Hannah P.S.Glascock   September 22,1841
Sec. William H.Francis.   Will Glascock, father of girl, auth. license.
Wit. John R. Carter

Benjamin B.Beard   Eleanor Frere of   June 23,1841
Sec. James Keen   Cameron Parish
Barron Frere, father of girl, consented.

Jacob R. Shepherd   Nancy Roszel   October 29,1841
Sec. Gunnell Saunders.

James Jennings   Ann Moxley   December 9,1841
Sec. Abigil Moxley. (Moseley?) (William Jennings in body of bond)

James S. Frazier   Mary Grubb   October 26,1841
Sec. William D. Grubb, who test. girl's age. John Frazier, father
of groom, auth. license. Wit. Josiah Frazier, James C.Frazier.

S. A. Roszel   Louisa D. Tebbs   November 2,1841
Sec. Chs. G. Eskridge

John P. Smart   Mary E. Wherry   October 12,1841
Sec. Robert G. Bowie

William Burke   Mahala Wright   September 23,1841
Sec. W.G.Wright.

John War   Caroline Emberson   September 17,1841
Sec. Judson Emberson

Daniel B. Humburg   Charlotte Chambers   April 13,1841
Sec. D.L.Crawford

Leander Carter   Elizabeth Beatty   September 6,1841
Sec. Joshua Pancoast, who test. girl's age. Susan Beatty, mother
of girl.

Landon Jones   Sarah E. Wynkoop   December 13,1841
Sec. Garret Wynkoop, who test. groom's age. Elizabeth Wynkoop, mother
of girl, auth. license. Wit. Cornelius Wynkoop.

William White   Elizth. Yakey   December 13,1841
Sec. Spence Minor

John Barnhouse   Sarah M.Johnson   December 13,1841
Sec. John Johnson, father of girl, who also test. ages.

William Rian   Elizabeth Yabower   March 9,1841
Sec. Johan Gebauer, father of girl

Name of Groom	Name of Bride	Date of Bond

John M. Filler   Emily Ann Divine   July 24,1841
Sec. William Divine, father of girl, who also test. ages.

Parkison D. Shepherd   Mary Ann Margaret Jennings May 11,1841
Sec. Sanford Rogers.

Thomas Burnes   Sarah Ann Waller of   April 7,1841
Sec. George Waller,   Cameron Parish
father of girl.

Eli Anderson   Sarah Frances Stillings May 10,1841
Sec. Jefferson Anderson, who test. groom's age. Benjamin Stillions,
father of bride, auth. license. Wit. James E. Slack

James Allder Jr.   Amanda E. Marshall   May 19,1841
Sec. Joseph W. Allder, who test. ages. R. Marshall, father of girl,
consented.

John Marts   Christena Miley   April 2,1841
Sec. Vincent Miley, who test. ages.

Washington Goodheart   Sophia Smith   March 8,1841
Sec. Frederick Eamich, who test. ages.

John Butler   Sarah Hamilton   March 26,1841
Sec. Thomas Littleton, who test. ages.

Robert James   ?   December 31,1841
Sec. John Simpson, who test. ages. (John Simpson entered in body of
bond for bride's name)

Hannibal James   Charlotte P.Bradfield   February 4,1841
Sec. Jefferson C. Thomas, who test. ages.

William Silcott   Frances Eliza Downs   August 30,1841
Sec. James H. Silcott, who test. ages.

James Minor   Nancy Shreve   September 13,1841
Sec. Francis Shreve, who test. ages. Benj. Shreve, father of girl,
auth. license. Wit. Presley Carr Lane.

Logan Osburn   Margaret C. Osburn   May 10,1841
Sec. Balaam Osburn, father of girl.

John Randolph White   Sarah G. Janney   December 6,1841
Sec. D. Shawen

Name of Groom	Name of Bride	Date of Bond

Thomas Hensey   Eliza Jane Harrison   August 16,1841
Sec. James Harrison, who test. ages.

John Roberts   Lydia Boothe   August 23,1841
Sec. Simon Mathew, who test. groom's age. John Boothe, test. age
of girl.

Hezekiah Davis   Frances Brooks   June 2,1841
Sec. Sampson Harper, test. ages of both.

Sampson Harper   Susannah Davis   August 24,1841
Sec. Jeremiah Davis, who test. ages of both.

Samuel A. Tillett   Caroline S. Dennis   June 1,1841
Sec. Joseph S.Harden, who test. girl's age. Elias Pool test.
groom's age.

Joseph Wildman   Charlotte Turner   April 16,1841
Sec. John Turner, who test. ages.

Armistead Orem   Mary Jane Clip   October 13,1841
Sec. Geo. Wm. Fairfax, who test. groom's age. John Clip, father of
girl, auth. license. Wit. Louisa Clip.

Stephen D. Farr   Mary Ann Barden of   May 15,1841
Sec. F.J.Stanhope.   Cameron Parish
James Barden, father of girl, auth. license. Wit.John B.Farr.

John L. Gill   Mary Todd   June 16,1841
Sec. William Beatty.

James H. Muse   Ann Eliza Seeders   March 18,1841
Sec. William Seeders, father of girl.

William H. Schooley   Hannah Stocks   January 11,1841
Sec. Stephen S.Stocks. William Stocks, father of girl, auth. license &
test. ages of both. Sec. Mahlon Stocks.

Mortimer Osburn   Mary Summers   January 14,1841
Sec. William Summers, who test. groom's age.

William Wood   Mariah Robinson   January 14,1841
Sec. John G. Hoge. Pricilla Robinson, mother of girl, auth. license.
Wit. Thos. P. Matthews.

Joseph V. Bemusdaffer   Mary E. Hardy   January 2,1841
Sec. John G. Lester. John Hardy, father of girl,auth. license.
Wit. Joshua Hardy.

Name of Groom	Name of Bride	Date of Bond
Isaac Moore	Catharine Ann Kent	March 8,1841

Sec. John Beavers, gdn. of girl.

Daniel Munday	Mary Ann Taylor	March 9,1841

Sec. George W.Johnson, who test. ages.

James Boles	Nancy Updike	March 8,1841

Sec. Thomas Rogers, who test. ages.

John W. Stallings	Mary Ann Dickey	March 10,1841

Sec. William Hixon, who test. ages.

Jacob F. Gillespey	Susan W. Bennett	March 9,1841

Sec. Nimrod Cummins, who test. ages.

Lewelin Hutchison	Julia Ambler	February 8,1841

Sec. F. Littleton. Vincent Ambler test. ages.

Ferdinand Clapsaddle	Mary Ann Glasgow	March 9,1841

Sec. F.M.Weadon, who test. ages, and also test. that Catharine
Glasgow, mother of girl, consented.

Addison Campbell	Susan Snoots	June 5,1841

Sec. Christian Comphar. Margaret Campbell, mother of groom, auth.
license. Wit.James McKim. Mary Snoots, mother of girl, auth. license.
Wit. John Wire and John Shafer.

Augustine McDaniel	Elizth. Lamb	December 30,1841

Sec. William S. Harrison, who test. ages.

William Gore	Sarah Ann Swan	March 1,1841

Sec. James M. Swann, who test. ages.

Charles W. Ellmore	Mary Rose of	February 11,1841

Sec. John Ellmore   Cameron Parish
Rich'd Rose test. ages and that John Ellmore, is father of groom.

William Poulton	Anna Jared	June 14,1841

Sec. Joshua Nichols, who test. ages.

Samuel Magaha	Pricilla Cloud	March 22,1841

Sec. Joel Hunt, who test. ages. Sidney Cloud of Lovettsville, mother
of girl, auth. license. Wit. Jonathan Wenner.

Luke S. Forrest	Mary Kendle	May 10,1841

Sec. French Thompson, who test. ages.

Name of Groom	Name of Bride	Date of Bond

Fenton Holmes   Sarah E. Simpson   February 8,1841
Sec. John Simpson. John G.Hoge test. groom's age.

John Urton   Nancy Weadon   January 22,1841
Sec. Horatio Drish, who test. ages.

William H. Smith   Emily Grimes   January 11,1841
Sec. John Butler, gdn. of groom. Ryland P.Jacobs, test. girl's age.

Richard W. Wade   Mary Elizabeth Myers   January 11,1841
Sec. John F. Barrett & Robert J. Saunders.

William McPherson   Diana Finnacom   January 19,1841
Sec. Silas Garrett, who test. groom's age. Diana Finnacom, mother
of girl, auth. license. Wit. George Finnacom.

Beverly T. Gill   Emily E.Saunders   August 31,1841
Sec.John Surghnor, gdn. of girl (Elizab. E. Summers).

Bernard Charlton   Mary Mills   March 8,1841
Sec. Thomas Cornell, who test. groom's age. Chloe McDuffy, mother
of girl, auth. license. Wit.Caleb Russell & Jos. Cornell.

Daniel H. Sowers   Frances Ann Oden   February 9,1841
Sec. William Sowers. Nathaniel S.Oden,father of girl, auth. license.
Wit.James S.Oden, Geo.W.Spooner and Wm.A.Lanham.

Richard Alexander   Mary E. Brabham   February 18,1841
Sec. William Alexander, who test. ages.

Thomas Cornelle   Harriet Ann Hawes   March 8,1841
Sec. Thomas P.Matthews & Bernard Charlton. Thomas Mills test. groom's
age. Asa Haws, father of girl, auth. license.

Lambert Myers   Rachel Eveland   October 20,1841
Sec. Sydnor Bennett, test. age of girl.

Edgar S. Bentley   Helen Mary Wilson   September 8,1841
Sec. Geo. Richards. Charlotte Wilson, mother of girl, auth.license.
Wit. Anna B. Richards.

- - - -   -   - - - -

John J. Sellman   Ann E. Belt   November 28,1842
Sec. Alfred Belt. Thomas Dorell, test. ages.

Richard James   Sarah Ann Waltman   November 5,1842
Sec. Jacob Waltman.

Name of Groom	Name of Bride	Date of Bond
Robert Dawson Sec. Isaac Leedom	Harriet Leedom of Cameron Parish	March 14,1842
John Hammerley Sec. Abraham Hewett	Catharine Ann Zellers	December 26,1842
Thomas Spates Sec. Nicholas Money, father of girl, test. ages.	Mary E. Money	September 15,1842
Lawson Wadsworth Sec. Presley Davis, who test. ages.	Catharine Gladdin	October 12,1842
George W. Rupp Sec. Richard B.Birkby, test. girl's age. James A.Barnhart test. groom'	Sarah Birkby	November 14,1842
John J. Wynkoop Sec. Landon Simons. Elizabeth W.Wynkoop, mother of groom, auth. license. Wit. W.H.Wynkoop.	Matilda Jane Simons	July 28,1842
William Bleakly Sec. Nathaniel Nichols. Enos Nichols (may be father of girl)	Emily A. Nichols	November 24,1842
Henry Virtz Sec. John V. Brown, test. ages.	Esther R. Brown	September 12,1842
Alfred Fox Sec. Henry Parker	Sarah Ann Lucas	April 28,1842
James S. Harris Sec. W.P.Harris	Mary A.Sutherland	September 13,1842
Charles F. Fadely Sec. Wm.D. Drish	Orra Moore Drish	September 7,1842
John A. Spilman Sec. James Daniel, who test. groom's age, Wm.Rogers test. girl's.	Susan Rogers	November 16,1842
John Weadon Sec. Daniel, who test. ages. (James Daniel)	Nancy Boland	September 28,1842
David Ruse Sec. George W. Wynkoop, test. ages.	Catherine Wynkoop	July 25,1842
Edward Owens Sec. William Lewis, who test. age of girl.	Eliza Jeffres	January 1,1842
Lorenzo D. Walker Sec. Ashford Weadon, who test. age of girl.	Elizth. Bemusdaffer	November 7,1842

Name of Groom	Name of Bride	Date of Bond
George Hawk	Mary Allen	August 25,1842 (Mar.)

George Hawk   Mary Allen   August 25,1842 (Mar.)
Sec. James Allen, father of girl, test. ages.

Newton Michie   Lalla Gray   November 21,1842
Sec. John Gray, father of girl.

Samuel Overfield   Mary P. Osburn   September 5,1842
Sec. Richard Osburn.

Charles E. Paxson   Eleanor Hough   January 15,1842
Sec. Benjamin Hough, who test. ages.

John W. Webb of   Sarah Ann Dorrell   May 17,1842
Jefferson Co. Harpers Ferry.
Sec. James T. Dorrell, who test. that groom was born Feb. 1821.

John H. Crim   Mary Hickman   February 7,1842
Sec. M.L.Arnold test ages of both.

James Clark   Martha J. Hart   August 22,1842
Sec. Jonathan Hart, father of girl, test. ages.

Samuel Carter   Jane Rivers   December 12,1842
Sec. Thomas Phillips, who test. ages.

John R. Hibbs   Catharine A.Gochnauer   April 6,1842
Sec. Jacob Gochnauer, test. groom's age.

Benjamin Franks   Nancy Ellen Gochnauer   April 30,1842
Sec. Jacob Gochnauer

William Wissinger   Elizabeth Parmer   January 22,1842
Sec. Stephen Parmer who test. ages.

John Crim   Catharine Everhart   June 28,1842
Sec. William Carroll, who test. ages.

Samuel Cooper   Mary Umbaugh   February 15,1842
Sec. John Umbaugh, who test. ages.

Samuel Clendening   Elizabeth Thomas   March 22,1842
Sec. James W. Nixon, who test. ages.

Michael Cooper   Mary A. Hunter   March 14,1842
Sec. William Hunter, father of girl.

William Selby   Eliza Noggle   February 17,1842
Sec. George Whitmore, who test. ages.

Name of Groom	Name of Bride	Date of Bond

Henry H. Nichols Maria White March 14,1842
Sec. Levi White

Charles Griffin Martha M.Brabham December 28,1842
Sec. James Smitson. Jesse Griffin,father of groom, auth. license.
Mary Brabham,mother of girl, auth. license. Wit.William Alexander.

Eli Heater Cornelia Ann Cost December 30,1842
Sec. Jonathan Cost, test. ages.

Charles F. Anderson Mary F. Hough January 15,1842
Sec. Benjamin Hough. Eleanor Anderson, mother of groom,auth. license.
Wit. E. Thompson and Mahlon Stocks.

John A. McDonough Elizth. King February 2,1842
Sec. Washington Jarvis.

Arthur Orrison Elizth. Hickman January 18,1842
Sec. William Hickman, who test. ages.

Samuel Carter Matilda Dennis February 5,1842
Sec. James E. Stonestreet, who test. age of girl.

William Ellmore Maria Lemon February 19,1842
Sec. Joseph H. Bodine

Samuel S. Palmer Nancy Thrift March 7,1842
Sec. James H. Chamblin, who test. girl's age.

Silas H. Feagans Sarah I. Wilder July 11,1842
Sec. John W. Shipley who test. groom's age. Wit. Henry Wilder.

William Casey Sarah V. Perry April 26,1842
Sec. John D. Perry

Alexander Kidwell Amelia Gibson August 22,1842
Sec. Aaron Gibson.

James Lacock Mary Ann White November 14,1842
Sec. James Higdon, who test. ages.

Samuel Beans Harriet Newhouse September 22,1842
Sec. Enos Pursel, who test. girl over 21.

Mahlon Tavenner Susan Ann Nichols April 2,1842
Sec. Jonah Nichols, who test. ages.

Name of Groom	Name of Bride	Date of Bond

Daniel Boyd — Catharine Minor — December 12,1842
Sec. Nathan Wisener.

James W. Monroe — Caroline D.McPherson — July 1,1842
Sec. Benj. C.Barton, who test. girl's mother is Mary, widow of
Maddison McPherson. She auth. license. Wit. William H.Gill.

James Trahern — Francis A.Overfield — December 12,1842
Sec. William McPherson. Anna Overfield, mother of girl, auth. license.
Father of girl dec'd. Wit. George Finacum.

Thomas W. Edwards — Sarah E. Chichester — November 1,1842
Sec. Charles B. Tebbs

Samuel George — Eliza C. Grubb — November 10,1842
Sec. Ebenezer Grubb. Curtis Grubb test. groom 21.

Jacob B. Ritter — Margaret Jenkins — September 12,1842
Sec. William Jenkins, father of girl, test. ages.

John P. Dickey — Eliza Ann Mosburg — February 7,1842
Sec. Otho Riggs, who test. ages.

Alexander Cockrell — Catharine F. Rose — December 14,1842
Sec. B.D. Cockrill

Washington Vandevanter — Cecelia E. Braden — April 11,1842
Sec. Oscar S. Braden, who test. ages.

Bushrod Washington Muse Thornton
Louisa Jackson — October 10,1842
Sec. Seth Smith

William Quail — Susan Shipman of — October 11,1842
Sec. Landon Shipman — Cameron Parish

Charles Riticor — Susanna Moss — December 13,1842
Sec. John Moss

Mathew W. Royston — Minerva C.Carpenter — September 5,1842
Sec. Robert Carpenter, who test. ages. Harriet Carpenter, mother of
girl, auth. license. Wit. R.D.Carpenter.

Thomas Needham — Ann C. Evans — August 9,1842
Sec. Harvey Evans, who test. ages.

John W. Win — Mary A.Derry — January 1,1842
Sec. Michael Derry, who test. ages.

Name of Groom	Name of Bride	Date of Bond

John M. Athey   Ann E. Edwards   April 14,1842
Sec. J.S.Edwards, who test. groom's age.

James W. Hummer   Frances Rollison   June 30,1842
Sec. Silas Havener

Wilmon P. Cole   Mary E. Cox   June 6,1842
Sec. J.F.Newton, test. ages. Samuel Cox,father of girl,auth.license.

David Alexander   Sarah S.Brabham   August 9,1842
Sec. Richard Alexander. Mary Brabham auth.license for her dau. Sarah
Susannah. Wit. Basil Gaines.

Harmon Reed   Rosanah Birkett   August 8,1842
Sec. John Birkit, who test. ages.

Mathias Prince   Mary Merchant   September 8,1842
Sec. John Merchant, who test. ages.

Thomas Jenkins   Sarah E.Jenkins   March 29,1842
Sec. Herod Jenkins, who test. ages.

Samuel Ropp   Rachel Beamer   November 7,1842
Sec. George Beamer, who test. ages.

Howard Hough   Phebe Ann Moore   March 5,1842
Sec. Garret Hough, who test. ages. Mary (Moore) Hough, formerly wife
of Abner Moore,dec'd, now wife of Garret Hough, father of Howard,
consented.

Sanford P. Rogers   Susan E.Simpson   April 4,1842
Sec. Friench Simpson. Sanford Gulick test. ages.

Jefferson Lane   Milly Gantt   June 29,1842
Sec. Presley Saunders. Lucy Gant, mother of girl consented.

Richardson Kent   Louisa A.Lowe   May 2,1842
Sec. Henry Lowe. Henry Lowe Sr., father of girl test. groom 21.

William Gibson   Sarah N. Smith   May 23,1842
Sec. Lloyd Noland

Jackson Hogeland   Amanda Malinda Hart March 30,1842
Sec. Daniel Hart. Jonathan Hart, father of girl, auth. license.
James Hogeland test. ages. Wit. William T.Hart

George Mull   Mary Filler   January 21,1842
Sec. William A.Hamilton, who test. girl 21.

Name of Groom	Name of Bride	Date of Bond

David Russell   Esther Ann Coe   February 28,1842
Sec. Elijah Coe, who test. ages.

Lewis Legg   Susan Cummings   February 7,1842
Sec. Thomas Cummings, who test. to cert. of Delilah Cummins, mother
of girl, who auth. license. Wit.Harrison Cummins.

Armistead T.M.Hough   Hariett Elizth.Elliott   March 1, 1842
Sec. George N. Tracy

Samuel A. Spring   Mary A. Stream   March 8,1842
Sec. Peter Myers, who test. ages.

George W. Johnson   Nancy Wright   March 2,1842
Sec. William Wright, father of girl, who test. ages.

Presley Hamilton   Ruth H.Russell   January 24,1842
Sec. Thomas Russell, father of girl, test. ages.

- - - -   -   - - - -

John E. Anderson   Amanda M.Carpenter   November 25,1843
Sec. John A.Beavers, who test. groom's age. Elizabeth Carpenter,
mother of girl, auth. license. Wit. John Thomas.

Elijah P. Myers   Margaret C. Monroe   November 28,1843
Sec. Columbus Jones, who test. ages. Catherine Flowers, mother of
girl, auth. license. Wit. Noble S. Braden.

Aquila Baughman   Emily Campbell   January 31,1843
Sec. John Campbell, father of girl, test. ages.

John F. Thompson   Mary E. Kidwell   November 29,1843
Sec. Joshua Kidwell, who test. ages.

John Lewis Turnipseed   Amelia Garrett   October 28,1843
Sec. Adam Cordell

William Forsythe   Louisa Jane Steadman   December 19,1843
Sec. T.J.Stedman, test. ages. John Stedman, father of girl, auth.
license. Wit. Uriah Stedman.

Elijah Coe   Adaline Smallwood   February 10,1843
Sec. William Smallwood, who test. girl's age.

James W. Rutter   Jane E. Handy   November 2,1843
Sec. Alfred Megeath, who test. ages.

Name of Groom	Name of Bride	Date of Bond

Joseph A. Hains   Mary Ann McGeath   July 25,1843
Sec. J.D. Burk, who test. ages.

Craven A. Copeland   Cynthia M. Cunnard   September 16,1843
Sec. George N. Tracy, who test. girl's age.

John T. Lynn   Nancy H.D.Currell   November 25,1843
Sec. William M. Lynn. Joseph R.Lynn, father of groom, auth. license.
Wit. Pammelia R. Currell

David T. Gulick   Mary Simpson   November 13,1843
Sec. Sanford Gulick. French Simpson, test. girl's age.

Samuel Carr   Elizabeth Brocon   February 7,1843
Sec. James Williams, who test. ages.

Joseph Compher   Susan Smith   January 10,1843
Sec. Jacob Smith, father of girl,test. ages.

Job Miller   Caroline Vincel   November 25,1843
Sec. Jacob Shafer, who test. ages.

James Slack   Ann Maria Kepler   January 17,1843
Sec. James Chappell, who test. ages.

William B. Vinson   Louisa M. Oxley   October 27,1843
Sec. Chs. Gassaway. John T.Vinson test. ages.

John W. Fenton   Frances C. Barton   May 22,1843
Sec. John Weadon, who test. groom's age. Sarah Barton, mother of
girl, auth. license. She a widow of Jim Barton. Wit. Thomas E.Gibson.

Arthur C. Johnson   Mary Jane Clowes   October 23,1843
Sec. A.M.Vandevanter, who test. girl's age.

Wellington Gordon   Far's A. Powell (?)   June 5,1843
Sec. William H. Gray

James Silcott   Eleanor J. Hough   September 25,1843
Sec. Samuel P. Thompson, who test. ages.

John Wade   Susan Wade   September 3,1843
Sec. Martha Wade, who test. groom 21, and she widow of george,dec'd.,
and consented to license for her son.

Charles Lewis   Mary A. Linch   June 5,1843
Sec. Washington Lewis, who test. ages.

Armistead Havener   Sarah A. Walter of   October 18,1843
Sec. John Walter   Cameron Parish

Name of Groom	Name of Bride	Date of Bond

John E. Green   Mary J. Insor   November 18,1843
Sec. C.C. Hinton. A.S. Tebbs test. girl's age.

William S. Harrison   Catharine Whitmore   February 15,1843
Sec. Michael Whitmore.

James Macdaniel   Rosana Osburn   April 15,1843
Sec. Joel Osburn

Alfred Lyons   Mary E. Perry   July 8,1843
Sec. Manly R. Perry. Hezekiah Perry, father of girl, auth. license.
Wit. Wm.Taylor. John Lyons,father of groom,auth. license. Wit.Cuthbert
Powell.

William W. McDonough   Harriet H.Donaldson   August 7,1843
Sec. James McDonough. Elizabeth C.Donaldson, mother of girl, auth.
license. Wit. Noble S. Braden.

William Hough   Sarah N. Love   January 21,1843
Sec. E. A. Love, who test. ages.

William Varney   Maria Cummings   March 20,1843
Sec. G.W.Noland, who test. girl's age.

James White   Ann C. Poulton   February 27,1843
Sec. Adin White. Both fathers present, and auth.license. (unnamed)

Joseph A. Curry   Leah Ann Conard   June 19,1843
Sec. David Conard, who test. his age.

Harrison S. Monroe   Julia Ann Jenkins   May 27,1843
Sec. William Jenkins, father of girl, auth. license.

Alfred Dulin   Margaret Beveridge   September 13,1843
Sec. E. Hammat

Thomas Palmer   Elizth. G. Tippett   April 19,1843
Sec. John C.Tippett, father of girl, who test. ages.

John W. Shipley   Susan M. Cranwell   April 18,1843
Sec. Carey C. Gover, who test. groom's age. Susan Cranwell, mother
of girl, auth. license. Wit. George W. Cranwell.

Ewell N. Byrne   Harriet P. Jeffries   February 15,1843
Sec. B.P.Jeffries, who test. ages.

Name of Groom	Name of Bride	Date of Bond

Jerome B. Young   Mary E. Sterrett   October 18,1843
Sec. R.H.Hoffman, who test. ages and that the bride's mother in person,
consented.

William Hunt   Mary Jane Bolon   May 31,1843
Sec. Aquila Mead,Jr., who test. ages.

John Ingram   Margaret Magaha   August 14,1843
Sec. George Wilt, who proved groom's age. David Miller test. girl's ag

John F. Poston   Mary C. McAtee   May 30,1843
Sec. William W. Poston. Harrison McAtee auth. license. Wit.John Beaver

David Carlisle   Mary Ann Boggess   August 14,1843
Sec. Reed Poulton, who test. ages.

Noble B. Peacock   Lucinda Beans   January 17,1843
Sec. Henry Verts. Wesley J.Saunders test. groom's age. David Reece,
gdn. of girl (and others) orphans of Aaron Beans,dec'd. auth. license.
Wit. James A. Cox.

Joseph Campbell   Ruth Thompson   May 19,1843
Sec. Elcanor Thompson, father of girl, test. ages.

Samuel Crim   Amanda White   August 14,1843
Sec. Thomas White. Jacob Crusin test. Sameul Crusin 21(signature
definitely Crim)

John Lowe   Ann Dawson   August 14,1843
Sec. Rich'd Dawson. Wm.Franklin test. groom's age.

Wesley S. Saunders   Elizth. Crim   August 14,1843
Sec. John Crim, father of girl, test. ages.

Henry Peyton   Susan Jett   September 8,1843
Sec. Burkett Jett, father of girl who test. ages.

Orlando K. Sheid   Amanda M.F.Geaslin   October 31,1843
Sec. Chas. A. Johnston

Martin Gant   Tacey Jane Hixson   October 30,1843
Sec. Benjamin Hixson

John McNealey   Susan C. Miller   February 6,1843
Sec. Gideon Housholder, who test. ages.

Name of Groom	Name of Bride	Date of Bond

William Worsley   Virginia Edwards   November 4,1843
Sec. Chs. Gassaway, who test. girl's age.

John A. Washington   Eleanor Love Selden   February 15,1843
Sec. W.C.Selden

Lewis Taylor   Ruth W. Bradfield   November 6,1843
Sec. Timothy W. Taylor, who test. girl's age.

David L. Beales   Catharine A.Wynkoop   March 31,1843
Sec. Samuel C. Wynkoop, who test. girl's age. Elizabeth Beales,
mother of groom, auth. license. Wit. Calvin F. Beales.

William P. Ryan   Margaret A. McFarland   May 6,1843
Sec. James A.McFarland   of Cameron Parish

Ephraim Smith   Julian M. Wissinger   April 25,1843
Sec. Bernard Goslin, who test. ages.

Edward Simons   Ann Magaha   September 13,1843
Sec. Hiram Hardy, who test. groom's age. Nancy Miller, mother of girl,
auth. license. Wit. Adam Cooper.

George H. Bozzall   Emily Elgin   December 18,1843
Sec. James A. Foster, who test. ages.

Samuel Verts   Duanna Harper   December 11,1843
Sec. Truman Gore, who test. ages.

Lewis Cator Jackson   Ann Gilbert   December 29,1843
Sec. G.W.Paxson, who test. ages.

Joseph Waller   Priscilla C. Shores   December 30,1843
Sec. B.B.Jeffries, who test. ages.

Elijah Tabler   Caroline A.Johnson   November 1,1843
Sec. Robert Johnson, father of girl, who test. ages.

Rodney Craven   Sarah E. Jones   June 26,1843
Sec. Alexander Johnson. John Jones test. girl's age.

James M.Kilgour   Louisa McIlhany   November 24,1843
Sec. Robert T.J.White. James McIlhany, father of girl auth. license.
Wit. Orra McIlhany

Elcanor Thompson   Jemima Pettitt   August 22,1843
Sec. John Clare, who test. ages.

Name of Groom	Name of Bride	Date of Bond

John G. Whaley   Lydia Presgraves of   December 11,1843
Sec.Melville Hutchison   Cameron Parish

Jacob Nollner   Mary Elizabeth Taylor   November 24,1843
Sec. Chs. G. Eskridge. William A.Harris test. girl a dau. of William
Taylor of Loudoun and is 21. William Taylor, auth. license. Wit.
Joshua Taylor.

Peter Kearnes   Mary Smith   August 26,1843
Sec. Margaret McCarty, formerly Mary Smith, mother of girl, and
auth. license.

Washington Wine   Ann Eliza Greenlease   February 13,1843
Sec. John H. Greenlease, who test. ages.

James S. Bascue   Sarah C. Hummer   August 28,1843
Sec. Thomas Hummer, who test. ages.

Cornelius Wynkoop   Mahala Lacey dau. of   December 14,1843
Sec.Israel Lacey   Israel Lacey

James W. Hamilton   Caroline A.Householder December 6,1843
Sec. Gideon Housholder, father of girl. Amos Janney test. groom's
age and that Gideon is father of girl.

Robert S. Wright   Sarah C. Carter   May 17,1843
Sec. R.R.Carter

John F. Milburn   Joanna Carruthers   September 11,1843
Sec. Calvin F. Beales

Edward Renehan   Sarah Carroll   February 25,1843
Sec. William Carroll, who test. ages.

John Cridler   Rebecca Gibbins   June 22,1843
Sec. George Survick, who test. ages.

Jonathan Ewers   Nancy McDaniel   March 13,1843
Sec. Thomas Rogers and William Ewers.

Elijah Hawke   Eliza Waters   March 15,1843
Sec. Jacob Waters, who test. ages.

Alfred B. Powell   Hannah Smith   March 31,1843
Sec. C. F. Anderson, who test. ages.

Gabriel Vandevanter   Jane Cecelia Heaton   April 10,1843
Sec. John T.W.Heaton, who test. girl's age.

Name of Groom	Name of Bride	Date of Bond

Samuel Tinsman — Mary Triplett — August 12,1843
Sec. George Tinsman, who test. girl's age.

George P. Virts — Martha E.Conner — November 27,1843
Sec. James Thomas, who test. ages.

William Rogers — Ruth White — March 13,1843
Sec. T.M.McIlhany

John Russell — Ellen Amanda Hartman — June 23,1843
Sec. Nelson Everhart, who test. ages.

John Clare — Elizth Hall — June 15,1843
Sec. Elcanor Thompson, who test. girl's age.

- - - -   -   - - - -

John Arnold — Elizabeth Case — May 20,1844
Sec. Samuel Case

John Aldridge — Mary E. Moffett — January 4,1844
Sec. Robert Moffett

Jonathan T. Birch — Lucinda I.Franklin — June 30,1844
Sec. George W.Hummer   of Cameron Parish

Michael Beamer — Julian Morrison — January 15,1844
Sec. Edward Morrison

Samuel Beavers — Martha M. Mouldin — December 21,1844
Sec. Joseph Beavers

Jesse Blockley — Manda E. Beaninger — May 4,1844
Sec. John H. Beaninger. Henry W.Beaninger, father of girl.

John Beamusdaffer — Nancy Alexander — June 17,1844
Sec. Mahlon Baldwin. John Alexander, father of girl.

Jeremiah Balthrop — Margaret E. Edison — December 30,1844
Sec. W.H.Edison. J.Edison, father of girl, gave her name as
Margaret Eidson.

William Bergess — Martha A.Campbell — February 19,1844
Sec. Charles Brooks and S.B.T.Caldwell

James P. Brandon — Catherine H.Williams — September 12,1844
Sec. Hiram Opie Williams, father of girl.

Name of Groom	Name of Bride	Date of Bond
Thomas P. Bayley Sec. Robert P. Bayley.	Mary Elizabeth Bayley of Cameron Parish	October 7,1844
Isaac Butts Sec. Colin C. Campbell	Lydia Ann Hart	July 15,1844
Samuel Craig Sec. Wm.S.G.Craig. James D.McPherson test. ages.	Ann M. Gulick of Cameron Parish	July 15,1844
John W. Cross Sec. William Harper. Susan Cross, mother of groom, consented. Wit. Solomon Everhart and Julius Harper.	Margaret A. Harper	May 14,1844
William Cline Sec. S. M. Boss	Margaret Ann Boss	March 9,1844
Jacob F. Cost Sec. James M. Carr test. ages.	Amanda Davis	March 16,1844
Ebenezer Coe Sec. Richard J. Grubb, who test. girl's age.	Jane Grubb	September 16,1844
Edward P. Davis Sec. M.C.Klein, who test. ages.	Elizabeth Klein	February 16,1844
Peyton Davis Sec. Robert Carlisle, father of girl.	Lydia Carlisle	January 17,1844
Thomas Davis Sec. Samuel McCutchen	Barbara Kitzer	January 12,1844
George H. Divine Sec. William W. Myers	Tacey Myers	December 7,1844
Aaron G. Elwell (Ewell) Sec. Nathan H.Janney. Jacob Marshall, father of girl.	Mary Marshall	October 24,1844
John W. Franklin Sec. B. T. Franklin. Mary Driscol, mother of girl.	Martha A. Driscol	July 8,1844
William Frits Sec. John W. Hummer	Amy Ann Spates	August 12,1844
Ebin Furr Sec. Peyton Moore, father of girl.	Emily J. Moore	November 11,1844

Name of Groom	Name of Bride	Date of Bond
James W. Gelleher Sec. George Rhodes	Elizabeth B.Rhodes	April 22,1844
John F. Gantt Sec. T.W. Edwards. Charlotte F. Wilson, mother of girl.	Anna Bell Wilson	February 20,1844
Minor Glascock Sec. John Woolf.	Maria H. Keene	November 4,1844
Carey C. Gover Sec. James Fritts. Edward Rinker father of girl.	Susan Rinker	April 2,1844
Edwin R. Gover Sec. Joseph L. Rathie	Elizabeth Rathie	September 16,1844
Francis Gulick Sec. David F. Gulick	Nancy Craig	March 18,1844
James T. Hamilton Sec. John F.Poston, Harriston McAtee, fater of girl.	Rebecca J. McAtee	July 30,1844
Thomas L.Hammer Sec. William H. Gray	Harriott H.Wilson	January 24,1844
Mandly S. Hampton Sec. Samuel Moore, father of girl.	Emily J. Moore	April 16,1844
David Hawn Sec. Jonathan Hart, father of girl.	Sarah Hart	November 25,1844
John Hooff Sec. Chs. G. Eskridge	Martha J.Blincoe	November 29,1844
Samuel S.Harrison Sec. William J.Adams. Randolph Rhodes,father of girl, consented.	Sarah Rhodes	November 24,1844
Thomas H.Harrison Sec. S.D.Beech. James Harrison,father of groom. Levi Cook, father of girl, consented.	Priscilla E.Cook	June 27,1844
Julius Harper Sec. John Johnson. Catherine Harper, mother of groom and test. he almost 22. Wit. Margaret Harper and Samuel Virts.	Virginia Johnson	September 2,1844
Gustavus I. Heath Sec. John Heath. John C.Chappel,father of girl. Wit. Isaac Heath.	Eliza J. Chappel	February 7,1844
John Heath Sec. Samuel Goram	Sarah J.Goram of Cameron Parish	November 4,1844

Name of Groom	Name of Bride	Date of Bond
Charles W. Henderson Sec. John Campbell	Delila Campbell	July 22,1844
George C. Herrington Sec. Geo. W. Miskell	Sarah A.Milburn	August 13,1844
Isreal Hibbs Sec. John Wornal	Nancy Rhodes	March 11, 1844
Charles Hough Sec. Samuel Slater, father of girl.	Ary Ann Slater	November 9,1844
Daniel Howell Sec. Henry Read.	Elizabeth Monday	January 1,1844
William H. Hughes Sec. John Simpson	Emily Simpson	May 13,1844
Solomon Humphrey Sec. Thomas Birkby	Catherine J.Moss	September 2,1844
W.L. Humphrey Sec. L.Luckett. Craven Pearson, father of girl.	Jane A. Pearson	October 14,1844
Samuel Jenkins Sec. William Miskell	Frances C. Miskell of Cameron Parish	December 30,1844
Michael Kilroy Sec. Thomas S. Dornell	Catherine Beatty	January 6,1844
Edward Lay Sec. Peter Crim	Susan Wolf	October 16,1844
Richard E. Lee Sec. Tilghman Gore	Ann C. McDonald	December 30,1844
James Leeth Sec. Joshua G. Hoge. Samuel Cox, father of girl.	Virginia Ann Cox	November 15,1844
Lewis Legg Sec. James Whitacre	Malvina F. Finch of	September 11,1844
Richard C. Littleton Sec. John M.Orr. Mildred T.Thompson, mother of girl.	Catherine M.Thompson	April 29,1844
John W. Littleton Sec. (No signature) Samuel Carter, father of girl.	Emily Carter	March 2,1844

Name of Groom	Name of Bride	Date of Bond
James D. Love Sec. James Sinclair	Susan A. Shipman	November 7,1844
Josias C. Luckett Sec. James Graham	Mary A. Graham	January 20,1844
Roger C. Luckett Sec. Joshua White	Margaret H. White	October 4,1844
Henry M. Lyon Sec. Joseph Edwards	Eliza J. Walters	February 24,1844
Thacker Mahony Sec. William Merchant, father of girl.	Emily A. Merchant	September 20,1844
John McIntosh Sec. Catesby Jones	Clary Ann Jones	December 30,1844
James McKenney Sec. James Clarke	Susan Ann Clarke	October 5,1844
Thomas Mead Sec. Joseph Mead	Mary Ann Worsley	August 10,1844
James Merchant Sec. George Shumaker	Mary Ann Baker	August 27,1844
Harrison Mills Sec. Thomas H.Muse	Frances R. Muse of Cameron Parish	January 27,1844
Jonathan J. Moore Sec. James McKim. Groom signed Jonathan J.Muse. Margaret McKim, mother of girl.	Margaret Campbell	May 13,1844
Samuel Mullen Sec. Charles Tebbs.	Barbara Oden	December 30,1844
Jonah Nixon Sec. Levi White, father of girl.	Mary White	November 4,1844
Enoch W. O'Bannon Sec. William Person. Wesley Smallwood, father of girl.	Sarah Jane Smallwood	December 17,1844
William O'Connell Sec. John Wornel	Elizabeth Jinking	January 8,1844
William P. Orrison Sec. Jonah Orrison	Pamelia A. McGarvick	January 3,1844

Name of Groom	Name of Bride	Date of Bond
Thompson Osburn	Sarah Osburn	January 22,1844
Sec. Herod Osburn, father of girl.		
Edwin H. Potts	Jane E.Clendening	March 22,1844
Sec. John Clendening		
William A. Rickard	Catharine A. Wine	March 29,1844
Sec. George Henry Wine		
David James Rice	Elizabeth Bolan	September 5,1844
Sec. Ezra Bolan		
John Rose Richards	Mary E. Gantt	February 20,1844
Sec. T. W. Edwards		
Colbert Roby	Nancy Ross	December 31,1844
Sec. William Ross. John Ross, father of girl.		
William H. Russell	Catherine Fairfax	September 12,1844
Sec. Simpson Cooksey		
Perry H. Saunders	Sarah A. Russell	November 4,1844
Sec. Charles W. Russell		
William C. Shawen	Ann C. Taylor	November 14,1844
Sec. Timothy Taylor, father of girl.		
Manly Slack	Mahala J. Saunders	April 16,1844
Sec. James W. Saunders. MahalaSaunders, mother of girl.		
Samuel Simpson	Rebecca Shreve	March 18,1844
Sec. Benj. Shreve		
Usher Skinner	Scotty Sparks of	December 31,1844
Sec. George Hatton	Cameron Parish	
Bushrod W. Skillman	Sarah E. Goucheneaur	September 24,1844
Sec. John Jones. Elizabeth Goucheneaur, mother of girl.		
William Spring	Lydia Ann Compher	March 18,1844
Sec. John Compher, father of girl.		
William Smith	Caroline M. Wenner	March 18,1844
Sec. George Whitmore		
P.A.L. Smith	Amanda Hemston	February 8,1844
Sec. John Butcher		
Patrick H.F.Smith	Edmonia Hancock	January 30,1844
Sec. C.F.Hancock. George Hancock, father of girl.		

Name of Groom	Name of Bride	Date of Bond
Moses Scott Sec. P. H. Smith	Rebecca J. Peugh	December 10,1844
Presley Snoots Sec. Benj. Miles	Sarah Fry	March 18,1844
Arthur Sullivan Sec. George Tavenner	Emily A. Simpson	May 11,1844
John Shryock Sec. Richard H. Rose. John Ellmore father of girl.	Mary Catherine Ellmore	November 12,1844
George N. Tracy Sec. Thomas Tracy	Elizabeth A. Copeland	November 29,1844
William J. Tabler Sec. B.B.Jeffries. John Tabler, father of groom.	Catherine E.King	July 30,1844
Richard B. Tavener Sec. James A. Cox	Lucy E. Blaker	January 1,1844
Samuel H. Tavener Sec. James D.McPherson. William King, father of girl.	Ann Maria King of/	Cameron Parish October 7,1844
Enoch Tincmon (?) Sec. Squire Lee	Elizabeth Alexander	May 6,1844
Sanderson Thrift Sec. Benj. Shreve	Mary B. Shreve	October 21,1844
Townsend Tribby Sec. Reed Poulton	Jane Ann Copeland	February 12,1844
Jackson Underwood Sec. Burr A. Tarleton	Caroline Tarlton	November 21,1844
Joseph Underwood Sec. Jacob Eckman	Harriett Scott	January 12,1844
William Van Sickle Sec. Hector Peacock. Robert Coe, father of girl.	Eunicy Coe	December 30,1844
Solomon Vincell Sec. Mahlon Demory	Louisa Demory	March 28,1844
William K. Wicks Sec. Josiah R. White	Virginia A. White	June 3,1844
Charles W. Wildman Sec. H.M. Hardy	Elizabeth A. Hamilton	August 12,1844

Name of Groom	Name of Bride	Date of Bond
Michael Whitmore Sec. George Whitmore.	Louisa Duvall Harriet Duvall, mother of girl.	June 12,1844
John Wright Sec. Thomas Young	Margaret Brown	December 16,1844
Thomas M. Wright Sec. Hamilton Cross	Martha Brown	April 9,1844
George Henry Wortman Sec. William Lafever Jr.	Jane E. Snider of Cameron Parish	December 18,1844
Samuel C. Wynkoop Sec. Garrett Wynkoop	Susanna Hunt	September 18,1844
Thomas Young Sec. Robert E. Beal	Martha A.Wright	November 9,1844
- - - -	-	- - - -
John Baker Sec. John Spring, father of girl.	Mary Elizab. Spring	January 11,1845
Edward Brady Sec. George Dorrell	Margaret O. Lowe of Cameron Parish	April 24,1845
Peyton Brady Sec. Presly Sanders.	Frances Stewart	May 12,1845
Jacob Allen Sec. James Allen, father of groom.	Sarah Derry	December 27,1845
Simon Arnold Sec. Michael Frey	Catherine Frey	March 31,1845
Charles M. Ayres Sec. Giles Jackson Mrs. Matilda Carter, mother of girl.	Mary J. Dennis of Cameron Parish	February 3,1845
Renselaer Bassett Sec. John W. Shipley.	Eliza A. Cramwell Susan Cramwell, mother of girl.	March 11,1845
Isaac T. Bayles Sec. Alex. D. Lee	Sarah A. Piles of Cameron Parish	January 10,1845
John W.B.Beach Sec. James D. McPherson	Susan A.E.Higdon	November 17,1845

Name of Groom	Name of Bride	Date of Bond
Benjamin C. Barton Sec. William Monroe, father of girl.	Mary E. Monroe	September 20,1845
Newman Briggs Sec. Henderson Bishop	Sarah Jane Jones	September 22,1845
Jonah T. Brown Sec. Jonah T. Brown , Benjamin Stevens.	Alcey Jane Otley	June 8,1845
John V. Brown Sec. John Umbaugh, father of girl.	Harriet Umbaugh	December 8,1845
Joseph Blincoe Sec. Thomas L. Hoskinson	Mary Thomas of Cameron Parish	January 11,1845
James Cockerill Sec. Jacob Verts, and James Virts is the father of girl.	Sarah Jane Virts	December 9,1845
John Cooksey Sec. Oscar F. Reed	Elizabeth Ann Curry	August 11,1845
Raleigh Colston Sec. B.P. Noland	Gertrude Ann Powell	May 17,1845
Zachariah T. Chunn Sec. Bushrod Rust,Jr.	Mary S. Rust	May 10,1845
George H. Cumming Sec. W.H. Brown	Harriet E. Haislip	January 10,1845
James M. Darne Sec. John Nichols	Emily A. Nichols	December 1,1845
Lemuel Daniel Sec. John R. Hibbs. Elizabeth Gouchenauer, mother of girl.	Frances A.Gouchenauer	February 24,1845
Enos Darr Sec. James H. Sanders	Emily S. Speaks	April 10,1845
Robert E. Divine Sec. Alexander Johnson. William Johnson, father of girl.	Emily Johnson	September 29,1845
Thomas S.Davis Sec. John L. Davis	Margaret S. Davis	January 6,1845
John Everhart Sec. Solomon Everhart	Matilda A. Everhart	January 4,1845
William Ewers Sec. William H. Poulton	Eliza E. Thatcher	February 20,1845

Name of Groom	Name of Bride	Date of Bond
Franklin Ewers Sec. Jonah Tavener.	Emily J.G.Baldwin Ruth Baldwin, mother of girl.	May 12,1845
Jacob Fawley Sec. T. W. Edwards	Elizabeth Magaha	January 20,1846
Townsend Frazier Sec. R.C.Littleton.	Sarah E. Littleton John Littleton, father of girl.	November 10,1845
Sandford Fling Sec. Richard H. Presgraves.	Sarah Blincoe	March 3,1845
Asher W. Gray Sec. F. W. Luckett	Martha L. Luckett	May 28,1845
Thomas E. Gibson Sec. James Chappell.	Mary Jane Tinsman Nancy Tinsman, mother of girl.	November 24,1845
Horatio W. Hall Sec. Hezekiah Newman.	Sally Cox Patty Cox, formerly Newman, mother of girl.	August 18,1845
Henry H. Hamilton Sec. A. Gibson.	Maria S.Gibson Abner Gibson, father of girl.	January 16,1845
John W. Hammerly Sec. John W. Gover	Margaret Johnson	September 23,1845
James D. Henvey(Hensey) Sec. Thomas Littleton, father of girl.	Emma Littleton	November 24,1845
Benjamin Hartley Sec. John Jones Jr.	Dorothy Leslie	March 5,1845
Henry Hatton Sec. Isaac E. Steer	Ruth A. Taylor	December 16,1845
Thomas A. Havener Sec. Alexander Moran.	Mary C.Moran of/ Catherine Moran, mother of girl. Cameron Parish	September 10,1845
Michael Havener Sec. Isaac Workman, father of girl	Charlotte Workman of Cameron Parish	January 17,1845
John Haws Sec. William Alexander.	Elizabeth Haws Asa Hawse, father of Elizabeth.	November 10,1845
Robert Henderson Sec. William H. Henderson.	Elizabeth S. Hawk	November 18,1845

Name of Groom	Name of Bride	Date of Bond
John H. Hixson Sec. William M. Lynn	Maria V.Lynn of Cameron Parish	December 3,1845
Joshua G. Hoge Sec. David H.Plaster. Henry Plaster,Jr., father of girl.	Susan H. Plaster	April 10,1845
William H.Hough(of Benj.) Phebe Ellen Hough Sec. Joseph Hough		October 18,1845
Townsend Howell Sec. Joseph Frye	Ann C. Frye of Cameron Parish	November 19,1845
George H. Ish Sec. Francis T. Adams	Elizabeth M. Adams of Cameron Parish	November 10,1845
Isaiah Jackson Sec. John Young, father of girl.	Lucy M. Young	December 2,1845
John Jones Jr. Sec. Samuel D. Leslie	Lydia H. Potts	December 8,1845
Wm. L.H.Kendrick Sec. David Daniel	Louisa E. Swart	August 2,1845
Augustine King Sec. James Gibbs. Isaac Starkey, father of girl.	Elizabeth A. Starkey	January 8,1845
William Lafever Sec. James W.Wiley. Kitty S.Rose, mother of girl.	Mary F. Rose of Cameron Parish	December 9,1845
Lorenzo Luntz Sec. William Greenway	Jane Fred	January 8,1845
Richard McAtee Sec. Daniel Hart. Sarah Kidwell mother of girl.	Permilion Kidwell	February 3,1845
Alexander McFarland Sec. William A. Lanham, father of girl.	Bethany A. Lanham of Cameron Parish	January 1,1845
William F. Mercer Sec. David Carr	Hannah J. Carr	November 18,1845
Benjamin Mershon not signed.	Mahulda Cunningham of Cameron Parish	December 29,1845
John I. Miller Sec. William W. McDonough	Margaret Donaldson	April 10,1845

Name of Groom	Name of Bride	Date of Bond
Peter Moore Sec. Elias Pool	Susan Solomon of Cameron Parish	July 14,1845
George William Mann Sec. John Conard, father of girl.	Leanna Conard	May 9,1845
Joel L. Nixon Sec. James D. McPherson	Mary J. Turner	July 25,1845
William Norell Sec. Samuel Danniel	Mary Ann Daniel	May 15,1845
John W. Patton Sec. Richard Alexander	Mary Alexander	December 24,1845
James S. Payne Sec. Edward Brooks	Margaret Starkey	June 5,1845
Leonidas Peugh Sec. Thomas Rogers	Elizabeth McDaniel	December 8,1845
David T. Pierce Sec. Joseph Bradfield	Orpha A. Bradfield	October 4,1845
William Popkins Sec. - -	Elizabeth Russell of Cameron Parish	December 23,1845
James H. Purcell Sec. Joel Osburn	Patience Osburn	September 25,1845
Daniel W. Rector Sec. Thomas Keene	Sarah Keene	June 2,1845
Samuel M.H. Rector Sec. Norval Craig. (girl's name Catherine Ann)	C.A.Goodin	September 27,1845
Isaac M. Rice Sec. David J.Rice. Theresa Rice,mother of groom. Ezra Boland,father of	Eliza Ann Boland	January 18,1845
Conrad Roller Sec. Leona Frederick.	Mariana Frederick	December 29,1845
John C. Rose Sec. Edwin A. Stover	Mary F. Stover	September 8,1845
James W. Rust Sec. John Hickman,Jr.	Margaret Hickman	January 27,1845
Isaac Starkey Sec. James Gibbs. Isaac Starkey, father of Isaac Jr. and Harrison McAtee father of girl.	Eliza McAtee	January 8,1845

Name of Groom	Name of Bride	Date of Bond
William Stephens unsigned.	Catherine Dennis of Cameron Parish	March 13,1845
Albert Silcott Sec. John W. Hanking	Elizabeth Hutchison	April 21,1845
John W. Shipley Sec. Henry M. Hardy	Rebecca E. Hellriggle	December 24,1845
Daniel G. Smith Sec. D. G. Smith, Chas. G. Eskridge.	Eleanor E. Hamilton	April 28,1845
Job Smith Sec. Michael Fry	Lydia Fry	August 11,1845
James T. Simmons Sec. Jonas Money	Eliza Ann Money	March 15,1845
William Scott Sec. Benson Cornwell	Eliza Hart	July 7,1845
Henry Snoots Sec. D. Adams	Leanna Smith	December 22,1845
William Shry Sec. T. W. Edwards	Christena Fawley	January 2,1845
John H. Thomas Sec. John Lowe	Mary Fair	August 11,1845
John F. Thompson Sec. James W. Jones	Lucinda Jones	October 13,1845
Lewis Torreyson Sec. Washington Jones	Rebecca Day (bride and groom, widow and widower)	February 21,1845
A.B.Thruston Sec. H.D.Magill	Fannie B. Gordon	August 25,1845
Armstead Vandevanter Sec. Timothy Taylor	Patience Taylor	May 5,1845
Alfred Veale Sec. Elijah Peacock	Rebecca J.Peacock of Cameron Parish	March 26,1845
John Wire Sec. George Amick	Susan Amick	February 17,1845
Henry Wirtz Sec. John Leslie, father of girl.	Virginia Leslie	August 11,1845

- - - -   -   - - - -

Name of Groom	Name of Bride	Date of Bond

William Mathers   Margaret Brooks   May 21,1846
John W. Haines, test. ages.

Jacob Major   Sarah Snoots   December 19,1846
Sec. John Snoots, test. ages.

Armistead McPherson   Agnes E. Ridout   May 5,1846
Sec. Richard Tavenner. Juby & Sally Ridout parents of girl,consented.

William McCray   Elizabeth Hatcher,widow February 9,1846
Sec. Mahlon Gore, who test. ages.

Samuel W. Liggett   Catharine Wright   January 1,1846
Sec. Edward Rinker

Henry Lefever   Sally W. Hammerley   April 20,1846
Sec. William Lefever,father of groom test. his age. Her father,
unnamed, also test.

Daniel W.J. Kuhlman   Caroline Diederichs of   January 1,1846
Sec. Daniel Diederichs   Cameron Parish

George J.D.Kuhlman   Catharine Ann Truslow of November 12,1846
Daniel W.J.Kuhlman test.ages. Cameron Parish

Mandervell Pearce   Ann E. Pearce   January 19,1846
Sec. Hector Pearce, father of girl, test. her age.

T.V.B.Osburn   Harriet Osburn   October 9,1846
Sec. Joel Osburn,Sr., father of girl, test. ages.

John W. Payne   Jarusa Jinkins   August 31,1846
Sec. Travis Payne, who test. ages.

Joseph O.'Niel   Mary Dwyer   January 21,1846
Sec. Andrew Carroll, who test. ages.

William F. Pearson   Ann Elizth. Vanhorne   February 12,1846
Sec. Joseph F. Brown

John G. Phillips   Elizabeth J. Oxley   March 28,1846
Sec. Thomas Oxley, father, of girl test. ages.

Jesse L. Rice   Lucinda War   November 9,1846
Sec. William McDonough test. ages.

William Reeder   Mary Ewers   November 16,1846
Sec. Franklin Ewers test. ages. William Ewers,father of girl,consented.
Wit. Jonathan Ewers.

Name of Groom	Name of Bride	Date of Bond

Joseph M. Poston — Sarah Elizabeth Reed — December 1,1846
Sec. Charles M.Littleton. Presley C.Reed test. ages. Sarah Reed
consented for her dau. Wit. Cornelious Reed.

John L. Prince — Elizabeth Everhart — August 31,1846
Sec. Nelson Everhart. Daniel and Martha Hirst consent for their
dau. to marry.

George W. Ridgeway — Martha Bussey — May 29,1846
Sec. John T. Bussey

George M. Ritchie — Catharine E.Heffner — October 6,1846
Sec. A.H. Haines, test. ages.

William Richardson — Richardetta Sims — November 21,1846
Sec. Wm.Sims, father of girl, test. groom 24 yrs. old.

Isaac Roberts — Lucinda E. Wince — October 16,1846
Sec. Alfred Shields, who test. ages

Simon Smale — Elizabeth Lott — June 30,1846
Sec. Presley Saunders

Lafayette W. Swart — Huldah Gulick of — January 1,1846
Sec. James W.Taylor — Cameron Parish
John Iden test. her age.

Henry S. Swart — Elizabeth J.Jinkins of — May 21,1846
Sec. Wm. Foley — Cameron Parish

Hugh J. Sweeny — Eliza Frits — April 13,1846
Sec. Nathaniel W.Everhart, test. ages

George Sexton — Martha Tribby — March 9,1846
Sec. David Reece test. her age. Thos. Gregg test. groom's.

Meshack Silcott — Emily Dodge — March 6,1846
Sec. William Lodge test. ages

John C. Moss — Frances Wildman — August 20,1846
Sec. William Wildman, father of girl, test. ages.

Stephen F. Monroe — Sarah E.McPherson — February 2,1846
Sec. Benjamin C.Barton test. girl is dau. of Mary McPherson who is
the widow of Madison McPherson, and she consented.

Armistead M. Miller — Mary Ann Edwards — February 2,1846
Sec. Solomon Everhart test. ages.

Name of Groom	Name of Bride	Date of Bond
Aaron Midcalp Sec. Alex'r. Keyes, father of girl	Elizabeth Keyes	January 8,1846
Richard Meathrel Sec. Isaac Leedom, father of girl, test. room 35 and a widower.	Julia E. Leedom	June 22,1846
William Mavin Sec. Presly Saunders Geo. Adie test. (Mrs.) Anna B. Wampler is 21.	Ann B. Wampler of Cameron Parish	December 19,1846
Joseph Everhart Sec. Thomas Lambaugh test. ages.	Sarah Feitchter	October 21,1846
Joseph Arnold Sec. Simon Arnold	Martha A. Matthias	December 28,1846
Daniel Baker Sec. William Bitzer, father of girl, test. ages.	Lydia Ann Bitzer	August 24,1846
David Axline Sec. John Prince, who test. ages.	Catharine S. Coe	March 21,1846
Harrison Ballenger Sec. Richard Ballenger, who test. ages.	Caroline E. Brackenridge	May 16,1846
George Sargent Sec. Hanson Derry test. ages.	Mary Fillingim	December 30,1846
Joshua Stocks Sec. Thomas Davis. Samuel McCutchen consented to his dau.'s marriage.	Elizabeth Ellen McCutchen	April 27,1846
Joseph Snow Sec. Michael Wiard who test. ages.	Louisa Ann Wiard	March 31,1846
Philip L.W.Vermillion Sec. John C. Rose, who test. ages.	Jane W. Bazill	February 6,1846
Tilghman Vincel Sec. Peter Fry, father of girl, test. ages.	Susan C. Fry	December 8,1846
John Vincell Sec. John Davis, who test. ages.	Elizth.Ulam, widow	January 19,1846
Charles F. Wright Sec. John Hamilton, father of girl, test. ages.	Lydia J. Hamilton	February 20,1846
Johnson Wheeler Sec. William Burk. Sydnor B.Johnson test. ages.	Susannah Wright	January 12,1846

Name of Groom	Name of Bride	Date of Bond
Thomas A. Schooley	Hannah Hough	November 16,1846

Sec. Garret Hough, who test. ages.

Charles W. Reed — Isabella V.Green — February 9,1846
Sec. Henry Green, father of girl, test. ages.

William Lowe — Jane Pomeroy — September 14,1846
Sec. John H.Thomas test. ages. Jane Lowe,mother of groom,consented
Wit. John Lowe

James Mankins — Sarah Ann Havener — January 12,1846
Sec. William D. Havener, test. ages. Wit. W. Schooley

Joseph B. Hough — Elizabeth Hough — March 13,1846
Sec. Joseph Hough test. ages.

Daniel T. Fouche — Mary Margaret Hough — January 21,1846
Sec. Leven W.S.Hough. Mary Hough,mother of girl, consented.

William Giddings — Ann E. Moffett — July 4,1846
Sec. Robert Moffett who test. ages.

Joseph G. Gregg — Martha A. Shepherd — April 3,1846
Sec. Alfred Megeath, test. ages.

John B. Grayson — Mary Ann Tyler — January 12,1846
Sec. William B. Tyler

John H. Greenlease — Ruth Hannah Taylor — January 12,1846
Sec. Charles Taylor, father of girl.

Lewis J. Garrison — Martha Alexander — January 1,1846
Sec. Richard Alexander test. ages.

Francis W. Galliher — Emily E. Stover of — January 18,1846
Sec.Edwin A.Stover, — Cameron Parish
father of girl.

Armistead R. Mott — Virginia L. Bentley — December 15,1846
Sec. Robt. W. Gray, who test. ages.

Peter Hickman — Mary E. Kalb — November 28,1846
Sec. Samuel Kalb

Norval V. Heskett — Emily Howell — May 4,1846
Sec. Burr P. Chamblin, who test. ages.

William Haws — Elizth. Lanham — December 9,1846
Sec. James Haws

Name of Groom	Name of Bride	Date of Bond

Curtis Grubb   Rachel Ann Locker   December 5,1846
Sec. G. Locker, who test. girl's age.

Thomas Gore   Mary Ann Webb   July 28,1846
Sec. Peter Gore, who test. girl's age

Henry Goodheart   Mary E. Mason   October 24,1846
Sec. Adam Mason

G.W. Bradfield   Matilda E. Klein   January 12,1846
Sec. James J.Love who test. ages.

Robert Elgin   Margaret Elizabeth Lynn of   June 15,1846
Sec. Chs. G. Eskridge   Cameron Parish
Pammelia C.Lynn, mother of girl,consented. Wit.Gustavus L.Elgin and
John T. Lynn.

John G. Fletcher   Alice J. Fletcher   April 23,1846
Sec. Joshua Fletcher Jr. who test. ages.

Joseph Fawley   Ary Ann Catherine Cordell   November 2,1846
Sec. Adam Cordell, father of girl, who test. ages.

Nimrod Johnston   Alice A. Athey   October 27,1846
Sec. James W. Athey test. ages.

Jacob Howser   Sarah Catharine Fields   January 19,1846
Sec. Samuel Orison, who test. ages.

Jacob Allender   Eliza Ann Steward   July 23,1846
Sec. Charles E. Speaks test. ages.

John Wolfe   Mary A. Ney   November 23,1846
Sec. David Galliher test. ages.

Edward Wines   Ann Beach   October 24,1846
Sec. James M. Carr

John Henry Schooley   Maria P.Norris   March 3,1846
Sec. Charles W.Schooley. Presley Saunders test. ages.

Burr Brown   Mary Ellenor Nichols   February 20,1846
Sec. Jonah Nichols test. her age(father of girl) Joseph Brown test. gro

George M.Brown   Eliza B.Gibson   June 8,1846
Sec. J.C.Murray. Mahlon Gibson,father of girl,consented.

R.G.Bowie   Julia A.H.Wilson   June 23,1846
Sec. Chs. G. Eskridge

John Boothe   Emily Jane Owens   December 17,1846
Sec. Edward Owens, who test. groom's age.

Name of Groom	Name of Bride	Date of Bond
Henderson Bishop Sec. Henry Clapper, who test. ages.	Elizabeth Campbell	June 25,1846
Hardage Bridges Sec. Alex'r D.Lee, father of girl.	Margaret A. Lee of Cameron Parish	February 19,1846
John Davis Sec. John Vincell, who test. girl's age.	Martha Spring,widow	January 19,1846
John T. Crupper Sec. Wm.Beatty. Geo. W. Norris test. groom 21.	Cora Ann Beatty	October 12,1846
Abner A. Conard Sec. Jesse Near test. groom's age.	Ann S. Neer	February 24,1846
John Clothier Sec.John Iden test. her age. Cameron Parish	Margaret Ann Iden of	May 11,1846
John Compher Sec. Ebenezer Grubb test. ages.	Esther Ann Grubb	January 28,1846
Michael O'Bryan Sec. John Conner, test. age of girl	Elizabeth Spinks	April 14,1846
Robert Boyd Sec. William Palmer test. ages.	Elizabeth A.Palmer	March 2,1846
Joseph L. Wright Sec. Jonah Orrison. Margaret Orrison,mother of girl, consented. Wit.David Orrison,Sr.	Margaret Orrison	October 19,1846
James F. Ball Sec. Asher W.Gray. Fayette Ball test. groom 21. Horace Luckett,father of girl, consented.	Maria Louisa Luckett	December 9,1846
Troy Ballenger Sec. John Ballenger	Margaret Ann Brackenridge	January 22,1846
Henson Elliott Sec.S.B.T.Caldwell	Lucinda Orum, orphan of Henry dec'd.	April 13,1846
Stephen Downs Sec. John Ault. Presley Saunders test. ages.	Mary Ann Ault	March 23,1846

- - - -   -   - - - -

Name of Groom	Name of Bride	Date of Bond
William Allder Sec. Francis M.Bradfield	Jane Ann Orr	April 3,1847
Richard Anderson Sec. Jonathan Milbourn	Mary E. Milbourn	May 13,1847
Ewell Attwell Sec. A.K.Peiser	Mary A. Simpson	March 15,1847
Franklin Arundell Sec. James Wiley	Mary E. Houser	February 17,1847
Joseph C. Baker Sec. Peter Coe	Mary Jane Coe	November 8,1847
William H. Bates Sec. Joshua Lee	Hannah Lee of Cameron Parish	November 22,1847
Sydnor Bennett Sec. James Silcott	Mary M.Silcott	November 15,1847
Harmon Bitzer Sec. B.F.Franklin	Catherine Franklin of Cameron Parish	January 21,1847
Philip Brooks Sec. Samuel Lamb	Mary Lamb	December 6,1847
Nathan Brown Sec. Edmund Phillips	Sarah A.Phillips	January 11,1847
Daniel Carnes Sec. Michael Everhart, father of girl.	Anna E.Everhart	February 23,1847
John B. Campbell Sec. None signed.	Rachael Ann Grubb	August 9,1847
Looman Chancellor Sec. Rufus Smith	Margaret E. Smith	September 6,1847
Charles W. Clements Sec. Jacob Smith	Sarah Ann Filler	December 27,1847
Tholemiah Cochran Sec. Asa James	Hannah James	January 27,1847
Jesse Colbert Sec. Robert E.Beall	Christena Virts of Cameron Parish	December 24,1847
William Cooksey Sec. G.W. Mock	Mary C. Shrigley	January 16,1847

Name of Groom	Name of Bride	Date of Bond
Joseph Cooper Sec. John Jones,Jr.	Catherine Aslinger	May 10,1847
Samuel Dailey Sec. L.W.Worthington	Harriet R. Tucker	January 30,1847
John W. Dailey Sec. Thomas Green, father of girl.	Frances I. Green	December 11,1847
James W. Dodd Sec. Charles A. Ware	Elizabeth F. McClenahan	December 15,1847
George Donaldson Sec. David Reece	Patience Beans	October 23,1847
Noah Downs Sec. Edward Hains, father of girl.	Mary Jane Hains of Cameron Parish	March 6,1847
Enoch Fenton Sec. Thomas Nichols	Ruth E. Nichols	August 17,1847
William Henry Frizel Sec. James G. Otley	Mary C. Hutchinson	March 11,1847
Solomon Filler Sec. William Divine, father of girl.	Juliet F. Divine	February 16,1847
Allen Gibson Sec. William Stillions, father of girl.	Mahulda Stillions	November 1,1847
Eli J. Hamilton Sec. James Heaton	Virginia Heaton	May 10,1847
Charles M. Fauntleroy Sec. Thomas P.Knox, father of girl.	Janet P. Knox	January 18,1847
John W. Hankings Sec. Isaac Brown	Mary Wiley	February 18,1847
James M. Howell Sec. John Huffman, father of girl.	Martha C.Huffman	January 12,1847
Abraham Hewitt Sec. John Woody, father of girl.	Isabell Woody	September 1,1847
Thomas H. Hixson Sec. William Gulick	Sarah E. Gulick	January 15,1847
William S. Hogeland Sec. William S.Hogeland Jackson Hogeland and Samuel Ayres, father of girl.	Margaret M.Ayres of Cameron Parish	November 9,1847

Name of Groom	Name of Bride	Date of Bond
Philip H. Hoof Sec. Charles W. Blincoe	Elizabeth Blincoe	February 11,1847
Robert J. Hoskinson Sec. Thomas Rogers	Elizabeth Tavenner	November 24,1847
Abijah W. Hudspeth Sec. I.T. Massey	Sarah W. Hurst	March 1, 1847
Thomas L. Humphrey Sec. Harrison Osburn	Dorcas Osburn	October 20,1847
Abner G. Humphrey Sec. Joseph Lodge, father of girl.	Mary C. Lodge	May 26,1847
Pickering Hutchinson Sec. William Ambler	Sarah E.Hutchinson of Cameron Parish	August 25,1847
Giles T. Jackson Sec. William A. Dennis Matilda Carter, mother of girl.	Sophronia E. Dennis of Cameron Parish	April 20,1847
Nathan H. Janney Sec. James H. Purcel	Lydia Jane Purcel	May 31,1847
John G.R. Kalb Sec. William Slater, father of girl.	Ellen H. Slater	December 31,1847
Peter Karns Sec. Elias Jenkins	Sally Greenwell	November 20,1847
Philip Kesler Sec. Philip Derry	Mary Everhart	January 2,1847
John Kidwell Sec. John Kidwell	Susan Blundon	June 19,1847
Joseph Magaha Sec. William Magaha	Civilla Cooper	October 29,1847
Hugh McNulty Sec. William Carroll	Mary E. Dawes	December 9,1847
Jacob Mann Sec. George Whitmore	Anna Ruse	March 29,1847
Charles T. Lewis Sec. Henry M.Rust. Benjamin Rust, father of girl.	Ann S. Rust	May 4,1847

Name of Groom	Name of Bride	Date of Bond
Thomas B. Love Sec. Jno. D. Baldwin	Eliza H.Gibson	January 15,1847
Franklin Minor Sec. Francis W. Elgin	Eleanor Anderson	June 28,1847
Samuel Mullen Sec. Abraham Hewitt	Lydia Ann Zeller	July 5,1847
John Myers Sec. John Campbell, father of girl.	Mary A. Campbell	April 13,1847
Isaac L. Mock Sec. Benjamin Ogden, father of girl.	Lydia Ann Ogden	March 6,1847
John McNealey Sec. David Everhart, father of girl.	Mary C. Everhart	January 23,1847
William C. Miskell Sec. William Peacock, father of girl.	Catherine Peacock	January 1, 1847
Charles A. Newton Sec. Thomas Skinner	Lauretta C. Skinner	May 26,1847
John P. Phillips Sec. Charles F. Phillips	Mary C. Warner	February 1,1847
George H. Rector Sec. D.M.Divine. George Backhouse, father of girl.	Elizabeth A.P.Backhouse	October 11,1847
Alexander F. Roby Sec. William Ross	Mary Jane Ross	February 27,1847
Robert T. Rose Sec. John M. Spencer	Harriet M. Swart	September 16,1847
Jonathan Russell Sec. Joseph Edwards, father of girl.	Elizabeth Edwards	November 29,1847
Robert Russell Sec. Samuel J. Chamblin	Amelia S.G.Prints	March 22,1847
Lee A. Sanders Sec. Thomas A.Havener	Penelope M. Havener of Cameron Parish	January 30,1847
John Sanbower Sec. Jacob Stoutsenberger	Emma Stoutsenberger	September 29,1847
Lewis Steele Sec. James D. McPherson	Leah Hazard	May 18,1847

Name of Groom	Name of Bride	Date of Bond
William Senate Sec. Presley Sanders.	Eliza Whitty	August 11,1847
Elias Spring Sec. J.B.Schooley	Lydia Shaffer	November 1,1847
James W. Solomon Sec. William Dove	Caroline Dove of Cameron Parish	January 14,1847
George Shoemaker Sec. John Grubb, father of girl.	Sarah Grubb	January 21,1847
Mahlon Stocks Sec. George Townsend. David Daniel, father of girl.	Matilda I.Daniel	December 11,1847
Joseph Taylor Sec. William Fritts	Ann Fritts	September 13,1847
James F. Trayhern Sec. S.B.T.Caldwell	Sally Ann Caldwell	June 7,1847
Foushee C. Tebbs Sec. Edwin C. Brown	Maria Brown	September 13,1847
Moses Buckner Trussell Sec. George Young	Sarah E. Young	July 31,1847
Samuel E. Washington Sec. Jacob Shafer	Sarah J. Everhart	July 23,1847
John Francis Waters Sec. Christian Nisewaner,father of girl. John F.Waters.	Susan Nisewaner	January 15,1847
Jacob Waters Sec. John Mobley	Ellen Elizabeth Magaha	October 26,1847
John W. Webb Sec. Nelson Chamblin	Amanda Jacobs	May 24,1847
John W. Wenner Sec. Jacob Smith, father of girl.	Mary Jane Smith	December 21,1847
Charles Wildman Sec. John Benjamin	Henrietta Benjamin	May 11,1847
Tobias R. Williams Sec. Jacob Smith	Sarah Ann Amich	May 24,1847
William Wiley Sec. Joseph Taylor	Charlotte E.Taylor	February 1,1847

Name of Groom	Name of Bride	Date of Bond
Harrison Wiley Sec. Thomas Green, father of girl.	Mary Elizabeth Green	March 27,1847
Jacob Wilklow Sec. Wesley J. Sanders	Mary Ann Cooper	March 8,1847
James A. Wilson Sec. Charles Kendall, father of girl.	Harriet M.Kendall	May 22,1847

- - - -   -   - - - -

Redmond F. White Sec.Murphey C.Shumate,father of girl.	Maria L.Shumate	December 18,1848
A. M. Johnson Sec. John G.Huffman, father of girl.	Sarah C.Huffman	November 22,1848
Ignatius M. Knott Sec. James Sinclair. Sarah S. Seeders consented.	Mary Lee Seeders	November 20,1848
Henry W. Castleman Sec. David J. Castleman, who test. groom's age.	Mary E. Sinclair	November 8,1848
Joseph Thomas Wynkoop Sec. Philip Henry Wynkoop. Jane Lowe consented for her dau.	Elizabeth Lowe	November 29,1848
John Suddeath Sec. G. W. Dorrell	Eliza Kelly	December 11,1848
John M. Kabrich Sec. John Frye, father of girl. George Kabrich consented for his son.	Eve M. Frye	November 6,1848
John W. Martin Sec. I. H. Vandevanter	Mary E. Dulany	December 22,1848
Hamilton Householder Sec. Joseph E.Axline	Caroline M.Axline	December 4,1848
Thomas Hummer Sec. John E. Stewart	Joanna Saunders	December 23,1848
Levi W. Nixon Sec. James D. McPherson	Margaret Major	December 29,1848
William Graham Sec. C. F. Wright	Nancy Stone	December 27,1848
George R. Head Sec. Edwin R. Gover	Sarah Virginia Gover	November 14,1848

Name of Groom	Name of Bride	Date of Bond
William Kitchen	Eliza Shelby,widow	October 30,1848

Sec. John Noggle, father of girl

Andrew Seitz	Amanda Yakey	October 7,1848

Sec. Jno. W. Shipley

Jacob Leeman	Elizabeth Lewis	October 12,1848

Sec. Daniel Lewis, father of girl.

George Jackson	Margaret Megeath	October 30,1848

Sec. Alfred Megeath

Peter W. Johnson	Anna S. Drish	October 31,1848

Sec. William D. Drish, father of girl.

James E. McCabe	Amanda Littleton	November 22,1848

Sec. Erasmus H. Fox

Frederick Miller	Edney Fitcher	October 10,1848

Sec. George Fichter

Henry H. Gregg	Jane J. Osburn	November 28,1848

Sec. Richard Osburn,Sr.,(father of girl)

John D. Larue	Maria Osburn	November 30,1848

Sec. Joel Osburn,Senr.

Joshua Bailes	Mary A. Harper	November 13,1848

Sec. John Johnson. Catharine Harper, mother of girl.

John E. Mount	Mary J. Fitzhugh	November 13,1848

Sec. Samuel K. Jackson

George W. Russell	Elizabeth J.James	November 6,1848

Sec. Elijah James, father of girl.

George W. Hough	Jane Hurdle	October 23,1848

Sec. R.H.Edwards. Nancy C. Hurdle, mother of girl, consented.

Josiah G. Keese	Mary E. Oneal	December 4,1848

Sec. Thomas Oneal, father of girl.

Tholemiah R. Wilson	Maria L. Boley	July 27,1848

Sec. James D. McPherson

William S. Alder	Margaret E. Birkitt	August 14,1848

Sec. William Birkitt

Gustavus J. Heath	Ann M. Popkins	August 5,1848

Sec. James H. Popkins

Name of Groom	Name of Bride	Date of Bond

James Easton   Laura Ambrose   August 15,1848
Sec. Robert Ambrose,father of girl, and James McNeally

John W. Fairfax   Mary Jane Rogers   September 26,1848
Sec. M.M.Lewis. Jos. Janney, gdn. of groom, consented.

George W. Loveless   Eliza Hamilton   September 18,1848
Sec. Christopher Howser, gdn. of girl.

Jesse Williamson   Susan Stayley   September 22,1848
Sec. George Survick

John P.H.Green   Alverda Osburn   September 11,1848
Sec. George Moore. Richard Osburn, father of girl, consented.

Joseph M. Conard   Mary J.D.Potts   September 4,1848
Sec. Ezekiel Potts, father of girl.

John Randolph Tucker   Laura Holmes Powell   October 5,1848
Sec. Henry L. Brooke. H.B.Powell, father of girl, consented.

Robert Lewis   Caroline A. Lynnd   October 4,1848
Sec. Nicholas Lynnd

John Reed   Maranda Winecoop   October 12,1848
Sec. John M. Kabrick

John William Conard   Susan A. Grubb   October 30,1848
Sec. William Grubb, father of girl.

Jacob Stoneburner   Jane Campbell   July 5,1848
Sec. Alexander Poland

Peter Crim   Susannah Waters   July 29,1848
Sec. John Smith

Edward Tillett   Elizabeth Pearson   July 18,1848
Sec. John Pearson. Samuel A.Tillett test. groom in 23rd yr.

Hugh William Hardy   Louisa J.Hamilton   July 31,1848
Sec. James Benjamin. Wm.Jackson test. both 21 and up.

William T. Craig   Martha Ann Cockerell April 7,1848
Sec. John Cockrill.

Moses Lowe   Margaret V. Beales   January 4,1848
Sec. William Lowe. Richard White,gdn. of girl, consented.

Philip Derry   Rachel Dowling   January 31,1848
Sec. Ezekiel Potts, gdn. of girl.

Name of Groom	Name of Bride	Date of Bond

Richard N. Daniel   Missouri A.Cross   January 12,1848
Sec. S.L.Hodgson. Harrison Cross,father of girl, consented.

Robert Polen   Julia Frances Ann Cross January 12,1848
Sec. S.L.Hodgson. Harrison Cross,father of girl. John Polen,father of g

John W. Wildman   Anna S. Bentley   January 11,1848
Sec. Jared Chamblin

Alexander Brooks   Susan A. Love   January 13,1848
Sec. James D. McPherson

Adison Cochran   Sarah James   January 14,1848
Sec. Robert James, gdn. of girl.

Armistead J. Wine   Mary E. Cassaday   January 17,1848
Sec. George H. Wine

John W. Sinclair   Catharine Wynkoop   January 19,1848
Sec.Thomas Wynkoop,father of girl. Alsinda Wynkoop,mother.   John Sincla
father of groom.

Thompson B. Robey   Mildred A.Nalls   January29,1848
Sec. Carr B. Nalls,father of girl. Jane Robey, mother of groom

James Long   Sarah C.Carnine   January 10,1848
Sec. Eden Carnine, father of girl.

Joseph L. Rathie   Mary Ellen Garner   January 4,1848
Sec. Benjamin D. Rathie

Joseph L. Virts   Eliza Ann Baker   January 28,1848
Sec. George Baker, father of girl.

William Keys   Mary A. Tavenner   February 15,1848
Sec. Eli Tavenner, father of girl.

Martin L.Arnold   Elizabeth Smith   February 24,1848
Sec. Jacob Smith, father of girl.

Isaiah R. Kabrich   Amelia Morrison   February 26,1848
Sec. George Kabrich,father of groom. John Morrison,father of girl.

Hugh S. Thompson   Ruth H. Clendening   February 23,1848
Sec. James H. Clendening

William T. French   Rachel A. Hough   February 4,1848
Sec. William S. Wood

Name of Groom	Name of Bride	Date of Bond
James Carlisle Sec. John Wiley	Emily Wiley	February 7,1848
George Sullivan Sec. James Keene	Elizabeth James	February 25,1848
John Z. Carlley Sec. Jesse L. Rice	Eveline Warr	February 12,1848
Smith Anderson Bond unsigned. Nancy Anderson, mother of groom, consented.	Frances Ann Moore	February 14,1848
John W.Simpson Sec. French Simpson, father of groom. Richard Adams,father of girl,con	Mary Ann Adams	February 14,1848
Alpheus L. Edwards Sec. Presly Saunders	Mary S. Washington	February 2,1848
George Anderson Sec. James M. Carr	Catharine Wildman	March 7,1848
James B. Havenner Sec. Walker J.Muse. Sarah Ann Dawson,mother of girl, consented.	Hortensia Ellen Dawson	March 27,1848
James Bazill Sec. Joseph E. Bazill. Warner Hales, father of girl, consented.	Mary Frances Hales	March 21,1848
Eli H. Nichols Thos. Nichols, father of groom	Elizabeth White	March 13,1848
William Atkin Sec. Thomas Hensey	Elizabeth P.Clark	April 28,1848
Dawson Poston Sec. Isaac Starkey	Roberta Ann Skinner	April 22,1848
John T. Steele Sec. William Merchant	Martina McKim	April 5,1848
John W. Board Sec. Samuel C.E.Ramsey. John R.Ramsey, father of girl, consented.	Margaret Ann Ramsey	March 6,1848
Aaron Edward Orem Sec. John L. Prince	Mary Ann Prince	May 27,1848
Ellison A. Currie Sec. Asher W. Gray. Horace Luckett, father of girl, consented.	Sarah Frances Luckett	May 24,1848
William Cross Sec. Robert James	Mary James	June 12,1848

Name of Groom	Name of Bride	Date of Bond

Alexander Moran
Sec. Francis M.Brabham.

Vilinda C.Brabham
Mary Brabham, mother of girl, consented.

June 10,1848

Adam Hesser
Sec. Solomon Smith

Hannah Edwards

June 13,1848

George W.Henderson
Sec. Norval Craig

Lucinda Hunt

June 22,1848

Peter Etcher
Sec. Alfred Dulin

Nancy Fowler of
    Cameron Parish

June 21,1848

James Lanen
Sec. John W. Webb. Elizabeth Webb,mother of girl, & widow of Elisha Web

Elisabeth Jane Webb

June 19,1848

Samuel Baker
Sec. Samuel C. Luckett

Elisabeth Virts

June 5,1848

John Newton Ross
Sec.Benjamin J.Poston.
Leonard R.Poston,father of girl, consented.

Susan M. Poston
John Ross,father of groom,consented.

May 8,1848

James F. Trenary
Sec. W.G.Trenary. James Chappel,father of girl,test. she 21.

Letitia Chapell

May 24,1848

John Stone
Sec. John Wolford

Rebecca Wolford

May 15,1848

William Lloyd
Sec. Gideon Milbourn

Emily J. Milbourn

May 22,1848

James W. Stewart
Sec. Eden Carnine, father of girl.

Mary Jane Carnine

May 8,1848

Jacob Nichols
Sec. James Sinclair

Edith H. Nichols

June 14,1848

- - - -   -   - - - -

S. M. Alder
Sec. Francis M. Bradfield

Mary A. Marshall

May 16,1849

James Alexander
Sec. Mahlon Baldwin. Margaret Carlyle, mother of girl.

Lydia Jane Boggess

March 17,1849

Samuel Ankers
Sec. William M. Moran

Henrietta B. Edwards

October 31,1849

James Bagent
Sec. Benjamin Wigginton

Sarah Wigginton
   of Cameron Parish

July 23,1849

Name of Groom	Name of Bride	Date of Bond
Joseph Baldwin Sec. Richard H. Benton	Eliza H. Benton	October 1,1849
Joseph Barnhouse Sec. W.D.Drish	Margaret Jane Barnhouse	November 19,1849
John Bartlett Sec. Evert Tracy. Groom signed Johnson Bartlett	Ann H. Tracey	September 29,1849
James A. Baughman Sec. Casper Spring	Mary Elizabeth Spring	November 23,1849
William B. Benedict Sec. Samuel K. Jackson	Henrietta Henderson	July 18,1849
Charles E. Benedum Sec. S.M.Boss, father of girl.	Martena K. Boss	February 19,1849
William H. Boam Sec. Elijah P. Myers	Mary Ann Tucker	May 15,1849
Beverly Boley Sec. H. Feagans	Sarah Ann Figgins	March 7,1849
William Butler Sec. L.T.Beach	Harriet Dailey	December 29,1849
George F. Byrne Sec.John R.Skinner Elizabeth B.Bogue, mother of girl.	Eliza F. Bogue of Cameron Parish	September 8,1849
Nicodemus Cartwright Sec. John Smith	Ann Taylor	November 6,1849
George Washington Cheek Sec. John Umbaugh, father of girl.	Elizabeth Umbaugh	April 3,1849
Peter Compher Sec. Howson L.Hooe, father of girl.	Mary D. Hooe	May 22, 1849
Robert Campbell Sec. Robert Curry, father of girl.	Martha Ellen Curry	April 23,1849
Daniel Diederick Sec. Samuel Jenkins	Elizabeth Murray	December 29,1849
George H. Divine Sec. Samuel Gover	Eliza Hough	August 27,1849

Name of Groom	Name of Bride	Date of Bond
Charles W. Divine Sec. Robert E. Divine	Ann N. Hurdell	February 6,1849
James R. Durborow Sec. Draco Marlow. Thomas J.Marlow, father of girl.	Margaret E.Marlow	September 21,1849
James K. Elderkin Sec. David P. Conard	Sarah E.W.Conard	August 31,1849
Philip P. Everhart Sec.David T. Crawford, father of girl.	Mary E. Crawford	February 10,1849
George Feaster Sec. Robert Curry, father of girl.	Laura Jane Curry	March 8,1849
Armistead T.M.Filler Sec. S.E.Washington. Mary M.Stuck, mother of girl.	Lydia M.Stuck	December 24,1849
George W. Fling Sec. Joseph Blincoe,Jr.	Susan Tillett of Cameron Parish	January 4,1849
Richard Ford Sec. Levi White	Martha Thomas	November 3,1849
Kemp Furr Sec. Moses B.Furr. James Chappell, father of girl.	Mary Ann Chappell	March 2,1849
John Fry Sec.George Baker. George Baker father of girl. Peter Fry,father of gro	Sarah E. Baker	January 1,1849
Richard Henry Gantt Sec. Giles Jackson	Margaret McCarty of Cameron Parish	March 6,1849
George L. Garrett Sec. Oscar F. Reed	Elizabeth Rinker	September 10,1849
Edwin R. Gover Sec. Edgar Jarvis	Ellen Hammerly	April 17,1849
Sidney Hawling Sec. Richard Osburn,Jr.	Eliza Osburn	January 1,1849
Charles H. Higdon Sec. Aaron Beans. James Higdon, father of groom.	Eliza Ann Beans	April 21,1849
Thomas Hoskinson Sec. Henry Sanders Jr.	Ann Hoskinson	March 10,1849
John E.S.Hough Sec. James Sinclair	Eugenia T. Dawson	June 20,1849

Name of Groom	Name of Bride	Date of Bond
Derigo C. Hough	Eleanor H. Schooley	February 24,1849
Sec. Jonas P.Schooley,father of girl. W.H.Hough, father of groom.		
David L. Hughes	Margaret F. Simpson	January 22,1849
Sec. George R. Jackson. French Simpson, father of girl.		
George W. Hummer	Leah J. Tippett	January 17,1849
Sec. John C. Tippett, father of girl.		
George W. Hummer	Emeline C. Miller	September 28,1849
Sec. John L. Bascue		
Joseph E. Hunt	Elizabeth Talley	October 15,1849
Sec. Smith Reed		
Thomas W. Keene	Roberta E.A.Jacobs	December 28,1849
Sec. John W. Jacobs, Elam Jacobs, father of girl.		
Joseph B. Lacey	Fannie Richards	May 16,1849
Sec. John Wornal. Jesse Richards, father of girl.		
Nathan Loughborough	Annie H. Rose	November 13,1849
Sec. William A. Stephenson		
James J. Love	Sarah A. Hurst	March 12,1849
Sec. M. C. Klein		
George M.McCoy	Ann Rebecca Stream	May 30,1849
Sec. John Snoots Jr.		
John McGavack	Sarah Ann Wine	January 30,1849
Sec. George H. Wine		
James W. McKinney	Cornelia Brown	October 6,1849
Sec. Asa Brown		
James H. May	Sarah Jane Barnhouse	November 19,1849
Sec. Joseph Barnhouse. Jane Barnhouse, mother of girl.		
Jonathan Mead	Mary Jane Beatty	January 1,1849
Sec. Thomas Mead		
William H. Mitchell	Sarah F. Perry of	February 6,1849
Sec.John S.Smith	Cameron Parish	
John H. Moore	Amanda Tribby	September 24,1849
Sec. John B. Dutton		
James W. Moore	Matilda Dulin	October 25,1849
Sec. Wm. B. Jackson		

Name of Groom	Name of Bride	Date of Bond
James D. Morris Sec. Hugh S. Thompson	Ann Davis	February 12,1849
Peter K. Mossburg Sec. Philip L. Phillips, father of girl.	Margaret L. Phillips	May 24,1849
Charles F. Myers Sec. R.H.Edwards. Elizabeth E.Donaldson, mother of girl.	Susan H. Donaldson	August 13,1849
John M. Orr Sec. Charles Miller, William Rogers and John D. Powell.	Orra Lee	November 8,1849
Joshua Osburn Sec. Mortimer Osburn. Rich'd Osburn,Jr. is father of girl.	Alcinda Osburn	May 13,1849
Clement A. Peck Sec. Presly Sanders	Mary Jane Sanders	December 15,1849
Jesse Piggott Sec. William Silcott	Mary E. Florida	October 3,1849
Evan W. Powell Sec. Benjamin Davis	Elizabeth Everitt	September 15,1849
Smith Reed Sec. G.Butts. James Roach is father of girl.	Caroline E. Roach Oliver	January 15,1849
Thomas Roberts Sec. Stephen Roberts.	Mary S.A.Heskett	November 26,1849
William H. Russell Sec. Jonah Orrison, father of girl.	Sarah E.R.Orrison	December 3,1849
Thornton Spangler Sec. C.B.Wildman	Elizabeth Stewart	December 27,1849
Samuel Snoots Sec. H.S.Williams, father of girl.	Sarah E. Williams	November 5,1849
John Squires Sec. Wm. H. Squires	Sarah J. Carter	November 6,1849
James Sparrow Sec. Conrad Virts, father of girl.	Elizabeth C. Virts	October 8,1849
M. L. Settle Sec. James W.Moxley. H.M.Davis, father of girl.	Julia Ann Davis	March 29,1849

Name of Groom	Name of Bride	Date of Bond
Richard F. Simpson Sec. Wm. Noland	Maria Louisa Noland of Cameron Parish	May 3,1849
James Skinner Sec. John Beaty	Elizabeth Beaty of Cameron Parish	May 26,1849
Benjamin Scroggins Sec. Garret Walker	Jane McCaen	February 12,1849
George E. Shryock Sec. Richard Howser, father of girl.	Rebecca J. Howser of Cameron Parish	February 12,1849
John Thomas Sec. Samuel Carter, father of girl.	Martha C. Carter of Cameron Parish	October 17,1849
Chandler Thomas Sec. Joshua Nichols.	Jane Ann Brady Emily Brady, mother of girl.	February 12,1849
Robert W. Thomas Sec. W.H.Thomas. of girl.	Rebecca J. Wright Mahalah Burk,late wife of Joseph Wright,dec'd, mother	August 4,1849
Waters Thompson Sec. John James Rusk	Hulda A. Rusk of Cameron Parish	January 17,1849
Bennett Wright Sec. Richard White.	Elizabeth Wyne	October 30,1849
Benjamin Wigginton Sec. Mary Wigginton	Mary Brooks	January 17,1849
John H. Wiley Sec. Albert C. Davis	Elizabeth S. Davis	March 5,1849
Hillary Wilson Williams Sec. James D.McPherson.	Mary Washington Sanders Mahala Sanders, mother of girl.	January 3,1849
Daniel T. White Sec. Robert W. Gray.	Virginia Marlow S.N.C.White, father of groom.	December 5,1849
William W. Whitmore Sec. William W. Whitmore	Julia E. Beach	February 17,1849
George H. Wine Sec. John McGavack	Ann C.B.Cassady	December 7,1849

- - - -   -   - - - -

Name of Groom	Name of Bride	Date of Bond
Francis T. Adams Sec. Beverly C. Rousseau	Martha L. Rousseau of Cameron Parish	March 9, 1850
Amos Beans Sec. Joseph Lacock, father of girl.	Elizabeth Ann Lacock	March 25, 1850
Edwin Beaumont Sec. Ellen Shipman	Lucy Ellen Shipman of Cameron Parish	March 21, 1850
John V. Brown Sec. S. S. Stocks	Aseneth Stocks	February 12, 1850
Mason Buck Sec. Alexander Adams.	Amanda Eitzallen Adams Henry Adams, father of girl.	January 17, 1850
James H. Carson Sec. Thomas R. Sanders	Catherine A.R. Sanders	February 20, 1850
Eli S. Castle Sec. Joel L. Nixon	Rowena E. Drish	January 19, 1850
John William Conard Sec. Joseph D. Holmes	Mary Ann Nyswanger	February 25, 1850
James A. Cox Sec. Eli Tavenner	Lydia Garner	December 20, 1838
Philip Derry Sec. Jonathan Painter, father of girl.	Mary Elizabeth Painter	January 7, 1850
Thomas Dobson Sec. T.J. Stedman	Sarah McClenan	January 12, 1850
Joseph Edwards Sec. William Dove	Mary Dove of Cameron Parish	February 10, 1850
Franklin Ewers Sec. William G. Furr	Virginia Furr	April 8, 1850
Romulus Ferguson Sec. John F. Allen. Samuel Ayres, father of girl.	Catherine F. Ayers of Cameron Parish	May 21, 1850
Joseph C. Fry Sec. John Ruse	Mary Jane Ruse	March 18, 1850
Hiram Grubb Sec. T. R. Williams	Pleasant Hurdle	May 6, 1850

Name of Groom	Name of Bride	Date of Bond
Fenton Hampton Sec. John Cockrill, father of girl	Sarah A. Cockrill	February 13,1850
Robert Harper Sec. Charles B. Ball	Mary A. Newton	June 25,1850
William Hoge Sec. James Hoge	Rachel E. Janney	February 22,1850
Charles L.Hollingsworth Sec. Samuel S. Stone	Nancy C.Weatherille	March 19,1850
William H. Hough of B. Sec. Sydnah Williams, father of girl.	Hannah Ann Williams	February 21,1850
James Hutt Sec. Thomas J. Morgan	Alcinda Wyncoop	May 17,1850
Levi James Sec. Samuel Paxson, father of girl.	Martha Ellen Paxton	March 1,1850
William T. Jones Sec. George R.Donaldson. Rachel Morris, mother of girl.	Harriet I. Morris	March 7,1850
Thomas Kent Sec. Francis M.Carter. Eden Carter is father of girl.	Susannah A. Carter	February 4,1850
Alfred Megeath Sec. Thomas G.Humphrey, father of girl.	Margaret P. Humphrey	June 18,1850
William A. Nisswarner Sec. John M. Conard	Barbara A. Conard	April 1,1850
William W. Painter Sec. Conrad Long, father of girl.	Ann E. Long	May 27,1850
Nathaniel Prince Sec. William N. Everhart	Mary Tavener	June 17,1850
Samuel Scott Sec. John E. Wright	Ann E. Wright	June 22,1850
Richard H. Turner Sec. A.T.M.McCarty. Catherine Simpson, mother of girl.	Ann Eliza Simpson	January 15,1850
Brown Sudduth Sec. H.C.Freeman	Ann Sophia Harris	February 20,1850
Andrew J. Taylor Sec. Lewis French, father of girl.	Emily E. French	February 9,1850

Name of Groom	Name of Bride	Date of Bond
B. W. Welsh Sec. Joel Craven	Alvina Craven	May 3,1850
Richard White Sec. Joel L. Nixon	Mary Julia Nixon	May 11,1850
John H. Whitmore Sec. Henry Adams, father of girl.	Elizabeth Ann Adams	February 25,1850
John H. Wright Sec. John Hunt	Elizabeth Hunt	January 19,1850
William Wyne Sec. John Carruthers	Emily Carruthers	June 17,1850

- - - -   -   - - - -

Andrew Green   Mary Lucas   March 5,1799
Sec. Joseph Gore
Thomas Lucas, father of girl, req. license.Wit.John Drish

John Hunter   Nancy Neer   February 19,1799
Sec. John Neer
Henry Neer and Susanna his wife, agreed to "match".
Wit. Nathaniel Neer.

Caleb Hoskins   Sally Davis of   January 14,1799
Sec.Kelleb Hoskins   Cameron Parish
John Davis

Sanford Wrenn   Sally Dulin   → March 14,1799
Sec.Edward Dulin. William Dulin,father of girl, consented.

Andrew Garner   Hannah Milner   January 5,1799
Sec. Isaac Milner, who test. girl over 21.

Thomas Hough   Peggy Skinner   January 31,1799
Sec. Samuel Hough who test. girl's age.

Note: When shown on bond, Cameron Parish is noted. It may be assumed
that the others are of Shelburne Parish. This is important since the
Cameron Parish records are not extant.

The following are records of Marriage Licenses entered in Clerk's
Fee Books, 1762, 1764 and 1765, Loudoun County, Virginia.

1762
May 25
Nicholas Seward to Ann Sorrell, Spinster

September 3
John Squires to Elizabeth Taylor, Spinster

September 13
John Johnson to Mary Debell (widow)

1764
Feby. 14
Christopher Hopwood to Martha Combs

April 20
Simon Triplett to Martha Love, Spinster

May 9
Richard Stephenson Jr. to Elizabeth Summers, Spinster

June 12
Richard Eskridge to Elizabeth Read, Spinster

December 15
Robert Cavins to Ann Todd Marr

1765
Feby.
John Smith to Mary West (widow)

April 17
William Smith to Margaret Whittley

May 30
Enoch McKenzy to Elizabeth West, Spinster

August 6
Sanford Payne to Abigail Lay

September 23
William Cotton Jr. to Frances Taylor, Spinster

A

Abbot, William R. 50
Abel, George 18
Abel, Susana 18
Abraham, John 40
Ackers, Daniel 81
Adam, William F. 58
Adams, Alexander 152
Adams, Amanda Fitzallen 152
Adams, Ann Eliza 65
Adams, Catharine 31
Adams, D. 129
Adams, Daniel 47
Adams, Elizabeth Ann 154
Adams, Elizabeth M. 127
Adams, Francis T. 127,152
Adams, Henry 31,65,74,152,154
Adams, James 60
Adams, Jane E. 68
Adams, John 6,61
Adams, Josias 26
Adams, Mary Ann 145
Adams, Mason S. 92
Adams, Patty 6
Adams, Richard 68,78,145
Adams, Sarah 83
Adams, William 1,76,91
Adams, William J. 119
Addison, Anthony 54
Addleman, Eliza 2
Adie, George 71,81,132
Adie, William 50
Aduddel, Caleb 57
Akers, John 65
Albaugh, Eli C. 78
Alder, Albert 31
Alder, Elizabeth Ann 22
Alder, Emily Jane 74
Alder, George 25
Alder, Joseph W. 70
Alder, Lucy A. 70
Alder, S.M. 146
Alder, William S. 142
Aldridge, Eliza 44
Aldridge, Harriet A. 23
Aldridge, John 23,44,117
Aldridge, Joseph W. 64
Aldridge, Sarah W. 64
Alexander, David 18,110
Alexander, Elizabeth 123
Alexander, James 78,146
Alexander, John 117

Alexander, Mary 128
Alexander, Martha 133
Alexander, Nancy 117
Alexander, Richard 105,110,128,133
Alexander, William 105,108
Allder, Albert 70,90
Allder, George H. 24
Allder, James Jr. 102
Allder, John 22,31
Allder, Joseph 42
Allder, Joseph W. 102
Allder, Latimer 74
Allder, Leonidas 74
Allder, William 74,136
Allen, Edmund 40
Allen, Jacob 125
Allen, James 107,125
Allen, John F. 152
Allen, Mary 107
Allen, Samuel C. 23
Allen, Teresa 23
Allen, William 38
Allender, Jacob 134
Allison, Cassander 10
Allison, John 86
Allison, Richard 10
Amblar, Lewis 3
Amblar, William 85
Ambler, Julia 104
Ambler, Vincent 104
Ambler, William 48,60,138
Ambrose, Laura 143
Ambrose, Robert 143
Amich, Mary 82
Amich, Sarah Ann 140
Amick, George 129
Amick, Michael 96
Amick, Susan 129
Anders, John 66
Anders, William 24
Anderson, A.L. 20
Anderson, Alfred 67
Anderson, C.F. 94,116
Anderson, Catherine 44
Anderson, Charles F. 108
Anderson, Christian 76
Anderson, Delilah 67
Anderson, Eleanor 108,139
Anderson, Eli 102
Anderson, Elijah 44
Anderson, Elizabeth E. 83
Anderson, George 85,145
Anderson, Harrison 44

Carter, Catharine 9
Carter, Charles 47
Carter, E. 29
Carter, Eden 153
Carter, Edmonia R. 81
Carter, Edward 25,78
Carter, Elizabeth 48,51
Carter, Emily 120
Carter Ferdinand A. 85
Carter, Francis M. 153
Carter, George 67
Carter, Joanna A. 81 James S.96
Carter, John A. 57
Carter, John R. 101
Carter, Joseph 77
Carter, Keturah R. 25
Carter, L.L. 75
Carter, Landon 29
Carter, Landon C. 24,26
Carter, Landon L. 60
Carter, Leah 18
Carter, Leander 101
Carter, Martha C. 151
Carter, Martha E. 29
Carter, Mary 15,16
Carter, Matilda 124,138
Carter, Oswell 85
Carter, Peter 95
Carter, R.R. 116
Carter, Rhoda 19
Carter, Richard 9,18,34,47,95
Carter, Richard H. 78
Carter, Robert 78
Carter, Ruth 7
Carter, Samuel 40,48,107,108,120,151
Carter, Sarah 95
Carter, Sarah C. 116
Carter, Sarah J. 150
Carter, Susannah A. 153
Carter, Thomas 16,17
Carter, William 18,19
Cartwright, Nicodemus 147
Case, Benjamin 54
Case, Elizabeth 117
Case, John 12
Case, Samuel 117
Casey, John 19
Casey, William 108
Cassaday, Mary E. 144
Cassady, Ann C.B. 151
Cassady, W.H. 63
Cassady, William 79
Castle, Eli S. 152
Castleman, David J. 141
Castleman, Henry W. 141
Catlett, Charles S. 90

Catlett, Louisa 90
Catlett, Mary E. 88
Cavins, Robert 155
Chambers, Charlotte 101
Chambers, William 18
Chamblin, A.G. 56,74,80
Chamblin, Aaron 61
Chamblin, Albert G. 74
Chamblin, Alfred G. 68
Chamblin, Angelina 61
Chamblin, Burr 32
Chamblin, Burr P. 37,133
Chamblin, Charles 32
Chamblin, Edith 56
Chamblin, Elenor 28
Chamblin, Elisha 76
Chamblin, Elmina L. 32
Chamblin, George 1
Chamblin, James H. 46,108
Chamblin, James Heaton 89
Chamblin, Jared 144
Chamblin, John 12,27,28
Chamblin, John L. 40,60
Chamblin, Leven P. 92
Chamblin, Mary 56
Chamblin, Mason 32
Chamblin, Nelson 140
Chamblin, Rebecca 37
Chamblin, Samuel J. 139
Chamblin, Stephen T. 68
Chamblin, William 44
Chambling, Ezekiel 18
Chancellor, Looman 136
Chappel, Eliza J. 119
Chappel, Ezekiel 18
Chappel, John C. 119
Chappell, Addison 66
Chappell, James 44,94,112,126,:
Chappell, Letitia 146
Chappell, Mary Ann 148
Charlton, Bernard 105
Cheek, George Washington 147
Chenoweth, James B. 27
Chew, Nancy 100
Chew, Roger 64,67,100
Chichester, George M. 48
Chichester, Sarah E. 109
Chilton, Elizth. 63
Chilton, Elizabeth A. 25
Chilton, William O. 21
Chin, Nancy 100
Chin, Roger 100
Chinn, Benjamin T. 81
Chinn, Charles E. 87
Chinn, Lucy 6
Chinn, Rawleigh 6

Chinn, Susannah 5
Chinn, Thomas 5
Chunn, Zachariah T. 125
Church, Catharine M. 62
Clagett, Thomas H. 27
Clapham, Elizabeth 41
Clapper, Henry 34,36,135
Clapper, Susan 36
Clapsaddle, Ferdinand 104
Clare, John 115,117
Clark, Elizabeth P. 145
Clark, James 107
Clark, John H. 82
Clark, Malinda 27
Clarke, Addison H. 34
Clarke, James 121
Clarke, Martha Margaret 82
Clarke, Polly 1
Clarke, Susan Ann 121
Claspey, Nimrod 55
Clawson, Sarah 10
Claxton, Thomas 93
Clayton, Eliza 46
Clements, Charles W. 136
Clendening, James H. 144
Clendening, Jane E. 122
Clendenning, John 122
Clendening, Ruth H. 144
Clendening, Samuel 107
Clendening, Sarah Ann 75
Clendening, William 19
Clendening, William Jr. 75,99
Clever, Catherine 50
Clifford, Obadiah 4
Cline, William 16,118
Clip, John 103
Clip, Louisa 103
Clip, Mary Jane 103
Clothier, John 135
Cloud, Jeremich 14,19
Cloud, Lydia 64
Cloud, Pricilla 104
Cloud, Sidney 104
Clowe, Amanda I. 70
Clowe, William H. 70
Clowes, Elizth. V. 87
Clowes, Mary Jane 112
Clowes, Nancy 56
Clowes, Thomas J. 87
Clyce, Catharine 17
Clyce, John 17
Coats, Agnes 62
Coats, Calvin 78,79

Cochran, Adison 144
Cochran, Edward 34
Cochran, Mary R. 67
Cochran, Nathan 37
Cochran, Richard 33
Cochran, Sarah Ann 75
Cochran, Susan R. 33
Cochran, Tholemiah 67,136
Cochran, William B. 75
Cocke, William C. 84
Cockerell, Julia Ann 85
Cockerell, Martha Ann 143
Cockeril, Harley 76
Cockerill, Amanda F. 86
Cockerill, Huldah 85
Cockerill, John H. 86
Cockerill, Joseph 22
Cockerill, Mortimer 95
Cockerill, Sanford F. 86
Cockerille, Thomas 10
Cockran, Benjamin D. 62
Cockrel, Isabella 61
Cockrel, Joseph 61
Cockrel, Sanford I. 63
Cockrell, Alexander 109
Cockrell, Hiram 59
Cockrell, Lee 14
Cockrill, B.D. 109
Cockrill, Elias 14
Cockrill, James 125
Cockrill, John 143,153
Cockrill, Joseph Marmaduke 5
Cockrill, Kelly 5
Cockrill, Reuben 54,76
Cockrill, Sarah A. 153
Coe, Catharine S. 132
Coe, Ebenezer 118
Coe, Elijah 111
Coe, Emily Jane 76
Coe, Esther Ann 111
Coe, Eunicy 123
Coe, John 89
Coe, Mary 51,54,76
Coe, Mary E. 54
Coe, Mary Jane 136
Coe, Peter 136
Coe, Robert 123
Coghlan, Edward 30
Cogill, Rachel 34
Colbert, Catharine 87
Colbert, Jesse 136
Colbert, Nancy 79
Cole, Eliza jane 74

Copeland, Sidney 70
Copeland, William 14
Copeland, Zillah 34
Cordell, Adam 13,111,134
Cordell, Ary Ann Catherine 134
Cordell, Helen A. 61
Cordell, Elizabeth 13
Cordell, M.E. 31
Cordell, Presley 31,61
Cordell, Samuel 25,48
Cordell, Susan 95
Core, Samuel 63
Cornell, Joseph 105
Cornell, Nancy 38
Cornell, Thomas 105
Cornelle, Thomas 105
Cornwell, Benson 129
Cornwell, Isaac 33
Cornwell, Josiah 33
Cornwell, Loveless 33
*Couper, Alexander 4
*Couper, Betsey 4
Cost, Cornelia Ann 108
Cost, Elizabeth 82
Cost, Jacob F. 118
Cost, Jonathan 108
Cost, Mary 82
Cost, Nancy 61
Cost, Peter 82
Costelo, James 99
Costelo, Robert 99
Cotton, William J. 155
*Cox, James A. 123,152
Cox, Mary E. 110
Cox, Patty 126
Cox, Polly 64
Cox, Sally 126
Cox, Samuel 110,120
Cox, Virginia Ann 120
Craig, George 52
Craig, Harriet 76
Craig, James 86
Craig, Nancy 119
Craig, Norval 128,146
Craig, Samuel 118
Craig, William S.G. 118
Craig, William T. 143
Crain, Bailey 85
Crain, Catharine L. 54
Crain, John 72
Cramwell, Eliza 124
Cramwell, Susan 124
Cranwell, George W. 113
Cranwell, Jane S. 60

Cranwell, John 60
Cranwell, John S. 16
Cranwell, Susan 113
Cranwell, Susan M. 113
Crawford, D.L. 148 *
Crawford, David T. 148
Crawford, Mary E. 148
Craven, Abner 6 *
Craven, Alvina 154
Craven, Edith 27
Craven, Eleanor H. 28
Craven, Eleanor V. 72
Craven, James 66
Craven, Joel 154
Craven, John 2
Craven, Lavina 47
Craven, Moranda 66
Craven, Rodney 115
Craven, Samuel 84
Craven, Sarah 32
Craven, Sarah S. 32
Craven, Sinclair 28
Craven, Sophia V.32,84
Craven, William L. 28
Cridler, Andrew M. 93
Cridler, Ann Elizabeth 67
Cridler, John 67,116
Crim, Catharine 43
Crim, Charles 12
Crim, Christena 12
Crim, Elizth. 114
Crim, George F. 81
Crim, Jacob 18,43
Crim, John 67,107,114
Crim, John H. 107
Crim, Peter 34,120,143
Crim, Samuel 114
Crim, Sarah Ann 94
Crimm, John H. 96
Crissey, Frederick L. 97
Crist, John 80
Crombacker, Eve 7
Crooks, Lucinda 47
Cross, Alice Ann 78
Cross, Elizabeth 30
Cross, Hamilton 90, 124
Cross, Harrison 29,78,144
Cross, James 30,93
Cross, John 81
Cross, John W. 118
Cross, Julia Frances Ann 144
Cross, Lewis 75
Cross, Missouri A. 144
Cross, Susan 118

Davis, Jemima 6
Davis, Jeremiah 43,103
Davis, John 6,22,80,132,135,154
Davis, John L. 125
Davis, Joseph 75,92
Davis, Julia Ann 150
Davis, Lucinda 92
Davis, Malinda 77,80
Davis, Margaret S. 125
Davis, Mary 1
Davis, Mary Ann 21
Davis, Peyton 118
Davis, Presley 43,80,106
Davis, Sally 154
Davis, Samuel 8,94
Davis, Sarah 4
Davis, Susanna 65,103
Davis, Susanna E. 66
Davis, Thomas 6,15,46,52,95,118,132
Davis, Thomas S. 125
Davis, Van 1
Davis, William 19,41,43,46,52,76
Davison, F.A. 87,90
Davison, Nathaniel Jr. 2
Davisson, Frederick A. 45
Davisson, Theodore 57
Davisson, Theodore N. 39
Dawes, James E. 84
Dawes, Mary A.M. 84
Dawes, Mary E. 138
Dawson, Ann 114
Dawson, Elizabeth 6,53
Dawson, Eugenia T. 148
Dawson, Hortensia Ellen 145
Dawson, Richard 114
Dawson, Robert 106
Dawson, Samuel 41
Dawson, Sarah Ann 145
Dawson, William 6
Day, Jane 46
Day, Rebecca 129
Daymude, James 27
Daymude, Sophina 27
Deakins, Catharine 86
Deaver, Daniel 59
Debell, Mary 105
DeButts, Mary 57
DeButts, Mary Welby 78
DeButts, Richardetta 57
DeButts, Samuel 78
DeButts, Samuel W. 57,59

Delehan, Letitia 57
Demory, Louisa 123
Demory, Mahlon 123
Demory, Mary 39
Denges, Mary 83
Denham, Charles T. 49,87   Amey El
Denham, D.B. 79
Denham, Margaret A. 42
Denham, Mary Jane 79
Denham, Oliver 42
Dennis, Caroline S. 103
Dennis, Catherine 129
Dennis, Frances Jane 99
Dennis, Henry 99
Dennis, James B. 21
Dennis, Lewis 40
Dennis, Louisa 55
Dennis, Matilda 108
Dennis, Mary J. 124
Dennis, Olivia F. 40
Dennis, Sophronia E. 138
Dennis, William A. 40,138
Densmore, William 36
Derry, George 55
Derry, Hanson 132
Derry, Jacob 55
Derry, John T. 88
Derry, Lydia Ann 76
Derry, Maria 55
Derry, Mary A. 109
Derry, Michael 76,109
Derry, Morelles 4
Derry, Peter 30
Derry, Philip 138,143,152
Derry, Sarah 124
Derry, Solomon 55,65
Derry, Susanna 52
Derry, William 55,80
Dever, Daniel 59
Dickey, John P. 93,109
Dickey, Mary Ann 104
Diederichs, Caroline 130
Diederichs, Daniel 130
Diederick, Daniel 147
Dillehay, Lyda 82
Dilloe, John 15
Dishman, Marcus 69
Dishman, Samuel 20
Divers, John 18
Divine, Aaron 13,80
Divine, Charles W. 148

Dunn, Patk. 5
Durborow, James R. 148
Dutton, John B. 85,149
Duvall, Harriet 124
Duvall, Louisa 124
Duvall, Wilson C. 56
Dwyer, Mary 130
Dyer, Anna 78
Dyer, Catherine 23
Dyer, Israel 54

E

Eaches, Frances A. 96
Eaches, Thomas 96
Eakey, Catherine 29
Eamich, Frederick 102
Earnest, John 49
Easton, James 143
Eaton, David J. 27,42 Isaac 89
Eaton, Mary I. 42
Eckman, Jacob 123
Edelin, Nancy 3
Edison, J. 117
Edison, Margaret E. 117
Edison, W.H. 117
Edmonds, Alex'r 92
Edward, John M. 48
Edward, Oliver 86
Edward, Thomas W. 81
Edwards, Alpheus L. 145
Edwards, Ann E. 94,110
Edwards, Charles G. 46,94
Edwards, Elizabeth 139
Edwards, Frances 36
Edwards, Hannah 146
Edwards, Harriet 46
Edwards, Henrietta B. 146
Edwards, Israel 67
Edwards, J.S. 110
Edwards, James E. 23
Edwards, Joseph 67,121,139,152
Edwards, Mary Ann 131
Edwards, Oliver 74
Edwards, R.H. 142,150
Edwards, Richard H. 94
Edwards, Samuel M. 45
Edwards, Sarah Ann 67
Edwards, T.W. 119,122,126,129
Edwards, Thomas W. 109
Edwards, Virginia 115

Eidson, Joseph 62,85
Eidson, Margaret 117
Elderkin, James K. 148
Elgin, Ann 45
Elgin, Diadama 74
Elgin, Emily 115
Elgin, Francis 35,72
Elgin, Francis W. 139
Elgin, Gustavus 75
Elgin, Gustavus Jr. 30
Elgin, Gustavus L. 134
Elgin, Ignatious 25
Elgin, John 45
Elgin, John C. 21
Elgin, Margaret 35
Elgin, Mary B. 45
Elgin, Phebe 7
Elgin, Rebecca 66,87
Elgin, Roana 36
Elgin, Robert 134
Elgin, Walter 45
Elgin, William 7,20
Elliott, Harriot Elizth. 111
Elliott, Henson 38,135
Ellis, Hezekiah 23
Ellis, John 2
Ellis, Samuel 79
Ellis, William R. 54
Ellmore, Charles W. 104
Ellmore, Edward 3,55
Ellmore, John 53,104,123
Ellmore, Mary Catherine 123
Ellmore, William 108
Ellzey, Ann E. 25
Ellzey, Fanny W. 34
Ellzey, L. 25
Ellzey, Lewis 41,91
Ellzey, Mary Cecelia 41
Ellzey, Mary E. 58
Ellzey, Rosannah Mortimer 91
Ellzey, William 1
Elwell, Aaron G. 28,118
Emberson, Caroline 101
Emberson, Judson 56,101
Emberson, Mary 56
Emery, Christiana 14
Emory, Elizabeth 52
Emry, Adam 14
Emry, Stephen 8
Erskine, John 9
Eskridge, Alfred A. 22

Eskridge, Charles G. 21,33,39,45,
  56,78,85,89,99,101,116,119,129,134
Eskridge, Richard 155
Etcher, Peter 146
Evans, Adam 38
Evans, Ann C. 109
Evans, Elizabeth 38
Evans, Harvey 49,109
Evans, Jesse 14,69,95
Evans, Samuel 69
Evans, Sarah Ann 95
Evans, Thomas A.H. 79
Eveland, Rachel 105
Everhart, Ann Eliza 92
Everhart, Anna E. 136
Everhart, Catharine 107
Everhart, Charlotte 82
Everhart, David 139
Everhart, Elizabeth 30,131
Everhart, Israel 69
Everhart, John 96,125
Everhart, Joseph 132
Everhart, Mary 138
Everhart, Mary C. 139
Everhart, Matilda A. 125
Everhart, Michael 136
Everhart, Nathaniel 95
Everhart, Nathaniel W. 131
Everhart, Nelson 39,88,117,131
Everhart, Nelson B. 40,69
Everhart, Philip 56,82,86,92
Everhart, Philip P. 148
Everhart, Sarah Ann 56
Everhart, Sarah J. 140
Everhart, Solomon 56,67,118,125,131
Everhart, Solomon Jr. 65
Everhart, Thomas 65
Everhart, William 86
Everhart, William N. 153
Everheart, Luisia 23
Everheart, Martha 39
Everheart, Philip 23
Everheart, Sarah 46
Everitt, Elizabeth 150
Ewell, Aaron G. 118
Ewers, Franklin 126,130,152
Ewers, Izabella 13
Ewers, Jonathan 70,116,130
Ewers, Leonard J. 85
Ewers, Levi 48,77
Ewers, Levi G. 26,85
Ewers, Mary 71,130
Ewers, Robert 13
Ewers, William 116,125,130

F

Fadely, Ann E. 27
Fadely, Charles F. 106
Fadely, Jacob 99
Fadely, Sarah D. 99
Fadley, Jacob 1,27
Fadley, Sarah D. 99
Fair, Mary 129
Fairfax, Catherine 122
Fairfax, George William 103
Fairfax, John W. 143
Falley, Eleanor 59
Falley, Isaac 59
Falley, George 10
Falley, Jacob 10
Falley, John 10
Fally, Elizabeth 5
Fally, John 5
Farlow, John 11
Farnsworth, Daniel 10
Farought, Elizabeth 52
Farr, John B. 103
Farr, Stephen G. 103
Fauntleroy, Charles M. 137
Faver, Edward 11
Favor, Benjamin 11
Fawley, Christena 129
Fawley, Elizabeth 37,42
Fawley, Hannah 96
Fawley, Henry 37,49,73,96
Fawley, Jacob 96,126
Fawley, James 11
Fawley, John 11,13,25,29,31
Fawley, Joseph 134
Fawley, Margaret 25,49
Fawley, Mary 73
Fawley, Polley 13
Fawley, Susan 79
Fawley, William 73
Feagan, Nicholas 9
Feagans, Daniel 43
Feagans, H. 147
Feagans, James 69
Feagans, Silas H. 108
Feagens, Wilford 87
Feagins, Daniel 11
Feagins, James 86
Feagins, Martha 87
Feagins, Mary Francis 87
Feagins, William H. 86
Fearst, John 9
Feaster, George 148
Fechter, George 71

Feitchler, Ann 30
Feitchter, Sarah 132
Felby, Sally 72
Fenton, Enoch 137
Fenton, John W. 112
Ferguson, Romulus 152
Fernandis, Sarah 17
Ferno, John 86
Fichter, Caroline 93 Edney 142
Fichter, George 14,93,142
Fichter, Sarah Ann 97
Fichter, Susan 58
Fidler, John 11
Fiechter, Nancy 71
Field, John 11
Field, Margaret 63
Field, William 11
Fields, James 73
Fields, Luke 95
Fields, Marthy 73
Fields, Sarah Catharine 134
Figh, Torrance 8
Figgins, Sarah Ann 147
Filingame, Benj. F. 40
Filler, Armistead T.M. 148
Filler, Benjamin 44
Filler, Emeline 83
Filler, Frederick 13
Filler, Jacob 81,83,86
Filler, John 2,10,59
Filler, John C. 71
Filler, John M. 102
Filler, Margaret 25
Filler, Mary 110
Filler, Mary M. 82
Filler, Matilda 81
Filler, Sally 48
Filler, Sarah Ann 136
Filler, Solomon 137
Fillingim, Mary 132
Finch, Colvin 11
Finch, Malvina 120
Finch, Thomas 9
Finnacom, Diana 105
Finnacom, George 105
Firestone, Christiana 5 Robert 51
Fish, Henry 45
Fishback, James Neville 9
Fisher, Michael 8
Fisher, Nelson 57
Fisher, Sarah 12
Fitcher, Amanda 76
Fitcher, George 76,109

Fitzhugh, Lucian 76,89
Fitzhugh, Mary J. 142
Fitzhugh, Nathaniel 4
Fitzimmons, James 9
Flagg, Thomas 10
Flanegan, John 9
Fleetwood, Isaac 10
Fleming, Dinah 58
Fleming, Evelina 61
Fleming, George 53,58,67
Fleming, Jesse 99
Fleming, Joseph 53,99
Fleming, Rebecca G. 58
Fleming, Susan 67
Fleming, William 53
Fletcher, Alice J. 134
Fletcher, Harriet G. 74
Fletcher, John G. 134
Fletcher, Joseph 74
Fletcher, Joshua Jr. 134
Fling, Eliza Jane 88
Fling, George 10
Fling, George W. 148
Fling, Sandford 61,88,126
Fling, William 11
Flinn, George 26
Florance, Albert B. 50
Florida, Mary E. 150
Floriday, Pat'k 10
Flowers, Catharine 11
Flowers, Thomas 55
Floyd, William 10
Foley, Bailys 69
Foley, Enoch 99
Foley, William 131
Foly, William 63
Fontaine, Alice Virginia 35
Fontaine, Mary B. 24
Forbs, Martin 9
Ford, Richard 148
Ford, Valentine 16
Ford, William 10
Forgison, William 17
Forrest, Luke S. 68,104
Forrest, Mary Elizabeth 79
Forsythe, William 111
Fortney, John 7
Fossett, John 16
Foster, James A. 115
Foster, William H. 25
Fouch, Abraham 8
Fouch, Amos 49,72,75
Fouch, George 8

Greenlease, James 63
Greenlease, John H. 116,133
Greenlease, Mary E. 63
Greenlease, William S. 79
Greenway, William 127
Greenwell, Sally 138
Greenwood, Henry 24
Gregg, Adeline S. 47
Gregg, Ann 33
Gregg, Belsora 33
Gregg, Eleanor 20
Gregg, Elizabeth 94
Gregg, Elizabeth P.24
Gregg, George 20,94
Gregg, Gibson 67
Gregg, Guilford 21
Gregg, Guilford G. 38
Gregg, Henry H. 142
Gregg, Jemima 38
Gregg, Joseph G. 133
Gregg, Martha L. 36
Gregg, Nathan 24
Gregg, Peter 54
Gregg, Phoebe 70
Gregg, Samuel 8,19
Gregg, Sarah Ann 62,92
Gregg, Smith 33
Gregg, Stephen 77
Gregg, Susan B. 24
Gregg, Thomas 3,29,33,131
Gregg, Thomas C. 31
Gregg, William 35
Gregg, Wilson 42
Gregory, Lavinia 51
Griffin, Charles 108
Griffin, Jesse 108
Griffith, Israel T. 38
Griffith, John 5,43
Griffith,John Jr. 3
Griffith, Margaret 31
Griffith, Martha 5
Griffith, Mary 24
Grigsby, Bushrod 79
Grimes, Charlotte 45
Grimes, Daniel 57
Grimes, Emily 105
Grimes, George 86
Grimes, Henry 67
Grimes, Sarah 86
Grimes, Susan 36
Grimes, Sylvester 4
Grimes, William 10

Gross, John 49
Grubb, Benjamin 89
Grubb, Curtis 89,109,134
Grubb, Ebenezer 8,20,109,135
Grubb, Eliza C. 109 Esther Ann 135
Grubb, Henry 98 Hiram 152
Grubb, Jane 118
Grubb, John 49,85,89,140
Grubb, Mary 101
Grubb, Mary Ann 85
Grubb, Nancy 49,89
Grubb, Rachel Ann 136
Grubb, Rebecca 89
Grubb, Richard J. 118
Grubb, Sarah 20
Grubb, Susan A. 143
Grubb, William 3,20,143
Grubb, William D. 101
Grymes, Nicholas 4
Guest, C.A. 33
Guest, Cynthia Ariel 33
Guest, Job 33
Gulick, Ann M. 118
Gulick, David F. 119
Gulick, David T. 112
Gulick, Francis 119
Gulick, Huldah 131
Gulick, James 87
Gulick, James H. 68
Gulick, John 86
Gulick, Levi 56
Gulick, Louisa 86
Gulick, Margt. J. 92
Gulick, Sanford 110,112
Gulick, Sarah E. 137
Gulick, William 92,137
Gullat, Charles 67
Gullatt, Charles 15
Guy, Kessiah 5

H

Hague, Amos 7
Hague, James 37
Hague, Mary 8
Hague, Plezy 17
Hague, Rose Ann 37
Haig, James 22
Haig, Mary Ann 22
Haines, A.H. 131
Haines, John W. 130
Haines, Washington 95

Harned, William 14
Harper, Catharine 56,119,142
Harper, Duanna 115
Harper, Effamah 16
Harper, Elizabeth 16
Harper, James 56,59
Harper, Jonathan 75,87
Harper, Julius 118,119
Harper, Margaret 119
Harper, Margaret A. 118
Harper, Mary A. 142
Harper, Robert 153
Harper, Sampson 64,103
Harper, Samuel 65
Harper, Sarah 4
Harper, Stasee 64
Harper, Thomas 4,16
Harper, Washington 75
Harper, William 65,75,76,118
Harris, Ann Sophia 153
Harris, Catharine H. 15
Harris, Eleanor J. 50
Harris, Elizabeth 45
Harris, Enoch 22
Harris, Hannah Ann 41
Harris, James S. 106
Harris, Jeremiah 13
Harris, John A. 15
Harris, Mary M. 45
Harris, Richard L. 92
Harris, Sally L. 35
Harris, Samuel 35
Harris, Samuel B. 45,50
Harris, W.P. 106
Harris, William A. 93,116
Harrison, Eliza Jane 103
Harrison, James 94,95,103,119
Harrison, John M. 55
Harrison, Margaret L. 39
Harrison, Maria P. 62
Harrison, Mary Ann 95
Harrison, Samuel S. 119
Harrison, Sarah 9
Harrison, Thomas H. 119
Harrison, William 9,88,94
Harrison, William S. 104,113
Harrop, James 19
Harrop, Nancy 19
Hart, Amanda Malinda 110
Hart, Daniel 110,127
Hart, Eliza 129
Hart, Jonathan 107,110,119
Hart, Joseph 76

Hart, Lydia Ann 118
Hart, Martha J. 107
Hart, Sarah 119
Hart, Thomas W. 83
Hart, William 86
Hart, William T. 69,110
Hartley, Benjamin 126
Hartman, Ellen Amanda 117
Harvey, Fielding 44
Haslett, Harriet J. 40
Hatcher, Jonah 47
Hatcher, Thomas 21
Hatcher, Thomas E. 24
Hatton, Benjamin 55
Hatton, Edith 63
Hatton, Elizabeth 55,130
Hatton, George 122
Hatton, Henry 81,126
Hatton, Joshua 62
Hatton, Stephen 9
Havener, Armistead 112
Havener, Bozzell 39
Havener, Emily 98
Havener, James B. 145
Havener, Joseph 98
Havener, Michael 70,126
Havener, Penelope M. 139
Havener, Sarah Ann 133
Havener, Silas 39,110
Havener, Sidney Jane 70
Havener, Thomas A. 126,139
Havener, William D. 133
Havenner, Joseph 39
Hawes, Asa 126
Hawes, Harriet Ann 105
Hawk, Elizabeth S. 126
Hawk, George 107
Hawke, Elijah 116
Hawkins, Joseph J. 65
Hawley, Barton 3
Hawling, Martha 31
Hawling, Sidney 148
Hawn, David 119
Haws, Asa 105
Haws, Elizabeth 126
Haws, James 133
Haws, John 126
Haws, William 133
Hay, George 22
Hay, Hortensia M. 22
Hays, Matthew 19
Hazard, Leah 139
Head, Christopher 88

Janney, Amos 63,116
Janney, Eli 8,14
Janney, Elisha 74
Janney, Hester B. 34
Janney, Isaiah B. 71
Janney, Jacob 34
Janney, John 22,66,89
Janney, Jonas 74
Janney, Joseph 143
Janney, Josiah 64
Janney, Josiah J. 65
Janney, M. 42
Janney, Mahlon Jr.3,14,18
Janney, Nathan H. 118,138
Janney, Rachel E. 153
Janney, Sarah G. 102
Janney, Susan B. 89
Janny, Eli 44
Janny, John 44
Janny, Rosannah 42
Jared, Ann 104
Jarvis, Edgar 148
Jarvis, Washington 108
Jay, David 3
Jay, George 88
Jay, Henrietta 3
Jeans, Rebeccah 9
Jeffres, Eliza 106
Jeffries, B.B. 113,115,123
Jeffries, Braxton B. 75,96
Jeffries, Harriet P. 113
Jeffries, John William 75
Jenkins, Amos 24
Jenkins, Catherine 24
Jenkins, Delila 28
Jenkins, Edward 79
Jenkins, Elias 138
Jenkins, Frances Ann 49
Jenkins, Herod 110
Jenkins, Julia Ann 113
Jenkins, Margaret 109
Jenkins, Margaret B. 40
Jenkins, Mary Catherine 87
Jenkins, Reubin 48
Jenkins, Sampson L.65
Jenkins, Samuel 26,120,147
Jenkins, Sarah E. 110
Jenkins, Silvester 24
Jenkins, Thomas 95,110
Jenkins, Thomas F. 12
Jenkins, Washington 44,49

Jenkins, William 21,109,113
Jennings, Betsey 56
Jennings, Harriet 56
Jennings, Jackson D. 83
Jennings, James 101
Jennings, Mary Ann Margaret 10(
Jennings, William 101
Jett, Burkett 114
Jett, Peter 17
Jett, Susan 114
Jinking, Elizabeth 121
Jinkins, Elizabeth J. 131
Jinkins, Evaline 81
Jinkins, Jarusa 130
Jinkins, John 81
Jinkins, John T. 81
John, Richard W. 9
Johnson, A.M. 141
Johnson, Absalom 100
Johnson, Adelaide 46
Johnson, Alexander 115,125
Johnson, Alexander W. 97
Johnson, Amos 26
Johnson, Amos W. 79
Johnson, Arthur C. 112
Johnson, Baldwin 30
Johnson, Benjamin 47
Johnson, Caroline A. 115
Johnson, Caroline Eliza 79
Johnson, Emily 125
Johnson, Fenton 97
Johnson, George W. 104,111
Johnson, Hanson 1
Johnson, James A. 56
Johnson, John 3,60,92,101,119,
Johnson, Margaret 126
Johnson, Peter W. 142
Johnson, Rebecca 93
Johnson, Sarah 47
Johnson, Sarah Ann Rebecca 82
Johnson, Sarah M. 101
Johnson, Susannah 53
Johnson, Sydnor B. 87,132
Johnson, Thomas 43
Johnson, Virginia 119
Johnson, William 46,53,100,125
Johnston, Alexander 66
Johnston, Ann Maria 64
Johnston, Baldwin 75
Johnston, Charles A.64,84,114
Johnston, Nimrod 134

Johnston, Robert 82
Johnston, Thomas B. 75
Jolly, Jacob 47
Jolly, Landon 47
Jones, Abel 28,39,78
Jones, Alfred 27,31,95
Jones, Cageby 30
Jones, Catesby 75,40,121
Jones, Clary Ann 121
Jones, Columbus 111
Jones, Eliza 78
Jones, Elizabeth 11
Jones, Hannah 28
Jones, James W. 129
Jones, John 11,115,122
Jones, John Jr. 126,127,137
Jones, Lucinda 42,129 Landon 92,101
Jones, Mahala 35
Jones, Mary Catharine 99
Jones, Mary Jane 94
Jones, Nancy 3
Jones, Sarah E. 115
Jones, Sarah Jane 125
Jones, T.L. 56
Jones, Thomas 35,60,78
Jones, Washington 129
Jones, William T. 153
Jordan, Catharine A. 43
Jury, Lewis 18 Abner 70
Jury, Malinda 34
Jury, Mary 61
Jury, Townsend J. 36,61,70

K

Kabrich, George 63,141,144
Kabrich, Isaiah R. 144
Kabrich, John M. 141
Kabrick, John M. 143
Kaighn, John H. 41
Kalb, Absalom 70
Kalb, Andrew H. 70
Kalb, Eleanora M. 93
Kalb, Jesse D. 98
Kalb, John G.R. 138
Kalb, Mary E. 133
Kalb, Samuel 133
Karn, Adam 40
Karns, Peter 138
Kearnes, Peter 116
Keeble, Edwin A. 33
Keedar, Nicholas 11
Keedar, Susannah 11

Keen, Elizth. 54
Keen, Francis 20
Keen, George 97
Keen, Jacob 54
Keen, James 101
Keen, John Jr. 96,97
Keen, Richard 79
Keene, James 145
Keene, Maria H. 119
Keene, Martha S. 79
Keene, Newton 72,88
Keene, Sarah 128
Keene, Thomas 128
Keene, Thomas W. 149
Keene, Unity 97
Keese, Josiah G. 142
Keist, Joseph 45
Keist, Nancy 45
Kelley, John 55
Kelly, Eliza 141
Kelly, Lawson 70
Kelly, Mary 9
Kendall, Charles 141
Kendall, Francis W. 41
Kendall, Harriet M. 141
Kendle, Mary 104
Kendrick, L.H. 127
Kendrick, Mary 5
Kendrick, Thornton 5
Kent, Anna 2
Kent, Ann Elizabeth 95
Kent, Catharine Ann 104
Kent, Harrison 27
Kent, Richardson 110
Kent, Thomas 2,153
Kent, William 91,95
Kent, William G. 95
Kepler, Ann Maria 112
Keppler, Octavia 89
Keppler, Samuel 89
Kercheval, Robert H. 97
Kercheval, Willis A. 97
Kesler, Philip 138
Keyes, Alex'r 132
Keyes, Elizabeth 132
Keys, William 144
Kidwell, Alexander 108
Kidwell, Coleman 47
Kidwell, Elizabeth 89
Kidwell, Francis 89
Kidwell, Gabriel 49
Kidwell, Hezekiah 99
Kidwell, John 138

Kidwell, Joshua 111
Kidwell, Mary E. 111
Kidwell, Mary Jane 99
Kidwell, Permilion 127
Kidwell, Thomas 61,89
Kidwell, Zedekiah 40,89
Kile, Elizabeth Jane 90
Kile, George 90,92
Kile, Mary Ann 92
Kilgour, Alex'r 44
Kilgour, James M. 115
Kilroy, Michael 120
Kindal, William 17
Kindall, Mahala 24
Kinder, Azariah 99
King, Ann Maria 123
King, Augustus 127
King, Catherine E. 123
King, Elizth. 108
King, Francis F. 28,78
King, Mary Ann 65
King, Susan 81
King, Thomas 28
King, William 39,65,81,123
Kinjelo, Michl. 10
Kinsel, John 27
Kiphart, Thomas 12
Kirk, Elizabeth 30
Kirk, Hetty 86
Kirk, Malcolm C. 30
Kirk, Rebekah 36
Kist, Solomon 38
Kitchen, William 142
Kittle, James 43
Kitzmiller, A.M. 43,50
Kitzmiller, W.W. 58
Kitzer, Barbara 118
Kizer, Mar tin 26
Klein, Elizabeth 118
Klein, John A.34,58,72
Klein, Lewis 48
Klein, Louisa 48
Klein, M.C. 118,149
Klein, Maddison C. 34
Klein, Mary A.72
Klein, Matilda E. 134
Kline, Jn. Nicholas 55
Kline, Maria L. 55
Knight, Harrison 23
Knolls, Leven 10

Knott, Julia Ann. 93
Knott, Ignatius 141
Knotts, Leven 10
Knox, Janet P. 136
Knox, Thomas P. 136
Koist, Catherine 1
Koist, Cutlop 1
Koist, Cutloss 1
Koist, Peter 4
Kuhlman, Daniel W.J. 130
Kuhlman, George J.D. 130

L

Lacey, Israel 116
Lacey, John 55
Lacey, Joseph 1
Lacey, Joseph B. 149
Lacey, Mahala 116
Lacey, Meshec 1
Lacey, Orpah 1
Lacy, John 41
Lacy, Matilda W.87
Lacock, Elizabeth Ann 152
Lacock, James 108
Lacock, Joseph 152
Lafaber, Rosannah 18
Lafaber, William 16,18,42
Lafeber, William 91
Lafever, Honour 77
Lafever, William 77,127
Lafever, William Jr. 124
Lalor, Jeremiah 41
Lamb, Elizth. 104
Lamb, Mary 136
Lamb, Nancy 94
Lamb, Samuel 136
Lamb, William 94
Lambert, Rebeccah 11
Lambough, Thomas 132
Lane, Arthur F. 54
Lane, Frances 84
Lane, Hannah 4
Lane, Jefferson 110
Lane, Joseph 17
Lane, Lyman L. 61
Lane, Nancy 17
Lane, Presley Carr 102
Lane, Will 4
Lane, William 9

Littleton, Richard 29
Littleton, Richard C. 92,120
Littleton, Richard K. 25
Littleton, Sampson 5
Littleton, Sarah E. 126
Littleton, Thomas 43,102,126
Livingston, Lewis 67
Lloyd, Ann 43
Lloyd, Joseph A. 49
Lloyd, William 146
Locker, G. 90,134
Locker, Mary Catharine 90
Locker, Rachel Ann 134
Lockheart, Jefferson 68
Lockheart, Madison 68
Lockheart, William 68
Lodge, Joseph 138
Lodge, Laban 51
Lodge, Mary C. 138
Lodge, William 35,131
Logan, John 94
Logan, Samuel 94
Long, Ann E. 153
Long, Conrad 153
Long, James 77,144
Long, Phillip 16
Long, Sarah 96
Long, William 47,75
Longley, Joseph Jr. 19
Lott, Elizabeth 131
Lott, Frances 42
Lott, Parkerson L. 43,62
Lott, Parkinson L. 42
Loughborough, Nathan 149
Love, E.A. 113
Love, Fenton 78
Love, James D. 121
Love, James J. 134,149
Love, Martha 155
Love, Sarah N. 113
Love, Susan A. 144
Love, Thomas B. 139
Loveless, Alcinda D. 65
Loveless, George W. 143
Loveless, Jonathan 77
Loveless, Thomas 65
Lovett, Daniel 6
Lovett, David H. 62
Lovett, David Harrison 62
Lovett, Evelina 58
Lovett, James P. 63
Lovett, Thomas A. 63

Lowe, Edward T. 40
Lowe, Eliza Ann 70
Lowe, Elizabeth 23,93,141
Lowe, Henry 72,81,93,141
Lowe, Jane 15,133,141
Lowe, John 114,129,133
Lowe, Louisa A. 110
Lowe, Margaret 0.124
Lowe, Mary 72
Lowe, Mary Jane 90
Lowe, Moses 143
Lowe, R. 90
Lowe, Rector 90
Lowe, Thomas 15
Lowe, William 133,143
Loy, Adam 31
Lucas, Casey 7
Lucas, James 19
Lucas, Mahala 19
Lucas, Martha Ann 77
Lucas, Mary 19,154
Lucas, Sarah Ann 106
Lucas, Thessa 7
Lucas, Thomas 154
Luck, Drusilla Ann 66
Luck, Emily M. 90
Luck, Jordan B. 66,90
Luckett, F.L. 126
Luckett, Francis W. 70
Luckett, Horace 135,145
Luckett, Josias C. 121
Luckett, L. 120
Luckett, Ludwell 58
Luckett, Maria Louisa 135
Luckett, Martha L. 126
Luckett, Mary 12
Luckett, Roger C. 121
Luckett, Samuel C. 50,146
Luckett, Sarah Frances 145
Luckett, William C. 34,85
Ludwick, Christian Gottleib 52
Lum, Hester Ann 59
Lum, John 59
Lumm, John 51
Lumm, Mary Ann 51
Lumm, Samuel 30
Luntz, Lorenzo 127
Lybough, Joseph 10
Lybough, Susannah 10
Lynch, Jane 37
Lynch, Margaret 47
Lyne, Mary 23

McGeath, Mary Ann 112
McGeath, Stephen 14
McGurgan, William 4
McGuygan, Sarah 49
McIlhany, James 2,115
McIlhany, James W. 30
McIlhany, Louisa 115
McIlhany, M. 24,57
McIlhany, M.M.44
McIlhany, Mortimer 24
McIlhany, Nancy 2
McIlhany, Orra 115
McIlhany, Rosannah 2
McIlhany, T.M. 60,117
McIlhany, Taliferro 24
McIntosh, David 82
McIntosh, John 121
McIntosh, Margaret 51
McIntyre, Catharine 28
McIntyre, Robert 57
McKenna, Hiram 76
McKenney, James 121
McKennie, Matthew 67
McKenzy, Enoch 155
McKim, Alcinda 42
McKim, Effie Ann 79
McKim, George 94
McKim, George W. 98
McKim, James 13,79,104,121
McKim, Jams 42
McKim, Margaret 121
McKim, Martina 145
McKimmie, Eliza 5
McKimmy, Francis 5
McKimmy, John 75
McKinney, George 15
McKinney, James W. 149
McKinny, Thomas 2
McKnight, James F. 49
McKnight, Josiah 12
McKnight, Mason 59
McKnight, Nancy 7
McKnight, Uriah 7,12
McLenen, John 96
McLeod, Hester A. 48
McManaman, James 8,14
McManaman, Sarah 8
McManamay, George 6
McMullan, Archibald 3
McMullan, Nancy 3

McMullen, Andrew 19
McMullen, Daniel 12,64
McMullen, Elizabeth 19,97
McMullen, George 78
McMullen, Mary 97
McMullen, Robert 97
McMullen, William 12,64
McMullin, George 27
McNabb, William 23
McNealey, John 114,139
McNeally, James 143
McNealy, James 72
McNeeley, Sanford 46
McNelea, Sanford 46
McNeledge, James 1
McNeledge, Mary 1
McNulty, Hugh 138
McPherson, Armistead 130
McPherson, Caroline D. 109
McPherson, Catharine 140
McPherson, James D.118,123,124,128,13*
McPherson, Job 12   1
McPherson, Maddison 109
McPherson, Madison 131
McPherson, Mary 101,131
McPherson, Sarah E. 131
McPherson, Sebastion 40,72
McPherson, Stephen 44
McPherson, Wesley S.55
McPherson, William 69,105,109
McVeigh, Angeline 68
McVeigh, Francis 61
McVeigh, Hiram 57,80
McVeigh, James H. 22,33,61
McVeigh, Jesse 22,61,68,77
McVeigh, Jesse H. 68
McVeigh, Mary Ann 61
McVeigh, Nancy H. 68
McVeigh, Town'd 22

M

Macdaniel, James 113
Maddux, Eveline 74
Magaha, Ann 115
Magaha, Elizabeth 126
Magaha, Ellen Elizabeth 140
Magaha, John 32
Magaha, Joseph 138
Magaha, Margaret 32,114

Murray, Elizabeth 93,147
Murray, Emma 93
Murray, J.C. 134
Murray, Juliet A. 60
Murray, Samuel P. 69
Murrey, Samuel 1
Murry, Frances 93
Murry, John C. 81
Muse, Barbara 10 Edward 3
Muse, Frances R. 121
Muse, James H. 103
Muse, Jonathan J. 121
Muse, Thomas 70
Muse, Thomas H. 121
Muse, Walker J. 145
Myers, Amelia Ann 87
Myers, Charles F. 150
Myers, Elijah P. 111,147
Myers, Elizabeth 28
Myers, Hannah 18 Israel 74
Myers, John 6,26,139
Myers, Jonathan 39
Myers, Lambert 51,105
Myers, Mahlon 49,65,74,94,80
Myers, Mahlon Jr. 52
Myers, Martha 6
Myers, Mary Ann 49,69
Myers, Mary Elizabeth 105
Myers, Michael 9
Myers, Peter 66,111
Myers, Rachel 65 Rebekah 3
Myers, Tacey 118
Myers, Thomas 18
Myers, Washington 51,69
Myers, William 94
Myers, William W. 118

N

Nalls, Carr B. 144 C.B. 61
Nalls, Mildred A. 144
Neale, Harriet C. 30
Neale, Nancy 38 Ruth 32
Near, Conrod 17
Near, Elizabeth 52
Near, Jesse 135
Near, John 26,52
Near, Sarah 17
Needham, Thomas 109
Neer, Amos 15,75
Neer, Ann S. 135
Neer, Henry 76 John 154
Neer, Nancy 154
Neer, Nathaniel 154
Neer, Samuel 15,20
Neile, Jemima 38

Neldon, John 1
Nelson, William 53
Newhouse, Harriet 108 Sarah 27
Newlon, David 19
Newlon, Deborah 18
Newlon, George 7,86
Newlon, Jesse 18
Newlon, John 7,96
Newlon, Mason 86 Nimrod 37
Newlon, Samuel R. 59,86
Newlon, Sarah 86
Newman, Benja 63
Newman, Eliza 63
Newman, Hezekiah 126
Newman, Patty 126
Newman, William 78
Newton, Alexander 73
Newton, Charles A. 139
Newton, Charles C. 44
Newton, Henry 51   J.F. 110
Newton, John C. 44,73
Newton, Joseph T. 16
Newton, Mary A. 44,153
Newton, Susan 16
Ney, Mary A. 134
Nicewanger, Juliann 58
Nichols, Abraham E. 68
Nichols, Dolphin 31
Nichols, Edith H. 146
Nichols, Eli 15, Eli H. 145
Nichols, Emily A. 106,125
Nichols, Enos 31,38,47,49,106
Nichols, Hannah 29 Hannah J. (
Nichols, Henry H. 108
Nichols, Isaac 29,31
Nichols, Isaac G. 82
Nichols, Jacob 70,79,146
Nichols, Jacob Jr. 70
Nichols, James 31
Nichols, John 125
Nichols, Jonah 78,134
Nichols, Jonathan 70
Nichols, Joseph 69
Nichols, Joshua 51,66,104,151
Nichols, Mary Ann 70 Mary Ellen
Nichols, Nathaniel 25,75
Nichols, Patience 75
Nichols, Pleasant 25
Nichols, Rebecca M. 85
Nichols, Ruth E. 137
Nichols, Samuel 79,85,97
Nichols, Thomas 64,82,137,145
Nieswaner, Christian 140
Nieswaner, Susan 140
Nieswanger, Christian 15 John 1
Nieswanger, Mary Ann 15

Nisewanner, John 58
Niswanger, Catherine 15
Nisswarner, William A. 153
Nixon, Ann 78
Nixon, Asbury M. 98
Nixon, George 18 James 37
Nixon, James W. 46,107
Nixon, Joel 64
Nixon, Joel L. 128,152,154
Nixon, Joel S. 96
Nixon, John 37,65
Nixon, Jonah 121
Nixon, Jonathan 94 Levi W. 141
Nixon, Lorenzo D. 47
Nixon, Malinda E. 64
Nixon, Mary Julia 154
Nixon, Nathaniel 106
Nixon, Pleasant 18
Noble, Dorothy R. 82
Noble, John S. 82
Noble, Thomas 54
Noggle, Eliza 107
Noggle, John 142
Noland, B.P. 125
Noland, Charles 35
Noland, Emily A. 32
Noland, G.W. 113
Noland, George W. 74
Noland, Lloyd 27,110
Noland, Maria Louisa 151
Noland, W. 28
Noland, William 24,35,151
Noland, William H. 38
Nollner, Jacob 116
Norell, William 128
Norred, William 65
Norres, John 45
Norris, George W. 135
Norris, Maria P. 135
North, William D. 54
Norton, Caroline 77
Nutt, Joseph 13
Nutt, Rebecah 13
Nutt, Thomas 13
Nyswanger, Mary Ann 152

O

Oatyar, Peter 16
Oatyer, Mary 16
O'Bannon, Enoch W. 121
O'Brien, Peter 72

O'Bryan, Michael 135
O'Connell, William 121
Oden, Ann 54
Oden, Barbara 121
Oden, Frances Ann 105
Oden, James S. 105
Oden, N.S. 50
Oden, Nathaniel S. 50,55,105
Oden, Solomon 17
Oden, Thomas 45,54
Offutt, Alfred D. 25,53
Offutt, Eli 15,25
Offutt, Thornton F. 46
Ogden, Andrew 76
Ogden, Ann 76
Ogden, Benjamin 139
Ogden, David 40
Ogden, Lydia Ann 139
Oliver, Caroline E.Roach 150
O'Neal, Mary 142
O'Neal, Thomas 142
O'Neale, Conn 9
O'Niel, Joseph 130
Oram, Henry 49
Orange, James 58,97
Orem, Aaron Edward 145
Orem, Armistead 103
Orison, Arthur 72,81
Orison, David 26
Orison, Samuel 134
Orison, Samuel Jr. 86
Orr, Ellen R. 25
Orr, Harrison 23
Orr, Jane Ann 136
Orr, John M. 120,150
Orrison, Abel 84
Orrison, Ananias 66
Orrison, Arthur 45,100,108,135
Orrison, Catharine 94
Orrison, David 28,100
Orrison, Eliza Ann 94
Orrison, John 57
Orrison, Jonah 121,135,150
Orrison, Joseph 62,69
Orrison, Margaret 28,100,135
Orrison, Mathew 6
Orrison, Presley 43,68
Orrison, Samuel 63
Orrison, Sarah 26
Orrison, Sarah Ann 100
Orrison, Sarah E.R. 150
Orrison, William P. 121
Orum, Emily 25

Sanders, Thomas R. 152
Sanders, Wesley J. 141
Sanders, Wilson C. 92
Sands, Alijah 18
Sangster, Charles F. 89
Sarbaugh, John 28
Sargent, George 132
Saunders, Benjamin 42,58
Saunders, Britton 36
Saunders, Crayton 29
Saunders, Curtis R. 60
Saunders, Edith 60
Saunders, Emily E. 105
Saunders, Gunnell,22,101
Saunders, James Jr. 39
Saunders, James W. 122
Saunders, Joanna 141
Saunders, John 60
Saunders, Lewis H. 78
Saunders, Mahala 22
Saunders, Mahala J. 122
Saunders, Mary A.L.58
Saunders, Perry H. 122
Saunders, Philip 37
Saunders, Presley 63,84,110,131,132,134,
Saunders,Presly 39   135,145
Saunders, R.G. 34
Saunders, Rachel Ann 22
Saunders, Robert J. 105
Saunders, Robert S. 28,87
Saunders, Sarah Ann 60
Saunders, Sarah H. 43
Saunders, Thomas 43
Saunders, Thomas R. 65
Saunders, Wesley J. 114
Saunders, Wesley S. 114
Saurbaugh, Jacob 60
Savage, John D.B. 46
Scanhan, John Henry 98
Scatterday, Pamelia 6
Schooley, Charles W. 134
Schooley, Charles William 99
Schooley, Eleanor H. 149
Schooley, Elizabeth 68
Schooley, Emma 85
Schooley, Ephraim 69
Schooley, J.B. 140
Schooley, John Jr. 8,34
Schooley, John Henry 134
Schooley, Jonas P. 149
Schooley, Presley Neale 68
Schooley, Thomas A. 133
Schooley, W. 133

Schooley, William H. 103
Schryock, Nancy 63
Scott, Charles 77
Scott, Gilbert 34
Scott, Harriett 123
Scott, Moses 123
Scott, Robert 10
Scott, S.S. 78
Scott, Samuel 10,153
Scott, William 129
Scroggins, Benjamin 151
Sears, Sarah 23
Seaton, Hiram 96
Seaton, James 1
Seaton, John W. 48,96
Sedgwick, Nancy 8
Seeders, Ann Eliza 103
Seeders, Mary Lee 141
Seeders, Sarah S. 141
Seeders, William 103
Seitz, Andrew 142
Selby, William 107
Selden, Eleanor Love 115
Selden, John 90
Selden, W.C. 90,115
Selden, W.C.Jr. 21
Sellman, John J. 105
Senate, William 140
Settle, Abner 64
Settle, Abner H. 92
Settle, Eliza 23
Settle, M.L. 150
Settle, Matilda 60
Settle, Nelson 60
Settle, William 67
Setzer, Philip 33
Seward, Nicholas 155
Sexton, Elizabeth 8,70
Sexton, George 131
Sexton, James 86,88
Sexton, John 70
Seygar, George 6
Seygar, John 7
Shackelford, Arthur 100
Shackelford, Warner W. 91,75
Shafer, Charles 22
Shafer, Jacob 38,71,112,140
Shafer, John 28,38,88,104
Shafer, Mary 88
Shaffar, Thomas 10
Shaffer, Jacob 27
Shaffer, Lydia 140
Shank, Andrew 65

Vermillion, Philip L.W. 132
Vermillion, Sarah 62
Verts, Conrod 9
Verts, Henry 114
Verts, Jacob 125
Verts, Samuel 115
Verts, William 29
Vickers, William 43
Vincel, Caroline 12
Vincel, George 76
Vincel, Tilghman 132
Vincell, George 82
Vincell, John 132,135
Vincell, Solomon 123
Vinsel, George 80
Vinsel, John 27
Vinsel, Philip 23
Vinsil, George 48
Vinson, John T. 112
Vinson, William B. 112
Violett, Asford 38
Violett, John 36,69
Violett, Mary 38
Violett, Mary Ann 69
Violett, Nancy L. 36
Virts, Christena 136
Virts, Conrad 150
Virts, Elizabeth 146
Virts, Elizabeth C. 146
Virts, George P. 117 James 125
Virts, Jane 43
Virts, John 85
Virts, Joseph L. 144
Virts, Mary 85
Virts, Samuel 81,94,119
Virts, Sarah Jane 125
Virts, William 43
Virtz, Catharine 9
Virtz, Conrad 98
Virtz, Henry 98
Virtz, Mary Eliza 98

W

Wade, Eleanor 12
Wade, George 112
Wade, Hez'h 12
Wade, John 18,112
Wade, Martha 112
Wade, Pricilla 8
Wade, Richard W. 105
Wade, Susan 112

Wadsworth, Lawson 106
Waggaman, John A. 67
Waid, Robert 8
Walker, Benjamin 19,94
Walker, Burr Smith 29
Walker, Eliza 4
Walker, Garret 151
Walker, Garrett B. 94
Walker, Lorenzo 99
Walker, Lorenzo D. 35,93,94,106
Walker, Mary 19
Walker, Mary Ann 94
Walker, Ruth Sarah 99
Walker, Thornton 74
Walker, William 15
Wallace, James M. 46
Waller, Elizabeth 76
Waller, George 76,102
Waller, Joseph 115
Waller, Sarah Ann 102
Walraven, Josiah 15
Walter, John 32,112
Walter, Sarah Ann 112
Walters, Eliza J. 121
Walters, Sarah 19,75
Waltman, Elizabeth 12
Waltman, Emanuel 50,84
Waltman, Jacob 12,105
Waltman, Margaret 68
Waltman, Mary A. 28
Waltman, Samuel 57
Waltman, Sarah Ann 105
Waltman, Susan A. 84
Wampler, Ann B. 132
Wampler, Anna B. 132
War, John 62,101
War, Lucinda 130
War, Mary E. 62
Ward, George 20
Ward, Henry 20
Ward, Thomas 73
Ward, William S. 71
Ware, Charles A. 137
Warford, Abraham 2,5,31
Warford, Catherine 5
Warford, Theodosia 2
Warner, George 9
Warner, George Jr. 65
Warner, Hannah 9
Warner, Israel 95
Warner, Mahlon 65
Warner, Mary C. 139

Warner, Massey 95
Warr, Eveline 145
Washington, Bushrod C. 62
Washington, E.S. 25
Washington, Edward S. 25
Washington, Elizabeth C. 25
Washington, George W. 53
Washington, John A. 44,115
Washington, Mary S. 145
Washington, S.E. 148
Washington, Samuel 140
Washington, Thomas B. 62
Waterman, A.G. 32
Waters, Eliza 116
Waters, Elizabeth 57
Waters, Ellmore 89
Waters, Jacob 39,57,116,140
Waters, John F. 140
Waters, John Francis 140
Waters, Mary Ann 39
Waters, Sophia 21
Waters, Susannah 143
Watkins, Bernard 60,61
Watkins, Catherine 49
Watkins, Eleanor 46,61
Watkins, James 10
Watkins, Margaret 10
Watkins, Sarah 2
Watkins, Sarah Ann 43
Watson, Egbert R. 22
Watson, Lemuel 45
Waugh, Alex. 1,2,6
Weadon, Asford 43,106
Weadon, Elizabeth 51
Weadon, F.M. 104
Weadon, John 80,106,112
Weadon, Nancy 105
Weatherill, Mary Eleanor 38
Weatherille, Nancy C. 153
Weatherly, David 39
Webb, Elisha 146
Webb, Elizabeth 146
Webb, Elizabeth Jane 146
Webb, John W. 107,140,146
Webb, Mary Ann 134
Weedon, Catharine 43
Weedon, F. 51
Weedon, William 76,87
Weeks, Burr 91
Welsh, R.W. 154
Welsh, James 19,99
Welsh, Sophia M. 49
Wenner, Caroline M. 122

Wenner, Charlotte 38
Wenner, Jacob 54
Wenner, John W. 140
Wenner, Jonathan 28,38,84,104
Wenner, Mary 40
Wenner, Mary Ann 65
Wenner, William 65
Wenner, William Jr. 10
Wenner, William W. 84
Wertenbaker, William J. 83
West, Elizabeth 155
West, James 67
West, John 6,15
West, Jonathan 36,91
West, Lydia 15
West, Maria 57
West, Mary 155
Westwood, Frances H. 1
Westwood, William 1
Wey, Peyton 21
Wey, Thomas H. 21
Whaley, Ann 95
Whaley, Ann M. 100
Whaley, Elizabeth 51
Whaley, Hannah 15
Whaley, James 24,69
Whaley, Jane E. 69
Whaley, John G. 69,116
Whaley, Levi 15
Whaley, Mary Ann 24
Whaley, William 15,51
Wheatley, Joseph 43
Wheatley, Nancy Ann 43
Wheatly, John 73
Wheeler, Johnson 132
Wheeler, Thomas T. 48
Wherry, Mary E. 101
Whistleman, Margt. 2
Whitacre, Amos 29
Whitacre, James 2,50,73,96,130
Whitacre, John 36,54
Whitacre, Lydia 50
Whitacre, Mary Ann 29
White, Aden 100,113
White, Agnes 60
White, Amanda 114
White, Ann Cecelia 87,90
White, Barsena 24
White, Daniel T. 151
White, Elizabeth 8,15,145
White, Hansford 45
White, James 55,113
White, James B. 60

White, Jane 1
White, Joel 80
White, John 57
White, John H. 49,59
White, John R. 30,41
White, John Randolph 102
White, Joseph 12
White, Josiah Jr. 10
White, Josiah R. 123
White, Joshua 121
White, Levi 89,108,121,148
White, Louisa 82,100
White, Mahlon 35
White, Maria 108
White, Margaret H. 121
White, Mary 121
White, Mary Ann 90,108
White, Mary E. 57
White, Mary I. 30
White, Nancy 90
White, Nathan 90
White, R.J.T. 90
White, Redmond F. 141
White, Richard 143,151,154
White, Rosanna M. 59
White, Ruth 117
White, S.N.C. 151
White, Sam C. 57
White, Sarah 32
White, T.J. 115
White, Thomas 8,15,114
White, Virginia A. 123
White, W.W. 92
White, Wesley 79
While, William 101
Whiting, George W. Carlyle 85
Whiting, Louisa 77
Whiting, Margt. 80
Whitmore, Catharine 113
Whitmore, Elizabeth 28
Whitmore, George 46,107,122,124,138
Whitmore, John H. 154 Michael 31,113,124
Whitmore, Margaret 31 William W. 151
Whitley, Margaret 155
Whitty, Eliza 140
Wiard, Jonathan 56
Wiard, Michael 20,132
Wiard, Louisa Ann 132
Wiard, Rachel 20
Wickes, Eliza D. 45
Wickes, William 45
Wicks, William K. 123

Widdicombe, John 62
Wiggenton, Benjamin 10
Wigginton, Benjamin 146,151
Wigginton, Mary 151
Wigginton, Sarah 146
Wilcoxon, Levi 15
Wilder, Henry 108
Wilder, Sarah I. 108
Wildman, Agnes 46
Wildman, Amelia 40
Wildman, Ann 64
Wildman, C.B. 150
Wildman, Catharine 145
Wildman, Charles 140
Wildman, Charles W. 123
Wildman, Dewanner 52
Wildman, Eleanor A. 70
Wildman, Frances 131
Wildman, Jacob 64 I.B.H. 70
Wildman, Jane D. 70
Wildman, John W. 144
Wildman, Joseph 16,103
Wildman, Juliet Ann 98
Wildman, Nelly 28
Wildman, William 131
Wiley, Ann 15
Wiley, Emily 145
Wiley, Harrison 141
Wiley, James 136
Wiley, James W. 127
Wiley, John 145
Wiley, John H. 151
Wiley, Kezziah 67
Wiley, Lavina 76
Wiley, Mary 137
Wiley, William 140
Wilkinson, Elizabeth 22
Wilkinson, Thomas 22
Wilkinson, William 33
Wilkison, William 51
Wilklow, Jacob 141
Willett, George 62
Willett, Linney 1
Willett, William 1
William, Charles 65
Williams, Catherine H. 117
Williams, Charles 72
Williams, Eleanor 50
Williams, H.S. 150
Williams, Hannah 91
Williams, Hannah Ann 153
Williams, Henry 93

Williams, Henry S. 95
Williams, Hiram Opie 117
Williams, Hillary Wilson 151
Williams, James 50,112
Williams, John 80
Williams, John C. 80
Williams, Margaret M.A. 42
Williams, Notley C. 42
Williams, Presley 13
Williams, Sarah E. 150
Williams, Sydnah 153
Williams, Sydnor 72
Williams, T.R. 152
Williams, Tobias R. 140
Williams, Washington 77
Williams, William 8,91
Williamson, Jesse 143
Willis, Elizabeth 46
Willis, Sally 5
Willis, William 46
Wills, Benjamin 18
Wilmarth, Jason 76
Wilson, Ann 57
Wilson, Anna Bell 119
Wilson, Archibald 9
Wilson, Charlotte 105
Wilson, Charlotte L. 119
Wilson, Edward 57
Wilson, Eleanor 46
Wilson, Evelina 26
Wilson, Harriott 119
Wilson, Helen Mary 105
Wilson, James 3,38
Wilson, James A. 141
Wilson, James P. 95
Wilson, John 26
Wilson, John M. 68
Wilson, Julia A.H.134
Wilson, Margaret 11
Wilson, Mary 1
Wilson, Moses 1,33
Wilson, Moses D. 44
Wilson, Nelson B. 79
Wilson, Rebekah 9
Wilson, Robert 9
Wilson, Susanna 3
Wilson, Tholemiah R. 142
Wilt, George 114
Wilt, Jonathan 91
Win, John W. 109
Wince, Lucinda E. 131
Wine, Armistead J. 144

Wine, Catherine A. 122
Wine, George H. 144,149,151
Wine, George Henry 122
Wine, John 44
Wine, Sarah Ann 149
Wine, Washington 116
Winecoop, Maranda 143
Winegardner, Adam 29,38
Winegardner, Mary 38
Winegardner, Sarah 29
Winegarner, Levi 46,47
Wines, Edward 134
Wines, John 95
Winn, Josiah 12
Winn, Thomas M. 36
Winn, Thomas W. 69
Winn, William 12
Winner, John 46
Winsel, George 30
Winsel, Louisa 30
Winsell, Samuel 54
Wire, John 104,129
Wire, Peter 84
Wire, William 23
Wirtz, Henry 129
Wise, Jane 49
Wise, William 49
Wisener, Nathan 109
Wissinger, Julian M. 115
Wissinger, William 107
Wolf, Adam 11
Wolf, Barbara 88
Wolf, Mary 10
Wolf, Susan 120
Wolfe, John 134
Wolfe, Mary 34
Wolford, John 146
Wolford, Mahala 91
Wolford, Mary Ann 34
Wolford, Rebecca 146
Wolford, William 34,91
Wood, Joseph 70
Wood, William 103
Wood, William S. 144
Woodard, J. 87
Woodard, Jabez 87
Woodard, Jane 87
Woodard, Julia Ann 93
Wooddy, Mary Jane 29
Woody, Isabell 137
Woody, James 45
Woody, John 137

Woodyard, Walter 51
Woodyard, William 17
Woolf, John 119
Woolford, Elizabeth 42
Workman, Charlotte 126
Workman, Isaac 24,29,126
Workman, Matilda 24
Wornal, John 24,26,40,120,149
Wornal, Rachel 70
Wornall, James 38
Wornall, Sarah 38
Wornel, John 121
Wornel, ·Mary Ann 121
Worsley, William 100,115
Worson, John 41
Worthington, Emily 59
Worthington, L.70
Worthington, L.W.137
Worthington, Landon 83
Worthington, Sarah 21
Wortman, George Henry 124
Wrenn, Sanford 154
Wrenn, Thomas M. 85
Wright, Albert 83
Wright, Alfred 40
Wright, Ann E. 153
Wright, Anthony 5
Wright, Bennett 151
Wright, C.F. 141
Wright, Catharine 130
Wright, Charles 38
Wright, Charles F. 132
Wright, John 2,53,124
Wright, John E. 153
Wright, John H. 154 Joseph 151
Wright, Joseph H. 71
Wright, Joseph L. 135
Wright, Jotham 53
Wright, Mahala 101
Wright, Martha 124
Wright, Mary 87
Wright, Mary Jane 99
Wright, Nancy 111
Wright, Ro. L. 77
Wright, Rebecca B. 83
Wright, Rebecca J. 151
Wright, Rebecca M. 77
Wright, Robert D. 53
Wright, Robert S. 116
Wright, Samuel 38
Wright, Sarah Ann 53
Wright, Susan 40
Wright, Susannah 132

Wright, Thomas 56
Wright, Thomas M. 124
Wright, W.G. 38,101
Wright, W.O. 83
Wright, William 19,59,111
Writt, Thompson 37
Wunder, Caroline H. 69
Wunder, H.S. 83
Wunder, Harry S. 69
Wyatt, Jacob 4
Wyatt, Thomas 3
Wylie, Hugh 15
Wyncoop, Alcinda 153
Wyne, Elizabeth 151
Wyne, William 154
Wyngrove, John 19
Wynkoop, Alsinda 144
Wynkoop, Catherine 106,144
Wynkoop, Catherine A. 115
Wynkoop, Cornelius 16,101,116
Wynkoop, Elizabeth 101
Wynkoop, Elizabeth W. 106
Wynkoop, Garrad 16
Wynkoop, Garret 96,101
Wynkoop, Garrett 83,124
Wynkoop, George W. 68,106
Wynkoop, Jane 16
Wynkoop, John 83,96
Wynkoop, John J. 106
Wynkoop, Joseph 89,94
Wynkoop, Joseph Thomas 141
Wynkoop, Margaret 35,89
Wynkoop, Philip Henry 141
Wynkoop, Richard 35
Wynkoop, Samuel C. 89,92,115,124
Wynkoop, Sarah E. 101
Wynkoop, Thomas 144
Wynkoop, W.H. 106
Wynkoop, William 50,94
Wynkoop, William B. 94
Wynn, John 17

Y

Yabower, Elizabeth 101
Yackky, John 30
Yakey, Amanda 142
Yakey, Elizth. 101
Yakey, John 83
Yaky, John 47
Yeaca, Martin 68
Young, Abraham 89
Young, Alfred 59

Z